D0849990

Self/Power/Other

Self/Power/Other

Political Theory and Dialogical Ethics

ROMAND COLES

Cornell University Press · *Ithaca and London*

First published 1992 by Cornell University Press.

International Standard Book Number 0-8014-2609-X
Library of Congress Catalog Card Number 91-55546

Printed in the United States of America

Librarians: Library of Congress cataloging information
appears on the last page of the book.

⊗ The paper in this book meets the minimum requirements
of the American National Standard for Information Sciences—
Permanence of Paper for Printed Library Materials, ANSI Z39.48-1984.

Contents

Preface

The coexistence between self and other is hell, or so Sartre once read the world. And if the theorists with whom I am most concerned in this book—Saint Augustine, Michel Foucault, and Maurice Merleau-Ponty—have diversely described the self and its relation with others in ways that avoid some of Sartre's most damning ontological assessments, all three would surely consent to Foucault's remark that in social existence "everything is dangerous."

In this book I seek ultimately to explore some of what seem to me the *highest* possibilities of our lives with others. Yet in a world as mired in senseless suffering as ours, a world where ideas offered to advance freedom so often contribute to the intensification of subjugative practices, the attempt to discern better possibilities must always be reflectively entwined with the effort to grasp both our most horrifying historical practices and our more banal evils. Hence in discussing each philosopher's thought, I begin by considering his critique of some of the central aspects of the violence of his day and then draw on this material to develop, analyze, and extend his ethical alternative.

I am interested in thinking about ethics in the setting of a modernity where God and the world created by him seem less and less able to secure our basic practices and thoughts; a modernity whose secular dimension has met with meager results as it has attempted to fill a post-

metaphysical void; a modernity that in some places has engendered
formal rights and constitutional democracies while simultaneously proliferating insidious modes of social control and exploitation, and in other
places has unleashed more brutish forms of power (often the first category of places uses political, economic, and military power in ways that
foster violence in the second). I seek to shed light on some of the ways in
which our very basic understandings of self, other, and their relationships
are entangled in this modernity, and to explore alternative ontological
and ethical positions that might encourage us to take up the tasks of
unraveling institutions of subjugation and replacing them with social
practices more conducive to freedom.

Insofar as this project is self-consciously situated in modernity, Augustine will perhaps strike the reader as an odd figure to engage. Yet I
find him fascinating in several ways. His reflections near Christianity's
dawn are relevant to those who wander in its dusk because they in-
sightfully examine problems that accompany the egoism of a decadent
non-Christian world in ways that I believe shed light on not dissimilar
problems in our own day. Augustine's critique of the Roman pagan self
can—among other things—draw attention to some of the dangers we
face as we attempt to "go it alone" without God. They are significant
dangers, and yet they are significantly underestimated by some thinkers,
for whom "postmodernity" signifies a human ability simply to leap beyond modernity's and premodernity's problems into a world of "play"
and "gaming." At the same time, Augustine's often suggestive alternative, the self whose very being rests on ceaseless confessions of deep
truths, is bound up with a new form of power that in some ways facilitates
a more thorough and endlessly proliferating control over selves. Foucault
argues that some of the basic contours of Augustine's confessing self live
on in modern versions of normalizing power that relentlessly attempt to
rout out otherness by constituting the ways in which selves subjectify and
objectify themselves and others. The contrast between Augustine's defense and Foucault's critique of confession as a basic form by which
selves are constituted allows us to develop a more subtle perspective on
the ethical implications of this practice than does either position alone.
The metaphysical and historical distance between these two theorists
facilitates a better grasp of both the plasticities and the continuities of the
effects of confession.

Yet what interests me about Foucault is more than his genealogical

critiques, for unlike most of his contemporary interpreters, I see emerging in his work a constructive ethical position that not only guides what
and how he criticizes but also provides a general vision of an alternative
(if loosely drawn) order of things. Much of my discussion of Foucault
attempts to pull together and develop this constructive dimension, which
lies scattered and often latent in his work. The effort is of great importance, for it allows us to pursue ethical thoughts that avoid both nihilism
and the totalizing dimensions of ethics rooted in the atomistic self, normalizing reason, and at least many versions of God. Foucault's ethics is
rooted in an esteem for the artistic fashioning of one's life, but he understands this project as inextricably linked to dialogue with, and affirmation
of, others who are different. Hence his notion of the self as a work of art
motions toward a significantly decentered ethic that implies care for
others and the fashioning of a social world where differences can be
affirmed and intermingle. In this manner he provides provocative ideas
for thinking beyond the arid antinomy between the atomistic individual
on the one hand and, on the other, the self that belongs to a community
through rigid identification. Foucault gestures toward a belonging in
difference.

Yet his ontology, with its nearly exclusive focus on violence, is, I believe, ultimately in problematic tension with his ethical position, for it
seems, if read literally, to condemn all action from the outset. Merleau-
Ponty provides insights that allow us to transcend these problems by
developing an ontology that understands our best relations with the
world to consist not merely of a transgressive dimension but of an expressive one as well. In so doing he returns to and substantially trans-
figures some Augustinian themes and enables us to strengthen and further elaborate the dialogical ethic we find in Foucault.

What I hope emerges in this book is an ethics that critically illuminates
some of what is hellish, while gesturing toward styles of coexistence more
conducive to the miraculous than to hell.

This work springs from the cacophony of conversations in which I
have with others questioned the world. Many people played vital roles in
the development of the ideas and interpretations herein. A decade ago,
Charles Fox guided me during my first forays into the texts of Merleau-
Ponty and Foucault. He, along with Maury Foisey, Tim Allen, Mitchel
Gray, and Russell White, created a stimulating environment for political

theory at Western Washington University. Tony Steinbock's work on Merleau-Ponty and his thoughtful efforts to elaborate Merleau-Ponty's conception of "depth" significantly influenced the development of this project. Bill Connolly read this work more than once and made innumerable suggestions, many of which found their way into these pages. Jean Elshtain's effort to read Augustine seriously in the midst of simplistic dismissals stimulated my engagement with his work. Hubert Dreyfus's insightful questions frequently forced me to rethink initial formulations in ways that affected the most essential dimensions of this book. Dennis Porter, Michael Shapiro, and Michael Gillespie each offered very helpful comments on this manuscript.

I also thank my parents, Jerry and Maria Coles and Chris and Dick Colvard, as well as my brothers, Terry and Jeremy Coles, and I hope some small fraction of what is wonderful about each of them finds its way onto these pages.

Kimberley Curtis shared with me the deepest frustrations and joys of this project. Our multiplicitous dialogue stretches over six years now, and her voice—both its agreements and disagreements—haunts this text.

The winds and images of the western Massachusetts landscape blow throughout these pages. They helped me remember that, as Merleau-Ponty writes, the earth is the soil of our thought as it is of our life.

ROMAND COLES

Durham, North Carolina

Self/Power/Other

1 · Introduction: From Edge of Darkness to Ecotone

Natural ecologists know that the boundaries between two different ecological communities—for example, between a forest and a meadow—often harbor a greater variety and density of life than either of the two distinct communities alone. These edges are, as Barry Lopez has written, "special meeting grounds," and "the mingling of animals from different ecosystems charges such border zones with evolutionary potential."[1] This fertility is often referred to as the "edge effect," and the edge itself wears the formal label "ecotone." The etymology of the latter word is of some significance, stemming from the Greek *oikos*, or habitation, and *tonos*, or tension. "Ecotone" and "edge effect" call our attention to the life-engendering character of the ambiguous tension-laden dwelling that emerges at the intersection between differently constituted regions: they speak of the pregnancy of edges.

This work is about edges, not those between forests and grasslands, but those between self and other, and those between differences within the self. The edges humans are most familiar with are often not pregnant with life, but rather zones of destruction, boundaries between warring

1. Barry Lopez, *Arctic Dreams: Imagination and Desire in a Northern Landscape* (Toronto: Bantam, 1986), p. 109. Cf. Peter Richerson and James McEvoy, III, *Human Ecology: An Environmental Approach* (North Scituate, Mass.: Duxbury Press, 1976); Robert Leo Smith, *Elements of Ecology and Field Biology* (New York: Harper and Row, 1977).

countries. Western civilization has a long and dark history with respect to edges; it tends to view them as indicative of an evil that lies on the other side; it constitutes them as regions to be forever thrust back and ultimately eliminated at the moment when we conquer the other. Yet it is not just specific edges that pose problems but edges per se; we are a civilization that on the whole, at least since Plato, dreams of a reality without wild edges, a world encompassed within one Reason. In the shadow of this dream it is little wonder that our approach to edges is obliterating and that when we are involved, edges are desolate rather than fruitful localities.

Yes, our often wretched edges and the social categories constructed on either side are a hauntingly ubiquitous phenomenon. Our history is marked by many barren boundaries; those between master and slave, capitalist and worker, humans and nature, male and female, white and black, "normal" and "abnormal." Of course, each of these oppositions is distinguished by specificities far greater than the thin breath of ink called "comma" which separates them might indicate. Yet there is sense in this sequence. In each case, the hegemonic category seeks to master and determine its other. The master masters the slave by ensuring both the distinction between the two and the former's rule over the latter. The "normal" masters the "abnormal" sometimes through categorization, condemnation, and ostracism, sometimes by "helping," "healing," and pressuring in ways that draw it into the circle of the same. In both cases, however, what is—or is to be—eliminated is the unmastered voice and being of the other. Thus, even where a difference is constituted and perpetuated as essential—for example, master and slave—the dynamic is fundamentally edge-denying insofar as it seeks to obliterate the other's otherness. (That is, here, constituting the other as other [slave] is at the center of the obliterative dynamic.) Hence even many of our socially constituted differences and the boundaries that emerge at the interstice operate to a very large degree to extend mastery, thrust back edges, and eliminate others' differences.

In contrast to what appears to me to be an important bent of our history, this book seeks the beginnings of an ethos attuned to the value of edges and to those differences whose communication makes them fertile. I seek a reevaluation of edges and difference—not simply a new conceptualization of edges, but a new reality as well, in light of a different conceptual approach to and participation in the formation of edges. It is my sense that the project of formulating an edge-affirming ethos and creating differences in light of this ethos must be one of the most fundamental dimensions of our efforts to reshape our contemporary social and political world. So long as edges and diversity remain anathema, we are doomed to a politics and life of explicit or insidious conquest, a politics that seeks to obliterate the otherness of others and in so doing devitalizes the human and natural world. Of course, I am not arguing that worldly change can be accomplished by the development of a new ethos alone. Our ideas, attitudes, and practices to a large extent take form within and are perpetuated by the institutions we inhabit, and change requires that careful attention be given to reality in all its dimensions. My argument is simply that the ethical dimension is critical, and in this discussion it is my primary focus. Let me begin by placing the current project in the context of some significant debates in political philosophy and then briefly sketch the contours of my argument.

In the terrain of contemporary political philosophy, two cleavages very often define the general features of present debates: that between various forms of individualism and communitarianism, and that between various forms of rationalism and relativism. Increasing numbers of theorists are finding this terrain and these debates inadequate insofar as they appear to close off important possibilities for thinking and being. Yet insufficient as these cleavages appear, it is not evident, on my reading, that viable alternatives have been convincingly formulated. To situate the project at hand—which I believe furrows through some of the important philosophical terrain in a way important for transcending these antinomies—I will briefly sketch some of the central aspects of the paradigmatic positions and point toward both the difficulties of these positions and the general direction this book pursues in order to formulate an alternative ethical perception of selves and social practices.

The position for methodological individualism finds one of its strongest expressions in John Rawls's *Theory of Justice*, which attempts to formulate principles that would determine rights, duties, and the division of social benefits and burdens.[2] Central to this project is Rawls's notion of a hypothetical situation he calls the "original position," the inhabitants of which are rational, equal, and behind a "veil of ignorance," knowing neither their place in the society whose principles they seek to establish

2. John Rawls, *A Theory of Justice* (Cambridge, Mass.: Harvard University Press, 1971).

nor their abilities or conceptions of the good. By imagining ourselves in this situation, we are supposed to be able, as rational individuals, to choose principles of justice in a rational and disinterested manner, seeking to further our own abstract interests, not those of others. Since each individual is unaware of the particularities of his existence, he will deliberate fairly. As Rawls reads the world, these principles of justice are the "first virtues of social institutions"; they are prior to and have primacy over any notions of the good.

Rawls clearly points out that his individualist departure is not necessarily opposed to arriving at communitarian values so long as they are in accord with what a rational *individual* in the original position could choose. Yet as Michael Sandel (with whom I represent the communitarian position) notes, this space for communitarianism within Rawls's theory does not lessen its very individualist philosophical bent.[3] For it gives priority to the choices of a self "individuated in advance." It assumes that the bounds that separate the self from others and the world are already fixed, for only within such bounds can we fully rationally and legitimately determine justice. We cannot deliberate in the original position with any conception of the good, because this would be an "attachment," and the purely rational individuated self has no attachments. A rational self may finally share values and aspirations with others and may join cooperative associations to further shared ends, but its choice to do so is that of an atomistic rational self, not a self partly *constituted* and *defined by* its relations with others and pursued ends. Given this essentially distanced self, right *must* have priority over the good, since an abstract individual can be only a bearer of rights (which protect its essential distance and boundaries) and not essentially committed to certain ends (since its relationships are simply choices). In Sandel's words, Rawls's ethic "means that what separates us is in some important sense prior to what connects us—epistemologically as well as morally prior. We are distinct individuals first, and *then* we form relationships . . . with others; hence the priority of plurality over unity."[4]

This priority, however, is precisely what Sandel seeks to question. In Sandel's view, we are not first rational individuals who then choose relationships, but rather beings essentially embodied in and constituted

3. Michael J. Sandel, *Liberalism and the Limits of Justice* (Cambridge: Cambridge University Press, 1982).
4. Ibid., p. 133.

by relations with others, values, and the world, into which we are born and by which we are significantly defined. The bounds of the self are not predetermined, but rather contingent products of history and our reflection. For Sandel's selves, as members of constitutive communities, values and intersubjective interested relations with others are not secondary qualities from which we should abstract in order to attain rational justice, but instead primary and significantly definitive qualities that must at least be reckoned with and sometimes must govern us, even when contrary to justice, since to act differently would be to cease being "who we are" as essentially and deeply attached and committed. The situated selves are not only capable of embracing communitarian values, but "conceive their identity . . . as defined to some extent by the community of which they are a part."[5] So in contrast to Rawls's methodological privileging of an abstract and atomistic self, Sandel gestures toward situated and connected selves who are "participants in a common identity." The existence of this common identity holds open the possibility of displacing the primacy of justice and making real communitarian politics (governance strongly defined by notions of a common good) both possible and desirable.

In spite of their important differences, Rawls's and Sandel's philosophical frameworks are similar insofar as they both harbor conceptions of the self that are substantially "edgeless." For Rawls, not only are there no constitutive relationships of commonality behind the veil of ignorance; neither are there *differences* and hence no possibility of dialogical interchanges across edges between different "others." Rational selves are prior to such a dialogue and uninterested in or "indifferent" to the value of dialogue with others' differences when considering the first principles of their social institutions. Such a self may later choose to value and enter dialogical relations with different others, but these relations do not enter into or well forth from the most basic understandings of self and freedom. Sandel's self is essentially related to other selves, but these relations are characterized by commonality and identity. The communitarian self is essentially connected with other selves through what it *shares* with them. It is constituted through communicative relations with others, yet these are understood primarily as relations that constitute "allegiances" continually "discovered" through our being with others.

5. Ibid., p. 150.

What is missing in Sandel, as in Rawls, is any notion of a self whose existence and freedom require dialogical relations with others not because they are equally abstract individuals or participants in a common identity, but because they harbor multiplicitous differences that, when dialogically engaged, make possible a creative freedom and perception of the world far richer than we could ever have alone or with others the same as us. Such a dialogical ethos would stress the essential interrelatedness of all selves but would accent the value of difference in these relations and the importance of creating and belonging to a diverse social fabric. These ethics of indifference and commonality would be displaced by an ethos that would encourage dialogical participation with differences and the creation of institutions and social customs that might make this more likely. This ethos—as I develop it through the works of Foucault and Merleau-Ponty—contains a notion of a common good from which we come forth and to which we contribute, yet it neither issues from nor requires our abstraction or sameness. Rather, the good in common consists of the establishment of a social world where diverse voices can develop in and through, as well as foster, dialogical relations. There is consensuality in this ethos and these relations, yet it is one that affirms the value of our differences and dialogue.

If this ethos seeks to shift toward a terrain different from the one on which individualists and communitarians have waged their debates, so too it strives to formulate a position that avoids the rationalist-versus-relativist swamp in some ways exemplified by the contrast between a self-proclaimed postmodernist and a second-generation critical theorist. The former, Jean-François Lyotard, argues that reason is a mythical and undesirable "metanarrative" with totalitarian implications. He urges us to abandon our search for a singular Reason that rises above the multiplicity and contingency of human life and instead affirm the incomparability and specificity of increasingly diverse language games, which develop not according to truths but by way of the creative impulses of sublime imaginations. He urges us to view our society as a "patchwork" of utterly heterogeneous games, games Samuel Weber describes as "incommensurable and non-communicating."[6] Indeed, in *Just Gaming*, Lyotard argues that these games should be kept "pure," that is, kept

6. Samuel Weber, "Afterword, Literature: Literature—Just Making It," in Jean-François Lyotard, *Just Gaming*, trans. Wlad Godzich (Minneapolis: University of Minnesota Press, 1985), p. 104.

from interfering with one another. This relative indifference coloring his writing makes him unable to address effectively the problems that arise when (because we are, with all our diverse language games and activities, embodied in the same social world) our discursive practices encroach on one another. Hence Hobbes rumbles in the final passage of *Just Gaming* as Lyotard backs into a corner where he finds lurking "the great prescriber himself."[7]

In contrast to this alternative, Jürgen Habermas sketches a vision of society as motivated and unified by efforts to achieve a rational consensus that legitimates the social system as a whole as well as its various subsystems and multiple public spheres. Far from being a dangerous myth, reason, for Habermas, is a barrier against injustice, rooted in the inherent interests of the human condition and the tacit telos of every effort to communicate. Rationality functions as a regulative principle rooted in the idea of an "ideal speech situation" (an idea that goes underground but still remains central to his later work) which would allow us to discriminate between tolerable and intolerable differences. Implicit and explicit in the rhetoric and logic of Habermas's texts is an imperative consensulism, an endlessly repeated assertion that our positions "must" strive to converge.

To distinguish the position I am offering in this text, I think it worthwhile to note the lack of edges in both positions. If Lyotard affirms "agonistics" within games, what is lacking within his work is an affirmation of dialogue between those more radically other—those in different games. Each language game becomes for him a pure, edgeless self-identity, utterly severed from different games and those outside a given game, both of which are placed in an abyss of irrelevancy with respect to the self-identical language game. If Habermas affirms rational critical debate, the edges he seems to tolerate, or at any rate find at all interesting, must fall within a still not entirely clear "rational discourse," where all differences acquire their initial legitimacy only insofar as they claim to be capable of motivating a rational consensus; and even these edges are a transient phenomenon, viewed only negatively, soon to be dissolved in a restless and imperative drive toward rational consensus. In contrast to Lyotard's relativistic, mutually indifferent different games, the ethos I attempt to develop affirms that a loose general ethic (or "metanarrative")

---

7. Lyotard, *Just Gaming*, p. 100.

is strongly suggested by the human condition as it is portrayed (somewhat variously) by Merleau-Ponty and Foucault. Yet it is not that of a
regulating "communicative rationality," but rather one that embraces the
sense, fertility, and value of the intermingling development of and communication among our *differences themselves*—differences not bound by
(or necessarily tending toward) a singular reason, but subject to the
preconditions and limits necessary to foster and protect our differences
and their dialogical entwinement. The artistic ethos fosters a communication among games, selves, and practices which transcends the limits
of each and calls for the diverse developments of each to acknowledge
and respect the dialogical interworld of differences to which they belong.
In short, the position I am proposing seeks to affirm difference without
falling into indifferent relativism, and maintain a general ethical position
without falling into the trap of a totalizing reason.

At first sight, the lineup of philosophers with whom I seek to pursue
this project will perhaps strike the reader as odd. Foucault and Merleau-
Ponty are not such an odd combination, but with the addition of Augustine we have a rather confusing and problematic—even weird—trio.
Is not the social, political, religious, philosophical context of late antiquity
simply too different from that of the contemporary world to allow us
legitimately to enter Augustine's writing into a constellation, albeit an
agonistic constellation, with Merleau-Ponty and Foucault? I do not wish
to deny the presence of an abyss between our world and the one that
possessed Augustine. And yet I think there are important ways in which
this specific distance adds to, rather than nullifies, the relevance of this
late antique voice. Augustine writes before Christianity has thoroughly
established its hegemony. He reflects as a Christian, but his reflections
are continually preoccupied with his own non-Christian past and a world
quite foreign to Christianity, however much different sects of the latter
owed substantial debts to the surrounding paganisms. Both many of the
problems of a world without a Christian God and many of the assumptions entwined with a world illuminated by such a God are addressed
with a kind of persistence and acuity that is perhaps only possible when
one lives a life so close to an "edge"—in this case, that between
paganism's decline and the rise of Christianity. I suggest that the owl of
Minerva sometimes spreads its wings at dawn as well as dusk; sometimes, if rarely, it traverses both in a single flight.

Yet it is not simply, or perhaps even primarily, the quality of Augustine's voice that makes him a seductive figure for me, but the likelihood that we live and write on the far edge of the phenomenon—the Christian world—with whose earlier edge he was preoccupied. Of course, "the Christian world" is a totalizing term for a multiplicitous phenomenon that spans a huge period of history. And yet there are important similarities between what Augustine meant by "Christianity" and meanings with which the term is entwined today. For example: a singular God that is the ground of all being; a morality that is true and the word of this God; an understanding of this world and ourselves as fallen; a belief that we must endeavor to align the depths of ourselves with the heights of God's word; a belief that to resist his word is to manifest an evil will worthy of punishment. In addition, the residues of this Christianity substantially color the often muddy and unstable world we call "secularized," even in places where we think we are furthest from God (for example, in the realm of "objective knowledge" and normal behavior). Much of this legacy, in both its religious and secular forms, is being challenged now, and there is a growing sense that it is nearing its end. Hence the amazing proliferation of the prefix "post-," which, when all posts are taken together, conjures a widespread cultural view that we are on the edge of something new. Whether or not we are in fact moving into a "new age" or the "postmodern" is a question I leave for the future-seers. What is more certain is that the current mixture of survival and erosion of Christianity and its secular legacy presents us with problems we must face. Augustine did not face our world and its problems, but his writings about a different world moving away from paganism toward "God" may help us shed some light on a world that seems to be moving away from that God and his legacy. Augustine's edge may help us consider our own.

Of course, our own world is my primary concern, and hence I have to some extent appropriated his voice for this project. Thus one will not find in these pages a very textured analysis of Augustine's historical context. Such an analysis would take me too far astray from my central focus. Yet if this reading "takes" something from Augustine (at least insofar as it historically situates him only with broad strokes of the pen), perhaps it "gives" something as well. Perhaps it requires a reading that dwells at our edge of the Christian world to illuminate and make sense of Augustine's sweat at an earlier border. Maybe it is precisely through our concerns that his voice can be heard profoundly in the modern world. This is my claim; let the reader judge.

The overlapping concerns of and substantial differences among Augustine, Foucault, and Merleau-Ponty can, when gathered together, shed an interesting and important light on the ethical issues at hand. Briefly, Augustine's critique of the pagans provides us with a penetrating analysis of one of the central dangers of our age: an obliterating egoism. The danger of this egoism intensifies with both the (partial) recession of God from much of the modern world and the development of capitalism. At the same time, however, Augustine's alternative to egoism, the confessing self bent on discovering and obeying deep truths, is, while helpful in some respects, the beginning of a new form of power intent on extirpating all that does not accord with the voice of the "one true God." Partially in spite of himself, Augustine formulates an ethic that is, in the vocabulary we opened with, edge-denying. This new form of power acquires further dangers when, in developments that follow the Cartesian *subiectum*, man himself becomes the origin of "deep truths" that he must ceaselessly attempt to discover and obey. Michel Foucault is a critic of this contemporary confessing self, which he argues is the central figure in what he refers to as "normalizing power." Modernity, on Foucault's reading, is characterized by a subjugating form of power that operates by producing "truths" and norms by which we must order our lives. I argue that far from being nihilistic—as many critics have maintained— Foucault's criticism is rooted in a dialogical artistic ethos that accents the value of dialogical differences. Yet Foucault's ontology, which focuses almost entirely on the discordant aspect of being, perception, and thought, while it provides important insights that give rise to his notion of the self as a work of art, is probably not sufficient to sustain such an ethos. Merleau-Ponty's ontology and epistemology allow one to refine many insights in Foucault's work on the "transgressive" dimension of being, yet Merleau-Ponty develops the "expressive" dimension of being as well. By so doing, Merleau-Ponty provides a position that calls attention to both the violence inherent in being in the world and that in life which is not reducible to violence. Some of the theoretical insights he establishes combine a sense of danger and possibility in a way that might sustain the dialogical artistic ethos, an ethos he too affirms and helps us further develop.

Augustine, whom I explore in Chapter 2, is a fascinating figure in light of these issues, for he has a heightened sense and provides a profound analysis of one important mode of being that transforms the edge into a war zone as it seeks to master all that is not the self: namely, that of the egoistic self of ontological conceit which takes itself as the ground of being. By carefully developing Augustine's critique of the Roman pagan self, we gain a critical elaboration of the dynamics and consequences of egoism which is extremely insightful and serves as a warning beacon of what we must avoid in our efforts to formulate an ethos with a greater appreciation of difference.

Augustine attempts, through his notion of the confessing self, to formulate an ethos that does not collapse everything to the self. The self turns away from the lust to dominate the world and toward the depths of its soul, where it seeks to fashion even its most fleeting desires in obedience to God's truth and morality. Augustine seeks to escape the tyranny of others' domination and conform to God in the depths of his soul, and this involves a profound recognition that others too are deep, diverse participatory signs of God's polyphonous voice rather than beings flattened to their "being-for-the-self." Yet if Augustine opens the space for an appreciation of others which appears to have been lacking in decadent Rome, his relation to what does not "face God" is (in a sense developed in the concluding section) monological: that which is not obedient to God is "nothingness," and hence we discover that the confessing self confronts its non-Christian other in a manner very different from, but every bit as relentless and extirpating as, the way the pagan self confronted its others. For all of Augustine's profound insights into depth, remembering, willing, and unifying the scattered self in confession, the edge where he faces the non-Christian—even within himself—is still a battlefield, not a region where fertile intermingling might be possible. Thus, in this respect, Augustine's confessing self inadvertently provides another beacon of warning of an ethos that still endlessly seeks to thrust back edges, one that proceeds not from the self, but from the one true God or, more generally, one truth.

In Chapter 3 I begin by elaborating Foucault's analysis of the "normalizing" tendencies that characterize much of the concrete functioning of power in modernity. I briefly summarize his critique of normalization as it operates through "panoptic power" and confessing practices that assert that we harbor "deep truths" within us which we must carefully decipher and follow. I then explore these themes at a metatheoretical level in his writing on the modern episteme in *The Order of Things*. When Foucault's more theoretical writing is read in light of his genealogies and vice versa, his work as a whole acquires a level of profundity missed by many of his interpreters. In contrast to Augustine, for whom depth is the dimension of freedom and truth, according to Foucault, depth is the dimension of subjugation. It is that dimension in which we rout out the other and constitute ourselves in light of hegemonic norms implanted deep within us. That we cannot "get to the bottom" of depth in modernity does not signify that we have somehow come to accept a degree of otherness; rather, it merely ensures the endlessness of subjugative interrogations.

Yet if Foucault's critique is extremely illuminating of modern approaches to edges, equally interesting is the alternative "ethos" that has guided most of his work. In contrast to most of his critics, who charge Foucault with nihilism, I argue that his work—the content of his critique, its style, and the positive directions toward which it gestures—is constituted around a dialogical artistic ethic that affirms the importance of difference and the desirability of giving shape to our individual lives and social milieu in light of a "limit attitude" that affirms edges and enriches human relations. Indeed, far from being a nihilist, Foucault offers us important insights into the possibility of ethics in a postmetaphysical age—a possibility I begin to develop.

Merleau-Ponty, to whom I devote Chapter 4, is a philosopher and political theorist for whom depth is a central concern. Yet depth is not a dimension that promises total identification, but rather a dimension of the concealed in which things always partially exceed and resist our gaze. Through an exploration of Merleau-Ponty's philosophy of depth (*Être profond*), I begin to articulate an ontology that harbors a profound awareness and reverence for the edge between the self and other as well as what inhabits the terrain beyond this edge. This insight acquires a particularly social significance in light of Merleau-Ponty's thoughts on the "intercorporeality" of depth. I attempt to gather these insights together and draw on his writings on art and politics as well, in an effort to develop an ethics and politics of depth and distinction which extend the dialogical artistic ethos initially formulated in the chapter on Foucault.

In the conclusion I contemplate the virtues and dangers of each theorist in light of the insights offered by the others.

This book contains long sections of exegesis. These may delay a direct integration of each thinker's positions with my own arguments and the agonistic constellation of the work as a whole. Nonetheless, such delay and the space it provides for each theorist's voice are essential to a textual practice that seeks to embody the ethos it explicitly articulates. This is a work about edges, difference, dialogue. Yet none of those things can exist without spaces in which real distinctions are nurtured and allowed to appear. A frequent integration of each theorist into the overall textual fabric seemed to me to violate the spaces where each achieves a radiance that makes him a worthwhile interlocutor. Meaningful dialogue requires not only proximity, but the latter's interplay with distance as well. Hence one of the intended textual effects is the juxtaposition of three intense "steepings" in the thinking of very distinct thinkers, followed by a discussion that presupposes that step.

The impatient reader is likely to ask, What is original in this work? I might point to several things. There is the reading of Augustine partially in light of questions raised by Foucault's interpretation of modernity—a reading that finds Foucault's questions to be unavoidable in our age, yet one that does not simply drown the metaphysician in postmetaphysics. There is the effort to draw an ethos out of Foucault's work which goes a good distance beyond what he was willing to formulate explicitly. There is a reading of Merleau-Ponty's ontology which accentuates intercorporeal depth, the interplay between expression and transgression, and an effort to gather and extend his thoughts on ethics and politics beyond his explicit statements. There are the particular hues each philosopher acquires in light of the concerns of the others.

Yet none of this is "original." At best what follows is a series of pregnant thoughts that formed in several dialogues, along several edges more powerful than any voice alone. We are, to paraphrase Merleau-Ponty, divergences of conversations—often too entwined in our differences to indicate clearly where the others end and we begin.

2 · Augustine

Dawning Confession

From unfathomable depths a question emerges whose answer lies most profoundly in the question itself. Augustine queries: "What then am I, O my God? What nature am I?"[1] This is the question through which the *Confessions* is created; the restless question through which Augustine is created; and hence the mysterious question that *transforms the self* as both the subject and object of the question. It is a question whose character and limits are defined by the height of the God he evokes—a God who guides the most sincere questioners. With a passion rarely equaled in the history of Western thought, Augustine pursues this question in search of the deep truths within himself. In his peculiar occupation of this question he signifies the dawn of the hermeneutic self. In his most revealing moment he answers the question thus: "I have become a question to myself" (*Confessions*, 10.33).

"What is Augustine?" Augustine is a being constituted through the restlessness and depth of his self-examination. Augustine is a confessing self; a self that continually faces itself in the endless task of discovering and telling the deepest truths about itself; a self that is itself a "soil" into which it continually delves; a soil "heavy with sweat."

1. Saint Augustine, *The Confessions*, trans. F. J. Sheed (Kansas City: Sheed, Andrews, and McMeel, 1942), 10.17. Further citations to this edition are given directly in the text.

Augustine's *Confessions* is an exemplary manifestation of a new way of being, the expression of a new form of self. Long before Michel Foucault, Augustine himself defined the Christian self in contrast to all previous forms of selves, largely through the act of confession. Even the Platonists, with so many insights that Augustine respected, inhabited a region far on the other side of a gigantic chasm with respect to the type of selves they were. "Their pages show nothing of the tears of confession" (*Confessions*, 7.21).

The confessing self is distinguished from previous selves in that it is constituted through a very peculiar movement: the movement of the self toward deciphering its own depths. In a most fundamental sense, the confessing self *is* this movement. It dwells at an edge within itself; an edge that ceaselessly retreats, shifts, moves into depth: the edge between light and darkness, between thought and the disparate and undermining impulses of unconscious desire. In its ceaseless journey to reveal and examine its interior, it becomes a being of depth. The confessing self dwells in its depth, the dimension that is simultaneously its most profound discovery and what makes confession both possible and necessary.

As we inhabit the movements of Augustine's heart and mind in his *Confessions*, we gain provocative insights into confession as a mode of being. Yet continual confession is not a way of being of which Augustine is merely an innocent and unwitting manifestation. As a particular expression of a new way of being, a way of being that one *is not* unless one chooses to become such through conversion, Augustine continually makes explicit and addresses the fact that he is a confessing self. Unlike modern "Western man," who inhabits a world that Michel Foucault argues has "become a singularly confessing society,"[2] a society in which confession is a constitutive element of so many of our secular practices, institutions, discourses, and ideals, Augustine inhabits a world in which nonconfessing modes of being have been hegemonic. Augustine's world is one in which people are for the most part born nonconfessors. Hence Augustine is quite aware that deep reflexivity is a "different" mode of being. (This is not to say that Augustine was one of the only confessing selves of his day. The early monastic self-examinations and the "self-publication" in penitential rites were both important mechanisms for

2. Michel Foucault, *The History of Sexuality, Vol. 1: An Introduction*, trans. Robert Hurley (New York: Random House, Vintage Books, 1980), p. 59.

producing confessing selves.[3] Further, as Peter Brown has noted, Augustine associated with a group of people concerned with "the events of their inner life."[4] Yet the techniques of confession were not nearly as pervasive or as dominant as they are today—and Augustine in any case was extreme in his confessing.[5]

Indeed, what makes the *Confessions*—this act of self-reflection—so fertile is that it is largely about deep self-reflection itself. Augustine confesses about confession. I know of few books that are so thoroughly about themselves. Hence the *Confessions* provides us with an opportunity to begin to apprehend deep self-reflection as a confessing self apprehended it from within confession, and to perceive the way in which a confessor at the dawn of confession could affirm confession as a mode of being.

Yet if we are to begin to experience and understand this early confessing self, it is insufficient to look merely at this self's-understanding. Augustine's conversion and subsequent life as a confessor welled forth from his perception of the late antique Roman pagan world and the type of selves he believed constituted that world. If it is true that Augustine was a confessing self because he thought confession was essential for human being, it is equally true and equally important that Augustine viewed the nonconfessing Roman self as the origin of *nonbeing*. Hence it is only through a textured understanding of Augustine's analysis of the way of being he rejected that we can comprehend the mode he affirmed.[6]

We begin with Augustine's critique of the Roman pagan self in an effort to situate the discussion of Augustine's confessing self which follows.

3. Michel Foucault, Lecture: "Christianity and Confession," Wesleyan University, November 24, 1980.
4. Peter Brown, *Augustine of Hippo* (Berkeley: University of California Press, 1967), p. 159.
5. Ibid., p. 160.
6. In the discussions of the Roman pagan self and the Christian confessing self which follow, one should note the specificity of and interrelationships between two dimensions that consistently characterize Augustine's analysis. One is the importance Augustine places on the attempt to understand both the implicit and explicit ontological framework within which different selves constitute themselves. Closely related to this dimension are Augustine's efforts to disclose the deep psychological characteristics of selves. Indeed, the ontological and psychological dimensions are generally so inextricably intertwined in Augustine's analysis that we might best describe his studies as "psycho-ontological." The salience of these two dimensions becomes clearer in light of the following discussion.

Augustine's Critique of the Roman Pagan Self

Augustine recounts the history of Rome as a long, dark succession of conquests, civil wars, tyrannies, rapes—a seemingly endless tale of subjugation. He describes a world of multiplicitous edges, yet they are sites not of being and life but of murderous lusts. It is a history of cruelty that was driven by the "lust for domination"[7] and the quest for glory. Even Rome's peace was structured around the dominion of some people over others. Yet domination is never primarily understood by Augustine to rise out of particular social and political organizations. Instead, Rome's social structures and the horrors so often associated with them are always perceived to originate fundamentally from the Roman pagan self's way of being. Slavery, poverty, bloodshed, and obscenities are simply manifestations of selves in error: selves of *civitas terrena.* How does Augustine understand this Roman pagan self—this self whose pervasive causality echoes so violently across the face of the earth?

Following scripture, Augustine argues that pride is the "start of the evil will [and] . . . of every kind of sin" (*City of God*, 14.13). Rome's lust for dominion originates in pride. Yet what is pride? Simply a moral error? Pride certainly has a moral and psychological character, but more profoundly, the psychological "longing for a perverse kind of exaltation" (14.13) is intertwined with an ontological error. Viewed ontologically, "this then is the original evil: man regards himself as *his own light*" (14.13; my emphasis).

For Augustine, God is the ground and origin of all being. He is the "light" that gives Being, Truth, and Goodness to all beings, and he illuminates his creation and thereby makes it perceptible to these beings. The ontological error committed by the proud appears to be that they view·themselves as self-originating light: self-originating being. Under the sway of this profound ontological error, people view themselves as the independent source of their own existence and as the source of the light in which the truth about other beings is illuminated as well. It seems that on Augustine's reading, the proud self believes that being and truth

---

7. Saint Augustine, *City of God,* trans. Henry Bettenson (Harmondsworth, U.K.: Penguin Books, 1972), 1.Preface. Further citations to this edition are given directly in the text.

originate in the self alone. Concerning the fall from the garden, Augustine writes that Adam and Eve "made themselves their own ground" instead of adhering to the "real ground of their being" (*City of God*, 14.13).

Already we begin to see the way in which psychology and ontology are inseparable in Augustine's analysis. He argues that this perverse "exaltation derives from a *fault in character*" (*City of God*, 14.13; my emphasis). The fault in character, however, is a very specific fault that refers to the ontological dimension—namely, the desire to be self-originating being. The essence of the conceit that is the origin of all evil is that it is *ontological conceit*. As the primordial conceit, ontological conceit is the origin and basis for all other conceit.

In taking itself to be the origin of its own being, the self of the purest form of ontological conceit seeks to renounce its relations of reciprocity with others and the world and its dependence on God. In pursuit of freedom from all necessary relationships with anything that is "other" than itself, the self strives to become conditionless and absolute, to live according to itself and grant itself universal status. In Augustine's words, the self lives "by the rule of itself" (*City of God*, 14.3).

Lest we fall prey to an oversimplification of Augustine's understanding of pagan selves and the possibility of a misleading anachronism, these lines should be read with caution and deserve further clarification. Augustine's description of the "origin of all evil" should not be construed in a manner that would establish an identity between Roman pagan selves and "modern subjects." If pagan selves could simply be reduced to the pure form of ontological conceit described above, such a comparison might be inviting. Modern subjects as we find described and criticized variously in many of Heidegger's, Adorno's, and Hegel's texts (among others) seem to exemplify some of the qualities that Augustine believed were most at the heart of evil: the self understanding itself as its own ground, living according to its own rule. Yet—with the exception of Augustine's analysis of the most wicked who seek to master the earth—his writing on the Roman pagan self reflects an awareness of the extent to which ontological conceit manifests itself in a highly differentiated world of beliefs, practices, and events; a world originating in, sustained, and exacerbated by ontological conceit, yet one in which this conceit frequently did not appear on the surface of beliefs and events in the pure form described here. More often than as an explicit set of beliefs, Augustine understands ontological conceit to be a deep truth animating and characterizing the desires and practices of the pagan self while remaining beneath the level of consciousness.

Certainly the selves Augustine describes are different from modern selves in important ways. Once humans take themselves to be their "own light," they lose the truths that Augustine believed only God's light could illuminate and fall into an extended progression of errors. Often these errors were purely self-centered, but often as well they were more complicated. In error, the Romans invented "false gods" and religious worship that connected them to a metaphysical world on which they were dependent. Augustine does not argue that in the complicated world of pagan cosmology all selves explicitly conceived of themselves as self-originating. Rather, he describes their metaphysics as "pitiable folly" (*City of God*, 1.3): pitiable not only for its falsity, but also because of the extent to which this metaphysics harbored and nurtured the germ cells of the ontological conceit that produced enormous cruelty and led them beyond all bounds, even those posed by pagan religion. According to Augustine, the behavior and exploits—the violence, cruelty, lusts—of the pagan gods was emblematic of and hence fostered the very ontological conceit and lust for dominion in which they originated. While the self was not the explicit center of Roman paganism in the large sense, nevertheless, on Augustine's account this paganism generated and encouraged thoughts, desires, and practices—*the self's mode of being*—that were purely self-aggrandizing. Hence most essentially, the pagan selves were for Augustine selves of ontological conceit. His discussion of ontological conceit is an attempt to capture the origin, essence, and driving force underneath and implicit in the desires, thoughts, and practices of Roman pagan selves—*not* a reductionistic attempt to *equate* all of their thoughts and practices with ontological conceit in its purest form.

When the self dwells in the ontology of conceit, its experience of the world—a combination of perception and judgment—is fundamentally erroneous. For Augustine, "it is the nature of things considered in itself, without regard to our convenience or inconvenience, that gives glory to the creator" (*City of God*, 12.4). Thus, "he lives in justice who is an unprejudiced assessor of the intrinsic value of things."[8] Just judgment is

---

8. Saint Augustine, *On Christian Doctrine*, trans. D. W. Robertson, Jr. (Indianapolis: Bobbs-Merrill, 1958), 1.27.

that which judges the intrinsic, which for Augustine always refers to God as the condition of all beings. Because we are finite beings with an incomplete perspective on the world, the intrinsic is always to a greater or lesser extent elusive. The world's meaning is rarely if ever simply identical with the meanings we discover. Hence for Augustine, the Christian self is always aware of the incompleteness that always points beyond to something "other" than itself and its own experience; an incompleteness that can be filled only by faith. Everything is part of that deep design that no human being can completely discover (*City of God*, 7.16).

For the purely self-originating self, beings in the world cease to have intrinsic value as diverse creatures of God and cease to be evaluated with respect to the ordered whole of creation. Instead, all beings are reduced to being experienced as objects that exist for this self that takes itself as the origin of being. The being of all that is not the self, all that is "other," is reduced to being a "being-for-the-self" of ontological conceit, to which everything refers. The salience of this problem is indicated in the first paragraph of the *City of God*, where Augustine characterizes the city of this world as a place where justice is absent from judgment. No one can be sure he judges justly, but Roman pagan selves are most deeply and persistently enmeshed in selfish judgment.

The proud self lives and experiences the world *according to the "flesh,"* by which Augustine refers not primarily to our physical flesh, but rather to the *self* as a whole, soul and body. Examining Saint Paul's "Epistle to the Galatians," Augustine notes that works of the flesh "include 'faults of the mind' such as enmity, animosity and envy as well as bodily lusts" (*City of God*, 7.2). To live by the flesh is to *"live by the rule of the self,"* and it is thus that man "becomes like the Devil" (14.3; my emphasis). To experience the world according to the flesh is to experience the world exclusively from the perspective of self-centered being, and this for Augustine is to live in "lust" in the worst sense of the word. Again, however, "lust" in this sense is meant to refer fundamentally not to the physical dimension, but rather to the *desire* of the self of ontological conceit for an *object*. Lust as conceited objectifying desire can take a bodily form (*libido carnalis*) or a more psychological form as in the lust for power (*libido dominandi*).

Lust is not a possibility for the proud self—it is a *necessity* imposed by the experience it has of the world. The self that strove for absolute freedom by taking itself to be the condition of its own being—its own light, its own ground—culminates in the most depraved state of slavery. It experiences around itself a world of beings that have been flattened out to its own singular perspective. This experience of the object flattens and drains the subject as well as the object, however. Each object, as for-the-self, demands that the self desire and appropriate it. The self is flattened to the single dimension of lust as it strives to conquer a world that invites—a world that *insists*—that the self subjugate it. And at the same time the subject is flattened, it is crushed and dispersed into as many objects as it desires.

Hence the world experienced through ontological conceit leads to life lived in "lust" according to the "flesh." The great intensity of this experience can be gleaned from Augustine's account of his attempt to overcome it before his conversion:

> When I rose against You in my pride . . . those lower things became greater than I and pressed me under so that I could neither loosen their grip nor so much as breathe. Wherever I looked they bore in upon me, massed thick; and when I tried to think, the images of corporeal things barred me from turning back towards the truth, as though they said: "Where are you going base and unclean?" All these things had grown out of my wound, for You humble the proud like one wounded; and I was separated from You by my own swollenness, as though my cheeks had swelled out and closed up my eyes. (*Confessions*, 7.7)

Augustine views this preconversion period as one when he was so enslaved by his experience of the world that despite his faith in holy scripture and Christ, he was still unable to free himself from its grip even though he longed to do so. In spite of his efforts to think, the world he experienced—a world revealed in ontological conceit—conscripted him into other forms of toil. The desire for the self's absolute hegemony over objects fostered a relentless and in some ways more profound hegemony of objects over the self.

Let us explore two of the most important and most "enslaving" lusts that Augustine addresses, to gain a more textured understanding of his interpretation of the Roman pagan self.

"The most pitiless domination," Augustine argues, "is that exercised by this very *lust for* domination" (*Confessions*, 7.7). It is this lust to dominate other people which dominates "the city of this world" (*City of God*,

19.16). The selves of ontological conceit view themselves, at least implicitly, as absolute beings and "live according to their own rule." The "proud self" seeks to impose its being and its standards on "others," for if others were to live according to "other" standards, the self's absoluteness and independence would be jeopardized. The only way this self, which Augustine describes as a "perverted imitation of God" (*City of God*, 1.Preface), can maintain the illusion of being independent and absolute in its involvement with others is by obliterating others' otherness. Hence the self "seeks to impose its own dominion on fellow men in place of God's rule" (19.12). "The wicked . . . desire to make all men their own people, if they can, so that all men can be subservient to one master" (19.12). Indeed, the only peace this "puffed up" self can accept is one in which it is absolutely hegemonic. Such a peace would confirm the illusions that arise from ontological conceit—all other peace mocks these falsehoods. Augustine asks rhetorically, "When can that lust for power come to rest until after passing from one office to another, it arrives at sovereignty?" (1.31).

Yet in attempting to impose its dominion, the self confronts other similar selves with antithetical objectives. "Hence human society is generally divided against itself" (*City of God*, 18.2). In absence of fear, the *libido dominandi* ran its unchecked course after the destruction of Carthage, resulting in "bloody insurrection . . . disastrous quarrels . . . the slaughter of civil wars . . . torrents of bloodshed . . . greed and monstrous seething cruelty" (1.30). The desire to impose the self's rule on others is the most pitiless lust, because it is the most impossible lust to satisfy and the most cruel.

Though Augustine sees the dynamic of *libido dominandi* play itself out time and time again throughout history, it is important to note that this dynamic is a tendency of, but not an absolute necessity for, the self of conceited ontology. There are times when these selves constitute situations in which this tendency is largely contained. Fear, for example, such as that which existed in the rivalry between Rome and Carthage, might produce "a period of high moral standards" (*City of God*, 1.30). Yet the fear on which these high standards were based was itself grounded in the unstable lusts of conceited ontology, lusts that could not rest long in a state of relative equality with others. The *libido dominandi* destroyed the unlikely preconditions of its containment and "first established victory in a few powerful individuals, and then crushed the rest of an exhausted country beneath the yoke of slavery" (1.30).[9]

Let us turn now to another lust one finds discussed in Augustine's writings: *libido carnalis,* or sexual lust. Here, I believe, Augustine is responding to another form of what he perceived to be flattening objectification. Without wishing in this work to explore the history of antique sexual practices in any detail, let me simply note some references that might caution us against a trite dismissal of Augustine's concern about sexuality on the basis of the belief that it was due *simply* to his weird personality, his personal obsessions, etc.

There are clear indications of objectifying sexual practices in Roman antiquity. Although in Book Two of *The Art of Love,* Ovid argues that "men and women should share the same pleasures,"[10] his instructions

9. Likewise, the passion for glory, which itself stems from and is "puffed up with empty conceit" (*City of God,* 5.20), may check the other lusts for a time. The object that glory seeks is "the judgment of men when they think well of others" (5.12). Here the self desires subjects more than objects for itself. The self that seeks glory depends on others to recognize it as the origin of the greatness that it continually attempts to demonstrate. Blinded by its conceited ontology, this self strives "to do things so that others will be 'converted' to itself" (5.14). In this sense, the desire for glory is another "perverted imitation of God."

Yet while Augustine states that glory is a vice, he recognizes that it can be regarded as a virtue as well, in the sense that it checks other vices. In its best form, glory, though it seeks "merely human praise, is anxious for the good opinion of enlightened judges" (*City of God,* 5.19). This desire for glory seeks to identify itself with a good that is not merely its own good, but a good for others as well. Augustine praises this glory in the early Romans: "They took no account of their own material interests compared with the common good . . . they resisted the temptation of avarice; they acted for the country's well-being with disinterested concern; they were guilty of no offence against the law, they succumbed to no sensual indulgence. By such immaculate conduct, they labored towards honours, power and glory, by what they took to be the true way" (5.15). This is an extremely interesting passage, because it illustrates Augustine's belief that the ontology of conceit could generate desires for social recognition which could actually give rise to what he considered to be altruistic, "praiseworthy" behavior. Yet like the situation of fear, the desire for glory, as Roman history itself attests, is an unstable basis for virtue, for it preserves a conceited ontology that constantly threatens to engender more depraved lusts. Hence at first the passion for glory gave rise to a love of liberty, "but when liberty had been won, such a passion for glory took hold of them, that liberty alone did not satisfy— they had to acquire dominion" (5.12). The conceit that had taken an altruistic form undermined this very altruism when freedom and altruism became mundane and insufficient to feed the thirst for glory. Thus Augustine writes that although there is a difference between the desire for glory and the lust for dominion, "there is a slippery slope . . . from the excessive delight in the praise of men to the burning passion for domination" (5.19).

10. Ovid, *The Erotic Poems,* trans. Peter Green (Harmondsworth, U.K.: Penguin Books, 1982), p. 211.

are aimed at teaching the reader how to find an "object for your love," and Ovid assumes and affirms that each person views others as potential objects for the self's pleasure and dominion. When the "other" is viewed as a subject (of pleasure, perception of action), it is almost always in an effort to enhance the self's dominion over the other. One finds evidence of the close association between sexual pursuit and domination in the metaphors and analogies employed in Ovid's poetry. The male who pursues women is continually equated with the soldier and the hunter. Indeed, "love is a species of warfare."[11] Ovid suggests that his poetic instructions on love should be used as weapons: "As Vulcan made arms for Achilles, so have I done for you: then use my gift, as he did, to conquer."[12] In both Ovid and Petronius, the male sexual organ is referred to as a weapon. In Petronius's *Satyricon,* Polyaenus attempts to apologize for his impotence and writes to Circe: "Remember this one thing, not I but my instruments were at fault. The soldier was ready, but I had no weapons."[13]

In short, sexual pursuit here seems to be entwined with struggle for dominion. The greater the intensity of struggle, the greater the pleasure of conquest. Perhaps Fellini's *Satyricon* provides us with an illuminating modern artistic rendering of the intertwining of sexuality, domination, and conceit in Rome—an illumination that might help us situate Augustine.

I have come across no passages where sexual lust is explicitly *identified* with the lust for dominion in Augustine's own writing. Rather, the closeness of the two seems to be an assumption that haunts his work. The arguments in the *City of God* shift to and fro between the two lusts with an ease that is often difficult for some modern readers (depending on his or her assumptions about sexuality) to follow. As G. I. Bonner argues, one area where sexuality and the lust for domination are brought into a particularly close relation to one another is in Augustine's discussion of Roman pagan religion. "In significant fashion . . . the twin *libidines* are brought together in the official worship of pagan Rome. . . .

11. Ibid., p. 198.
12. Ibid., p. 213.
13. Petronius, *The Satyricon,* trans. J. P. Sullivan (Harmondsworth, U.K.: Penguin Books, 1965), p. 148.

The glories of conquest are thought to depend upon ritual obscenities."[14]

According to Augustine, both lusts originate in ontological conceit and both are manifestations of the enslavement of others and the self which occurs as the result of our own "disobedience." It is this second point that Augustine finds most profound and seeks to elucidate throughout much of his discussion of *libido carnalis*. The ultimate irony of the self of ontological conceit's claim to be an independent and self-controlling being is that it initiates an atomization of itself which continues beyond the level of the self. In becoming a self of ontological conceit, the self becomes a kind of being that is unable to control—and falls victim to—a process of disintegration it sets in motion itself, one in which parts within the self make similar demands for autonomy and control which the self cannot resist.

Augustine writes that "the retribution for disobedience is simply disobedience itself. For man's wretchedness is nothing but his disobedience to himself. . . . He who in his pride had pleased himself was by God's justice handed over to himself. But the result of this was not that he was in every way under his own control, but that he was at odds with himself, and lived a life of harsh and pitiable slavery, instead of the freedom he so ardently desired" (*City of God*, 14.15).

It seems that Augustine has two (related) interpretations of man's fall into disobedience to himself. In one sense, this disobedience was inflicted on man by God as a form of retribution for man's pride. God transformed man's body—it became mortal, and certain parts of his flesh ceased to submit to his will. Henceforth, willing to face God became much more difficult than it had been in the garden: it would now require an endless effort to gather a disparate human self through perpetual confession. In another sense, however, Augustine views this disobedience as connected in a far more organic manner to the mode of being generated by the self of ontological conceit. As we have seen, the self of ontological conceit is trapped in an experience of the world which holds sway over it even when it tries to resist. Within this experience, the world

14. G. I. Bonner, "Libido and Concupiscentia in St. Augustine," *Studia Patristica* 7 (1962): 313. On the same page he also argues: "Augustine did not envisage any division such as developed in later Christian thought, where preoccupation with sexual concupiscence assumed preponderant . . . proportions."

demands that the self dominate it and hence the lust for domination becomes a form of compulsion in which the self is unable to control disobedient lusts within itself. Yet this slavery may or may not be apparent to the self, depending on the extent to which the self unquestioningly *affirms* its domination over others.

It is sexual lust that most undeniably announces the self's disobedience to itself. Even those who affirm this lust are continuously and obviously subject to it:

> In fact, not even the lovers of this kind of pleasure are moved . . . just when they have so willed. Sometimes the impulse is an unwanted intruder, sometimes it abandons the eager lover, and desires to cool off in the body while it is at boiling heat in the mind. Thus strangely does the lust refuse to be a servant . . . it is quite often divided against itself. It arouses the mind, but does not follow its own lead by arousing the body. (*City of God*, 14.16)

The self of ontological conceit is linked to the world in multiple ways through the immediacy of desires evoked by the self's erroneous experience, within which the world appears as an object-for-itself. The proud self is continually thrown *outside of itself* in its lust to appropriate the world. "It casts away what is most inward to it, and swells greedily for outward things" (*Confessions*, 7.16). Embroiled in the unmediated desire for the world around it, the self is consequently an unreflective self. Augustine describes his preconversion period as one in which he was "behind (his) own back" (7.7). It is at precisely this point that the proud self finds itself most enslaved by its demand to be a self-originating subject. For the type of self that results from this demand is so unreflective and beyond itself that it is unable to control the various parts of its own body and soul. The self's conceit incites the various parts of the self in such an immediate and powerful manner that they become autonomous, and the pagan self, as an unreflective conglomeration of these desires, is unable to control them. Those who attempt to "swell" disintegrate. The proud self becomes the locus of multiple lusts, each of which attempts to govern the whole. Sexual lust becomes uncontrollable and at its height leads to an "almost total extinction of mental alertness" (*City of God*, 14.16). The undeniable autonomy of the sexual lust, which originates in pride, leads to shame. Humans are, according to Augustine, universally "embarrassed by the insubordination of their flesh" (14.17).

Thus, Augustine tries to show not only that the self of ontological conceit objectifies and attempts to dominate the world around it, but further that it is an assemblage of self-defeating motives. Born in pride, this self ends in shame. Its quest for absolute freedom leads to slavery. Its attempt to be the self-centered locus of expansion culminates in the disintegration and dispersion of the self. In short, the attempt to live as a self-grounded being leads the self further and further away from being. "Vanity," says Augustine, "is nothingness" (*City of God*, 20.3).

And nothingness has a powerful inertia. For to the extent that the proud are absorbed in the external world, they are "behind their own backs," unreflective and victims of habit. Trapped in immediacy, the self of ontological conceit is "pressed under" by an experience of the world that is "massed thick" and provides exceedingly little room for self-examination, which might lead to self-criticism and change. Augustine laments, "I know how great is the effort needed to convince the proud of the power and excellence of humility" (*City of God*, 1.Preface). The ontology of conceit and the absence of self-reflection are inseparably linked in a mutually reinforcing dynamic.

As Augustine stared into the face of the darkness of his age, he saw at the origin of a multifarious evil a self that willed an ontology of conceit and was constantly outside itself in its relentless expansive appropriation of the world. Decadent Rome, on Augustine's reading, was the epitome of a type of being (and order of things based on this being) that, in my terms, turned edges into war zones or sought to constitute them from the perspective of and for the benefit of one side of the difference. His effort to transform this situation would consist in changing the self's trajectory; rerouting its outward course back toward the inner depths of the soul in search of the voice of God within. The self would become a problem for itself, and in the process a new self would be created: a confessing self. But what would remain hauntingly familiar in Augustine's portrayal of and his existence as a confessing self is a certain quality of relentlessness.

Augustine's Confessing Self

In opposition to a world that was "massed thick" with selves who were "outside themselves" and experienced others as objects-for-the-self—a world largely dominated by the lust for dominion—Augustine sought to nurture the *civitas Dei,* where spaces might appear for what was eclipsed by late antique Rome. In contrast to flattening pagan perception, Augustine yearns for a world of depth where the multiplicity of different beings might be appreciated, where those dimensions in others that exceed the self might be affirmed as diverse expressions of God. Instead of conquering the other, we might affirm God as the absolute Other and dwell meditatively with the beings of his awesome creation, seeking to discover and participate in his infinitely protean voice by unraveling the endless mysteries presented by his beings. The City of God would not be understood most fundamentally in terms of a different institutional structuring of life, however, any more than the problems of the city of earth were understood fundamentally to result from particular social arrangements. Rather, the City of God would represent a type of self (and relations between such selves) that stands in diametrical opposition to the self of the ontology of conceit. The difference between the two would be discernable regardless of social position: master, slave, ruling husband, obedient wife.

But what would this Christian self be like? Would it worship God and follow his commandments? Certainly, but the difference between Christian and non-Christian selves would run far deeper than a set of beliefs or a moral code. Augustine's conception of the Christian self was most essentially concerned with the trajectory of the soul. If the self of ontological conceit had engendered a way of being whose fundamental motion was one of "going outside itself" in its unreflective enslavement to the immediacy of lust, the new self would have to change this motion to recover a truer way of being and a truer ontology. Instead of moving away, the Christian self in Augustine's view would be fundamentally defined by its perpetual trajectory toward its own depths to rout out Godless desires and conform one's soul to the deep truths and will of God. In a most profound way, the Christian self would *be* this reflective trajectory. Its existence would be transformed by this motion, through which it would purify and create itself. This inward trajectory was the precondition for Christian activity.

For Augustine, to become a Christian is to be perpetually engaged in this hermeneutics of the self. To be a Christian self, that is, *to be,* is to be a confessing self: a self that has itself as an object of deep discernment. The confessing self has the perpetual task of finding and telling the truth about itself, for it is only through this ceaseless confession that the

Christian can be a being capable of *truly* embracing Christian meta-physics and Christian moral standards. Augustine believes that in absence of confession the ontology of conceit and the "slippery slope" toward the lust for dominion continually reemerge. Put simply, in absence of the practice of the deep self-reflection and self-discipline according to God's light in confession, vanity would assert itself and the self would be too dispersed and multiple to be a responsible, just, and charitable Christian human being.

To be just is not simply a matter of occasional reflection for Augustine. Instead, the self must strive to *be* a deeply reflective confessing being: always. To be a confessing self is an endless and demanding course requiring the continuous consumption of one's life and one's energy. Yet for Augustine, the life and quality and quantity of energy that one gains through confession far surpass what is expended. To put it in these terms of comparative cost and benefit, however, is much too modern. For Augustine, it was a question of *being or nothingness*. The trajectory of the soul—toward or away from itself and God—within one's daily life determined the larger trajectory of one's life: toward justice and Being on the one hand, or the "slippery slope" toward domination and nothingness on the other.

The slippery slope was far easier to follow in this fallen world than the ascending path toward justice and God. Slaves took the former direction, those struggling for freedom took the latter. The self as it occurred in the fallen world was, as long as it remained in an unreflective state, insufficient for the struggle for freedom. The confessing self was a creation that might make this struggle—this journey—possible, and this journey would eventually make confession easier. God was essential to both.

The fallen self, however, with its lusts and deeply buried dark drives, would never simply be transcended while humans lived on earth. Rather, it would always lurk in the background, a source of suspicion that always called for further reflection. Human evil was too ubiquitous, too deeply rooted, and too recalcitrant for the confessing self ever to cease its inward gaze.

Conversion: The Birth of the Confessing Self

Augustine's life before conversion was not completely devoid of self-reflection. For years he was aware of and disturbed by his sexual lusts.

Yet when reflection was not completely absent, it was at best intermittent and false in Augustine's view. Augustine the confessor reflects on his preconversion life as one in which he was a slave to his lusts and his pride. When he saw evil within: "I very much preferred to excuse myself and accuse some other thing that was in me but was not I" (*Confessions*, 5.10).[15] Of his iniquity Augustine writes: "I had known it, but I had pretended not to see it, had deliberately looked the other way and let it go from my mind" (8.7).

In short, Augustine had tried to avoid self-reflection, and where he could not avoid it, he attempted to view the origin of evil in such a way that he would not have to identify it as his own willful error and thus consider it more seriously. Augustine was reflective in the sense that he was consumed with questions on the nature of evil and God, but he was not truly *self*-reflective in the deep sense that would later seem so unavoidable to him. These former philosophical questions had a distance from his inner soul which they would never have after his conversion.

Augustine's conversion occurs after Ponticianus tells him and Alypius about the conversion of two officials prompted by a written account of the life of Saint Anthony. The experience of conversion as the birth of deep self-reflection is striking in the passage that follows:

> This was the story Ponticianus told. But You, Lord, while he was speaking, *turned me back towards myself, taking me from behind my own back* where I had put myself all the time that I preferred not to see myself. And you *set me there before my own face* that I might *see* how vile I was, how twisted and unclean and spotted and ulcerous. *I saw myself* and was horrified; but there was *no way to flee from myself.* If I tried to turn my gaze from myself, there was Ponticianus telling what he was telling; *and again You were setting me face to face with myself, forcing me upon my own sight, that I might see my iniquity* and loathe it. I had known it, but I had pretended not to see it, had deliberately looked the other way and let it go from my mind. (*Confessions*, 8.7; my emphasis)

Conversion, for Augustine, is not most fundamentally a change in "belief." Speaking to God of his thoughts before conversion, Augustine says: "I believed that You were . . . and that in Christ Your Son Our Lord, and in the Holy Scriptures which the authority of Your Catholic

---

15. Augustine's debate with the Manichees should be situated within the overriding issue of deep self-consciousness.

Church acknowledges, You had established the way of man's salvation" (*Confessions*, 7.7). Yet the explicit faith in Christianity was superficial insofar as it remained outside of the inner movements of his soul, movements that implicated the self at this deep and truest level in a very conceited metaphysics. If in conversion one comes *truly* to face God for the first time, the equally profound change underlying this experience is that the self comes *truly* to face *itself* in God's light: its "iniquity" and iniquity's implications. It is a fundamental change in the self's being which transforms the quality that God has for the self and the self's relation to God.

For Augustine, becoming a confessing self is the most traumatic experience of his life. At the age of thirty-one, he undergoes a transformation as profound as any transformation of the self in Western history. This is not to say that Augustine's conversion is a watershed event that marks the birth of the confessing self. Augustine was by no means the first confessor. Yet his own life is divided by this critical disjuncture: on one side Augustine dwells as a nonconfessing being, a type of being he would later despise; and on the other he is a confessing self, a self that earlier was incomprehensible to him. That he understood such a transformation as the beginning of a radically new life should not surprise us.

"The day was come when I stood naked in my own sight and my conscience accused me" (*Confessions*, 8.7). In the passage quoted at length above, Augustine declares repeatedly in astonishment the experience of becoming a deeply self-reflective being. These are the repetitious cries of one who confronts—in this case becomes—the unbelievable. At first Augustine felt horrified and trapped, but finally there was "no way to flee" from confession. Augustine has become a confessing self.

Being-as-Confession: "What Am I?"

Face to face with himself, Augustine asks, "What then am I, O my god? What nature am I?" (*Confessions*, 10.17). Augustine finds no simple answer to this question, and he continues to ask it in various ways throughout his life. At one point, however—a moment of considerable insight, as noted above—he discovers an answer that refers back to the question itself. At the end of a wrenching inner debate over whether the church should resonate with beautiful melodies or with bland monotonic psalms (to prevent ensnaring pleasures) as well as how his own desires might be implicated in the answers he offers, Augustine writes: "I have become a question to myself" (10.33). Augustine will ask the question "What am I?" endlessly, but each time he asks, the question will further illustrate the truth of this assertion. Augustine *is* as a question to himself.

This self-understanding gives rise to another question, however: *Why* does Augustine affirm being a confessing self? Why is Augustine a question to himself? Given the thoroughness of Augustine's confessions, his ceaseless efforts to uncover deep reasons or motives underneath each thought and action, it is not surprising that he addresses this question, or that this question leads him to explore other dimensions of the question "What am I?" For Augustine, the questions "what" and "why" endlessly refer to one another.

Hence, in trying to understand Augustine as a confessor, we must keep these questions in close proximity to each other and, further, recall the difference between the manner in which Augustine poses the question "What am I?" and the way it was posed by nonconfessing selves. With Augustine, the question, which had previously been predominantly ontological, becomes inextricably connected with a depth psychology of the soul. Unlike Plato's approach, Augustine's attempt to answer this question will be full of impassioned accounts of the soul's secret desires and hidden thoughts. Yet the ontological dimension of self-reflection remains strong in the confessing self's questioning. To confess thoroughly is constantly to shift back and forth between psychological and ontological questions whenever they lead to one another. Hence Augustine's understanding of confession moves to and fro, partaking in both of these spheres.

To the question "What am I?" Augustine answers: "A life powerfully various and manifold and immeasurable" (*Confessions,* 10.17). The fallen life, he discovers, is a multiplicity that is continually scattered in its involvement in the world. Be it food, sex, our desire for praise, or beautiful sights and sounds, our relationships with other human beings and things in the world cut through us, divide us, push us out of focus, and decenter us. In an unreflective state, we generally do not engage with other beings and things as whole human beings. Rather, the external world speaks to and incites various parts of the body and soul, generally at the expense of the self as a whole. Before becoming a confessing self, the self is constantly in a state of being "scattered abroad in multiplicity"

(10.29). And such a self tends to objectify and erode the integrity of the world.

Augustine examines his will and finds that even—indeed, *especially*—his inner dimension is discordant. Although most parts of the body obey the will on command, Augustine discovers that the will does not *obey itself*: "The body more readily obeyed the slightest wish of the mind . . . than the mind obeyed itself in carrying out its own great will which could be achieved simply by willing" (*Confessions*, 8.8). The problem is that the will "does not totally will" (8.9) because it is divided within itself. Arguing against the Manichees that there is one extremely divided will within us rather than simply two natures, Augustine says, "If there be as many contrary natures in man as there are wills in conflict with one another, then there are not two natures in us but several" (8.10). (Augustine and the Manichees reject the latter conclusion.)

For Augustine, the self as divided is "monstrousness" and a "sickness of the soul" (*Confessions*, 8.9). As we have seen, this division is rooted in the ontology of conceit in which all fallen human beings dwell before deep self-reflection. The divided self is bonded to the world in an immediacy of desire in which it enslaves, distracts, and weakens itself, and endlessly attempts to dominate the world around it. But in addition to the evil that it fosters, this self cannot face God, the condition of its being, in such an uncontrolled, dispersed, and impure state. The dispersed self is scattered in every direction except the one that faces God. Unable to face God, the scattered self moves toward nonbeing and eternal death.

The goal of confession—a goal that can never be attained completely and with certainty on earth—is to unify and purify this multiplicity: to prepare the self to face God. According to Augustine, the *very act of confession*, above and beyond the specific contents it addresses, is unifying.

The Unified Self: Confession as Re-Membering the Dismembered

To confess is to stand face to face with oneself, to search the depths of the self endlessly and proclaim the truths that one discerns. But one faces oneself not fundamentally to examine what one is in the pure present moment of the confession. For Augustine, the present is infinitely minute and has no duration. The present *is* as merciless "ceasing to be" (*Confessions*, 11.14), an infinitely rapid "becoming past." Only God is pure presence; humans are condemned on earth to be "divided up in time . . . and the deepest places in [their souls] are torn by it" (11.29). The infinitely fast, infinitely fleeting present moment scatters the self in relentless, uncontrolled change. Confession as a human act occurs in time, and hence if the self faces the self in the present moment, the self that the self reflects on has always ceased to be instantaneously. In confession one does not face the self in the pure present, however, because to do so would be to sacrifice the self further to dispersion in the cutting edge of time. Instead, confession makes the self present by holding its past more stably before itself.

The self confesses as a temporal being that has a history it *presents* to itself in memory. Indeed, the self *is* this history. Its action in the lightning-fast present is dominated and "weighed down by customs" (*Confessions*, 8.9). The self *is not* an ephemeral wisp existing solely in the present with "no duration," and hence it cannot know itself if it takes itself to be this sort of being. The self must know itself as a fundamentally temporally extended being, for although the self continually *ceases to be in the present moment* because the present moment continually ceases to be, the self that was present does not cease to exist altogether. Rather, it becomes lodged in the self's past, a past that is not only capable of being *presented* frequently in memory, but further presents itself indirectly through its uncanny propensity to *make the present* through the inertia of one's past being, customs, and habits. (Indeed, for Augustine, the extent to which the past makes the present "behind one's back" is inversely related to the extent to which it is presented in remembering.) Hence to face itself truly and stably, the confessing self must remember itself.

Confession as *remembering* the self partially escapes the tyrannical scattering of the present and thus begins to *unify* the self by transferring its attention and the trajectory of its being to the stabler presence of the self's past in memory. In remembering, the self that was tossed and torn helplessly in the violent waves of the sea's surface dives into the relative stillness of its depths where it can regain more composure and control. By remembering, the self—as much as is possible in this life—escapes the cutting edge of time. In memory, the self can abide and hence become an object for its own continuous considered reflection. One way Augustine escaped self-reflection before conversion was by dwelling in the fleeting presence of desire. When he had seen his iniquity, he "had deliberately looked the other way and let it go from [his] mind"—he did not remember it. When Augustine writes of being "turned back" on himself, he speaks of the reflective trajectory of the gaze within, but inseparable from this is a "turning back" on the self as a historical being. Turning back in the temporal sense is remembering: holding the past that one is present before oneself, so that one cannot flee from and hence avoid oneself.

That confession is to face, examine, and understand oneself as a temporally extended being is indicated not only by Augustine's theoretical insights, but by the biographical content of the *Confessions* as well, in which Augustine remembers himself beginning with his infancy and continuing through his ongoing struggles with pride. Augustine attempts to hold his whole life present before himself as a phenomenon for ceaseless overturning, inquiry, and suspicion. Hence it should be no surprise that he refers to confession repeatedly as an act of remembering. When asking God's help in confession, he says, "Grant me . . . to re-traverse now in memory the past ways of my error" (*Confessions,* 4.1). In proclaiming to confess for the love of God, Augustine writes that he is "passing again in the bitterness of remembrance over my most evil ways that Thou mayest thereby grow ever lovelier to me" (2.1). In proclaiming the integrity of his confession, Augustine writes: "Behold my heart, O my God, look deep within it; see how I remember" (4.6).

In addition to the notion that confession begins to unify the self by *present-ing* the self in memory—a present that is less victimized by the ceasing to be of the present moment—remembering unifies the self in another sense, which Augustine addresses in Book X of the *Confessions.* Augustine begins the first section of Book X with the plea, "Let me know Thee" (*Confessions,* 10.1). This, of course, is a reiteration of the plea of the *Confessions* and, more generally, the plea of Augustine's life. To know God, one must confess the truths of one's soul to him and will to extirpate what is evil in his light. Thus he writes: "He that does the truth comes to light. I wish to do it in confession" (10.1). Knowledge of God and self-knowledge are inextricably intertwined. Yet in his ceaseless questioning of both, he runs up against the problem of memory: for "how shall I find You if I am without memory of You?" (10.17). Similarly, with respect to the self, Augustine writes, "In my memory too I meet myself" (10.8). Indeed, everything the self knows lies there. If Augustine is to "do truth" thoroughly, he will have to examine the part of him that contains and recalls truths. Hence the examination of memory.

In Augustine's first attempt to grasp memory in Book X, he refers to it metaphorically as "the fields and vast palaces . . . where are stored . . . the innumerable images of material things brought to it by the senses . . . the thoughts we think" and "the affections of the mind" (*Confessions*, 10.8, 10.17). Augustine is overawed by memory: "Great is this power of memory, a thing, O my God, to be in awe of, a profound and immeasurable multiplicity. . . . In the innumerable fields and dens and caverns of my memory, innumerably full of innumerable kinds of things . . . in and through all these does my mind range, and I move swiftly from one to another and I penetrate them as deeply as I can but find no end" (*Confessions*, 10.17).[16]

For Augustine, memory is metaphorically conceived of as a spreading, limitless room within (*Confessions*, 10.8), which is impressed by sensations, thoughts, and emotions as they pass in the present (11.27). While things are kept distinct and those entering by different senses are stored apart in their right categories (10.8), for the most part things in memory are scattered and unarranged (10.11). For Augustine, the way in which things are contained in memory is primarily a result of the manner and order in which they were experienced. Hence their scatteredness corresponds to the scatteredness of the infinitely fast, infinitely fleeting present in which our experiences and we ourselves are scattered.

As brute storage alone, memory is of little use to Augustine, for it embodies the quality of dispersion that is so problematic for him. It is only in conjunction with its power of *thoughtful re-membering* that memory's value is manifested. When one remembers things in memory, one "places within reach," "collects out of dispersion," and "draws together" things that were scattered in the immeasurable depths of memory (*Confessions*, 10.11). Augustine makes explicit the relation between *cogito* (I think) and *cogo* (I put together) (10.11). Thus, when one thinks about the self, one collects the self out of its dispersed form in the depths of memory and places it together within reach. Augustine is quick to add, however, that "if I ceased to give thought to [things] for quite a short space of time, they would sink again and fall away into the more remote recesses of the memory" (10.11). For the drawing together to be effective, it must be continuous.

16. It is worthy of note that while spatial metaphors are important in Augustine's understanding of memory, he is explicitly uncomfortable with them as well. He says to God in 10.25: "And indeed why do I seek in what place of my memory You dwell as though there were places in my memory?"

Let us further explore this relationship between memory and the self. Is it simply that memory is a part of the self and the self is something that can be remembered? The relationship Augustine sees is much deeper than this, for indeed he identifies the self with memory: "This thing I am" (*Confessions*, 10.17). The self *is* the manifold and constantly expanding field of memory and the scattered sensations, thoughts, and feelings therein. One does not simply *have* a past, a memory, thoughts, and desires; for Augustine, one *is* these things. Thus to confess—to remember—one's thoughts and desires is not simply to collect *them* out of dispersion, but to collect *the self* out of dispersion, to draw the self together. As memory, the self is both the locus in which its existence is "impressed" as scattered and the possibility for purposively drawing together this scatteredness. It is this latter possibility that Augustine seeks to realize in confession.

The task of collecting the self is an endless process for Augustine. New experiences continually scatter the self, parts of the self that are placed within reach "fall away" if they are ignored for a "short period of time," and the self is immeasurably deep and can "find no end" to these depths. If one is to lessen the uncontrolled quality of being scattered, the evil that may lurk in the scattered depths of the soul, and the even greater evil of being behind one's own back, one must collect oneself and face oneself continually: one must remember. Remembering *as such* is a focusing, healing, strengthening, and disciplining activity in Augustine's view.

Humble Confession

Thus far we have discussed two ways in which remembering as such begins to unify the self: first, by partially decreasing the scatteredness that is generated when attention is on the fleeting present, and second, by collecting out of dispersion a self that is scattered. The substantive manner in which the confessing self is remembered is also extremely important to Augustine, however, for it *undermines the false ontology of conceit*, fosters a new understanding of the self, and constitutes a different type of self based on this understanding. Through his own confessions, Augustine shows that deep self-reflection leads to a very powerful comprehension of one's finitude, dependence, and iniquity. The conceited self was able to uphold an ontology in which it was the origin of being only by being "behind its own back." Facing itself in God's light, the self discovers a very different order of things.

In attempting to know and speak the truth about himself, Augustine immediately confronts his own finitude; he discovers that he is a life he cannot entirely know. Rather than being the origin of truth that the self of ontological conceit believes itself to be, Augustine realizes that he cannot even grasp *himself* totally and with certainty. Augustine's forgotten infancy is accessible to him only indirectly through the accounts of others and through his observations of other infants.

These limits have a powerful impact on Augustine: "I am loath, indeed, to count it [his infancy] as part of the life I live in this world. For it is buried in the darkness of the forgotten as completely as the period earlier still that I spent in my mother's womb" (*Confessions*, 1.7). Yet Augustine cannot simply discount his infancy any more than he can discount the forgotten depths of his soul which he discovers can never be rendered completely intelligible. For Augustine *is* this hidden depth, this partially hidden life, which demands to be known for the truths it reveals and the evils it hides. Even his prenatal life haunts him: "I was conceived in iniquity and in sin my mother nourished me in the womb, then where, my God, where, O Lord, where or when was I, Your servant, innocent?" (1.7).

The answer is nowhere and never. Through Christian self-reflection in the light of God, one discovers that instead of being the pure origin of morality that oneself and others should live by, the self is an actuality ridden with imperfection, impurity, and iniquity.

Just as Augustine is neither the origin of nor the complete possessor of truth and goodness, so too confession shows him to be a *dependent being* rather than self-originating. Recalling his infancy, he is in awe of his dependence on the miracle of his mother's nurturing. His account of his slow evolution toward conversion and fully embracing God is saturated with continual acknowledgment of the way in which the people and events around him allowed him to develop—often inadvertently through the invisible hand of God. For Augustine, to think deeply about the being of oneself and that of the surrounding world is to recognize an abundance of harmony and beauty which signifies a greater being on which all things depend. Of the things in the world Augustine says: "They cried out in a great voice: 'He made us.' My question was my gazing upon them and their answer was their beauty" (*Confessions*, 10.6). The final book of the *City of God* lists many of the miseries of human existence on earth, but it is also full of an appreciation of the world as overflowing with beauty and miracles. Not only the sky, the earth, the sea, food, health, and the "soothing coolness of breezes," but "even the body, which is something we have in common with brute creation . . . even here what evidence we find of the goodness of God, of the providence of the mighty creator!" (*City of God*, 20.24). For Augustine, to look deep within is to realize the overwhelming extent to which we depend on miracles that originate not in ourselves, but elsewhere. Only having grasped "the truth that is within them" can people see that God is the condition of all beings (*Confessions*, 10.6).

God of Self-Consciousness

This realization, which emerges with deep self-reflection, feeds and shapes an intensifying dynamic of confession. In his state of dependence, Augustine realizes that we must live in God's grace to be truly satisfied, strong human beings. Indeed, to live in any sense that is not dying we must live in his grace. To achieve God's grace, however, the self must *face God*. To turn away from God—his Truth, his Goodness—is to lose his light (e.g., *Confessions*, 5.3). Augustine's insight that "no man loses Thee, unless he goes from Thee" (4.9) provides him with a spring of hope to which he can and must constantly return. Yet the hope harbors an anxiety that fuels relentless and continual deep self-reflection. For how can a self that is a torn, scattered multiplicity face God? How can a self that is immeasurably deep and cannot grasp all that it is *know* that it faces God? The answer to both questions is that it cannot in any sense that is absolutely secure and final.

The hope springing from the insight that "no man loses Thee, unless he goes from Thee" would die in the despair of uncertainty were it not continually reborn in confession. Through perpetual confession, the self must draw itself together, place itself within reach, so that it can face itself toward God and conform to his will in as complete and unified a manner as possible. It cannot allow dispersed parts of the self to "fall away" from God in pride and lust. It must probe its depths endlessly for evil thoughts and desires that might turn the self unwittingly away from the Being to which it owes its being.

Yet the creation of the confessing self is not fundamentally a heroic feat of the self which must be accomplished in order to face God. For Augustine, God dwells too deeply within and is too thoroughly the condition of our being to be merely the goal or endpoint of the self's action. Rather, God is internal to the process of remembering. The Christian self's relationship to God is one in which *both* the self and God make the self more self-conscious.

The act that initiates the empowering self-God relationship is less the remembering than the *will to* tell the truth about the self and do nothing to deceive God. When Augustine exclaims, "Woe is me! See I do not hide my wounds" (*Confessions*, 10.28), he is not proclaiming a complete and "successful" confession, for there is always a surplus of truths and evils far exceeding those that can be discovered and disclosed. Rather, he is expressing his willful *desire* to reveal the truth about himself—as it appears in God's light—to himself and God. It is the purity of this desire to show God everything that is all-important. Thus Augustine asks God to "behold his heart" and see his will to confess.

When one wills to place himself before God, God participates in the development of the self's deep self-consciousness. "I entered into my own depths, with You as my guide; and I was able to do it because You were my helper" (*Confessions*, 7.10). Augustine's God is the God of self-consciousness. He makes the weak strong, not by bestowing on them an abstract power, but by facilitating the transformation of the nonreflective self of the ontology of conceit into a confessing self. It is in God's grace that "every weak man is made strong in that he is made conscious of his weakness" (10.3). When Augustine refers to God as "You in whom all that is scattered in me is brought into one" (10.40), he is not writing of an external power that comes out of the sky and carefully makes the self a unity, as if God were using his hands to reassemble a shattered egg. God is within, and he unifies the self by succoring self-consciousness, by turning the self's trajectory inward in deep Christian remembering.

Compulsive Confession

Thus we begin to see what is at stake and what is possible for Augustine's confessing self. For Augustine, the choice is between being a nonreflective self dwelling in a world that is falsely revealed through a conceited ontology, a self scattered in an immediacy of desire in which it enslaves and is enslaved; or a reflective way of being that tends toward increasing unity, strength, justice, and God. The choice is between non-being and being.

Out of Augustine's understanding of the self, the world, and God comes a deep and continuous self-examination that restlessly strives to collect, penetrate, and bring under control all parts of the self. Having confessed about his life from his infancy to the period following his conversion, Augustine proceeds relentlessly to examine his present condition according to the truths of Christian morality. Largely freed from the grasp of sexual concupiscence (though not in his dreams), he moves toward an increasingly meticulous study of himself. Nothing escapes his gaze:

> As for the allurement of sweet scents, I am not much troubled: when they are absent I do not seek them; when they are present I do not refuse them; yet at any time I do not mind being without them. At least so I seem to myself; *perhaps I am deceived.* For that darkness is lamentable in which the possibilities in me are hidden from myself: so that my mind, questioning itself upon its own powers, feels that it cannot lightly trust its own report: because what is already in it does for the most part lie hidden. (*Confessions*, 10.32; my emphasis)

The "hermeneutics of suspicion" passes from one thing to the next. Augustine examines the "pleasures of the ear" and discovers that while he is not held as persistently by them, he still "find[s] it hard to know what is their due place" (*Confessions*, 10.33). His description of the inner dilemma brought by this problem is amazing. Wondering if he may desire church melodies in the wrong way, he says:

> At times indeed it seems to me that I am paying them greater honour than is. their due—when, for example, I feel that by those holy words my mind is kindled more religiously and fervently to a flame of piety because I hear them sung than if they were not sung: and I observe that all the varying emotions of my spirit have modes proper to them in voice and song, whereby, by some secret affinity, they are made more alive. It is not good that the mind should be enervated by this bodily pleasure. But it often ensnares me, in that the bodily sense does not accompany the reason as following after it in proper order, but having been admitted to aid the reason strives to run before it and take the lead. In this matter I sin unawares, and then grow aware.
>
> Yet there are times when through too great a fear of this temptation, I err in the direction of over-severity—even to the point sometimes of

wishing that the melody of all the lovely airs . . . should be banished not
only from my own ears, but from the Church's as well. (10.33)

After more turmoil Augustine hesitantly and tentatively decides that
church music is probably for the better. But the outcome is really unimportant. What is important, and the reason I quoted the passage at such
length, is the extent to which Augustine has problematized all corners of
himself. The *act* of listening to church music is of relatively little importance compared to the problematic pleasures, desires, and motives that
may lurk beneath. The latter are buried deep; sometimes they are invisible. Always they are suspect. The slightest impurity threatens to scatter
the self back into the madness of conceit, far from itself, far from God.[17]

Gareth Matthews has made some interesting observations on the
important differences between Augustine's *Si Fallor, Sum* (If I am mistaken, I am) and Descartes's *Cogito Ergo Sum*.[18] And certainly Augustine's confessing self does not occupy the position of the *subiectum* in
the sense that Heidegger finds exemplified in Descartes's notion of
man.[19] Nevertheless, perhaps there are some dimensions of Augustine
which resonate deeply in the philosophical chambers of much of modernity. Perhaps it is not the *cogito*, but the broadest contours of *Confession
Ergo Sum*, which Augustine shares at a distance with modernity. We must
wait until the following chapter to decide with respect to modernity, but
for Augustine, confession is clearly the human condition for human
being. God, of course, is the ultimate Being of beings for Augustine, but

17. To view the passages above as stemming from "Augustine's hatred of worldly
existence" is an error. It is impurity within the self that is at stake here for Augustine. In
Augustine's view, beautiful colors, the sound of birds singing, delicious foods, etc., were
blessings (*City of God*, 22.24). Indeed, despite a highly developed sense of the miseries that
are a part of human existence, Augustine still views the world as "that miracle of miracles"
(21.19). Yet the world was most importantly a polyphonic *sign* of the God who created it.
When enjoyment of the world became an end in itself and obliterated the primacy of one's
awareness of God, Augustine sought to eliminate or contain it. Yet this is a problem of the
self, not of the world. The world could be loved, but it had to be loved "justly" with an eye
toward the "intrinsic value of things" (*On Christian Doctrine*, 1.27). Desires and pleasures
that aided one's awareness of God as the condition of all being were acceptable, but they
were always dangerous, for they harbored the potential to place the self unwittingly in
God's place as the origin and ground of things.

18. Gareth B. Matthews, "Si Fallor, Sum," in *Augustine: A Collection of Critical Essays*,
ed. R. A. Markus (Garden City, N.Y.: Anchor Books, 1972), pp. 151–67.

19. Martin Heidegger, *Nietzsche, Volume 4: Nihilism*, trans. F. A. Capuzzi (San Fran-
cisco: Harper and Row, 1982), chaps. 16 and 17.

we cannot face God and hence partake in his Being unless we confess continually. As we have seen, the vanity that leads one away from confession and God leads at the same time toward "nothingness."

Strangely located in a work that affirms confession as a way of being, however, one discovers the following: "God, hear me and look upon me and see me and pity me and heal me, Thou in whose eyes I have become a question to myself: and that is my infirmity" (*Confessions*, 10.33). Be it a moment of brilliance or a simple recognition of the obvious, in this concise statement Augustine appears—if only for an instant—to peer into the heart of the confessing self and see a problem. In the depths of his soul, Augustine comes face to face with the "infirmity" that arises when the will to truth of the Christian narrative confronts the ambiguous nature of a self that is of necessity largely invisible to itself (on earth). Augustine must know himself, but to an important extent he cannot. He must remain "a question to himself." Not a question that he can affirm as a mystery, but a question that is in large part an "infirmity"—a question he must work to eliminate. This deep question he is, this question that is the source of his strength and hope, is at the same time a problem for Augustine. Yet neither the questions nor the problem can be put to rest, since each question only leads to more questions. The Christian conception of the "disease of curiosity" limits in important ways the nature of the self's interrogation of the world around it. But with respect to itself, the questioning self is driven beyond all limits. For an instant Augustine seems to find the confessing self to be worrisome. What was to lead to health appears to be the cause of infirmity.

The infirmity does not pose a fundamental challenge to the confessing self for Augustine, however. Indeed, it appears that further confession is the only solution. A little later in the text, Augustine repeats: "Again, let me examine my self more closely" (*Confessions*, 10.37). The confessing self moves toward the God who will "heal." "I beseech You, O my God, show me to myself that I may confess" (10.37). As long as Augustine's God exists, the confessing self remains impervious to any fundamental and sustained problematization.

Confessing Self: Depth and Freedom

As the confessing self's trajectory is redirected from the world toward its inner depths, it comes to understand itself in light of the motives and desires that hide there. This self is defined no longer primarily in terms of its actions, but more important, by the motives buried below. It is the latter that must be surveyed, interrogated, and controlled in a manner every bit as relentless as the way the self of conceited ontology sought to dominate all that was "other." Yet the development of the confessing self should not be reduced to being understood simply as this persistent attempt to purify the self. To see it wholly in these terms is to obfuscate the more positive aims of the confessing self, which were at least as important to Augustine. For Augustine, self-consciousness was not of value merely because of what it could control or repress. Just as important, Augustine affirmed the birth of the confessing self because it gave rise to a set of possibilities for being in the world which he believed were never before possible. The confessing self was not simply a new way of controlling an old self. Certainly it was this, and the old self could never be entirely eradicated, yet deep self-reflection gave rise to a *new self* as well. Deep self-consciousness was accompanied by two interrelated qualities that Augustine thought were almost entirely lacking in the late antique pagan self: depth and freedom. These two elements not only gave rise to new possibilities for the self, but perhaps more essentially, constituted "possibility" in a new manner—allowed it to be.

Since freedom wells forth from depth in Augustine's thinking, let us explore the latter first. There are two senses in which depth is important for Augustine. In one sense, depth is an attribute of all human beings, yet in another sense, it is an achievement only of the confessing self.

For Augustine, all people are deep beings in the sense that he identifies them with the motives and desires that lurk below their actions. Under the surface of human activity is a largely invisible interior where the real truths of the self are born and lie. These depths are for Augustine what is most real about the self, while the surface is often determined and shaped by realities largely outside of the self. To know anybody—an impossible task to complete—is to know these depths.

Interestingly, however, Augustine's realization that we are all beings with a depth is accompanied by a continuous critique of nonconfessing selves as one-dimensional, flat beings that dwell "outside" of themselves in their compulsive relationship to the world. The nonconfessing self is flat because its life is one of denying its depths. In its claim (either explicit or implicit in its way of being) to be an absolute self-originating being, the self must deny these depths, for the invisibility and ambiguity disclosed by depth threaten the self's claim to omnipotence and certainty. Further, the evils lurking beneath the surface threaten the self's claim to be worthy of being "its own rule." For Augustine, the conceited self denies the depth that it *is* and hence lives outside of this depth: its *way* of being is flat.

Living in the immediacy of desire, the self of ontological conceit and the world toward which it lusts is as shallow as the fleeting present that consumes it. It is only the disciplined inward turn of continual confession that allows the self truly to become a deep being: a being that wills to inhabit its depth. What is this relationship between the depth one becomes through turning inward and the depth that as human beings we all are?

As discussed above, the turn inward is, for Augustine, essentially a remembering of the self. In remembering, the self recalls what is absent from its attention before remembering. It collects out of dispersion what was scattered in the depths of the self and places the "forgotten" within reach of the attentive gaze. It is precisely because all selves are largely deep interiors of thoughts, desires, and feelings not present at any given time that remembering can have any meaning. A self that was totally present to itself *would not have any need to* remember itself; its consciousness at any instant would be totally identical with its being. But neither would it *be able* to remember itself; for it is the depth below the surface of attention which makes memory as such possible. For Augustine, it is the nonpresent depth of selves—the partial absence of one's being to oneself—that establishes both the desirability of and the possibility of relating to oneself in self-remembering.

It is the distance, the difference within the self between its dark nonpresent depths and its luminous present attention—this ever-shifting interstice—which provides the space for the remembering act of confession. It is the interval between the thought and the unthought which the confessing self traverses, and in the process of traversing, it changes the boundaries of a difference that is ineliminable. Every depth exposed in remembering becomes the surface of another depth. "Know thyself! Know thyself!" yearns the confessing self as it attempts to pass out of the interstice and render its dark depths in God's light. Yet no matter how much it illuminates, it remains on the edge of a beckoning darkness.

In another work Augustine states: "Gaze at the sky, the earth, the sea, and all the things which shine in them or above them, or creep or fly or

swim beneath them. They have forms because they have rhythm; take
this away and they will no longer be."[20] The rhythm of the confessing
self is the constant unfolding of its movement in the region between its
light and its darkness; a movement that can never be completed, but that
must never be discontinued lest the self lose its rhythm and "fall back
into nothingness."

As we have seen, depth is of endless concern to Augustine because of
the fallen state in which he finds humanity, and it also provides the
possibility for remembering. Remembering is, for Augustine, a transformative activity in the sense that it creates a "collected," more controlled,
more Christian self. Yet memory is transformative in another sense
equally important to Augustine. In remembering, the self makes itself
present in such a way that it is not purely identical with the parts of the
self it remembers. When the self lives in the immediacy of desire, *desires
govern* the self's perceptions and actions, and render critical discernment
of the desire itself impossible. Desire becomes identical with the self in
that it has complete sway over the self. Remembering, in contrast, allows
the self to make dark elements of itself present, while simultaneously
establishing a distance between itself and those parts of itself it discovers.
Rather than being disguised in their own false light, in confession evil
desires are critically illuminated in God's light. For Augustine, the self
makes itself present in confession in such a way that as it identifies the
evil thought, desire, or emotion as a part of itself, it simultaneously
creates a germ cell of nonidentity between itself and what is illuminated.
The light of the will to God's truth vitiates the evil that is presented and
diminishes its power to hold sway over the self. The nonidentity occurs
not through a denial of the fact that the desire is a part of the self, but
through a particular affirmation of this fact. When the desire holds sway,
it is what *makes* other things *present* (or absent) to the self, but when the
desire is placed before the self in remembering, at least for that moment,
it is not hegemonic. It is *presented* as an object by another desire (the will
to God's truth). It is precisely this particular objectification of conceited
desire which establishes a distance between the desire and the self, and
allows the self the possibility of *choosing* to separate itself from the desire.
The light of the will to truth places desire within reach, but as *placed,* the

20. Saint Augustine, *On Free Choice of the Will,* quoted in Erich Przywara, *An Augustine
Synthesis* (New York: Harper and Row, 1958), p. 16.

desires can be dis-placed from the self. In short, to know oneself, one must make present parts of the inexhaustible depths that one is, and it is this presenting that allows the self to become other than these identified depths.

It is here that we begin to see a direct connection between confession and freedom in Augustine. It is only through remembering—presenting parts of itself to itself—that there is any hope for freedom in Augustine's view. For it is only in remembering the self, with God's help and in God's light, that the self can become an object of conscious choice for itself. In absence of truthful remembering, we are not free beings, but beings dominated by habits and lusts.

All people have free will in Augustine's thought, yet most people do not will freely. True living freedom is an arduous task that can be achieved only to the extent that the self remembers deeply, truthfully, and ceaselessly in light of the will to God's truth. Only the confessing self, the self that dwells in the deep, can be free, for only this self is sufficiently unified and self-conscious to carry out the work of freedom. Yet even the confessing self is in constant danger of forgetting and slipping back into slavery.

Humans are born with the capacity for freedom, but their fallen bodies and souls and their first choices enslave them to habits and lusts that henceforth tend to overshadow and conceal their freedom. It is only when the self is held face to face with itself in conversion that it begins to be released from the tyranny of habit. As the birth of deep self-consciousness, the conversion is the point at which the self *begins* a *new* mode of being, whose essence is precisely the ability to free oneself from the causality of unconscious habit and *begin*. Reading Augustine's account of his conversion, one is struck by the sense of sudden freedom that seems to overwhelm him. "Thou hast broken my bonds" (*Confessions*, 9.1). Of his life before conversion he asks: "But where in all that long time was my free will, and from what deep sunken hiding-place was it suddenly summoned forth *in the moment in which I bowed my neck to Your easy yoke?*" (9.1; my emphasis). Yet if this transformation brings a sudden freedom from many of the past lusts that haunted him, Augustine's exuberance is soon tempered with the realization that though his new life in communion with God delivers him from the worst cares that gnawed (9.1), it by no means delivers him to a life of pure and easy truth and freedom. As Augustine looks inward, the initial flash of God's light helps him truly see and transcend the most prominent lusts of his past. Yet at the edge of this radiance is a deep, dark, hidden region that demands further interrogation and illumination. God's freeing charitable light is infinite, but only for those who will join him in diligently extending his truths into the depths of their souls. God offers freedom, but it is a freedom marked by a strong awareness of one's own present finitude and a responsibility for expanding one's boundaries most fundamentally through ceaseless confession. The *sudden freedom* of conversion calls forth an inner *struggle for freedom* that is never finished. The confessing self is free precisely because it can partially release itself from its identity with unconscious habits and desires—from the past that it is—through reflection and begin to be otherwise. Released from this causality, the will in conjunction with God is its own beginning.[21]

As a confessing self, the self actualizes the freedom with which it is born. All selves are free from being totally passive objects of the world's chain of causes, but few are free of the causal dynamics within themselves, and they have achieved this freedom only through relentless remembering. Freedom for Augustine does not come lightly or easily out of the beings we are. It is not the effortless ability to put down our pencil and rise out of our chair at an unpredictable moment. True freedom is the most arduous task humans can accomplish. Freedom demands responsibility not only because through it we become the initiators of events with important consequences that elaborate Christian practice. More primordially for Augustine, freedom demands responsibility because it is only through responsibility (as continual will to truth about the self) that freedom is released into being. It is the depth of human being that provides the possibility of the confessing self, and it is the confessing self that frees freedom.

Thoughts of Another Hue

As we have seen, Augustine's critique of the pagans and his affirmation of the confessing self are tightly connected. They are, in a sense, anti-

21. Hannah Arendt emphasizes the importance of our essential capacity to "begin" in Augustine's work, yet she fails to recognize the incredible labor that such beginning entails. Cf. Hannah Arendt, *The Human Condition* (Chicago: University of Chicago Press, 1958), p. 177.

thetical types. The former is characterized by conceit, flattening, lust, dispersion, forgetting, and movement toward evil and nothingness; the latter by humbleness, a yearning for the depth of God's voice, gathering together, remembering, and movement toward goodness and Being. Yet the connection between these types in Augustine's thought is not merely one of external opposition. Rather, they appear in Augustine as *internally intertwined*. On the one hand, the confessing self harbors dimensions of conceit deep within. This conceit is what the confessing self must always be on guard against and ceaselessly attempt to rout out of its depths. The confessing self's being is defined by this project. On the other hand, the pagan self, and more generally the nonconfessing self as it appears in Augustine, is essentially defined by its struggle with the confessing self. The pagan existence is characterized by an effort to turn away from God, willfully to deny goodness and being—his light within. This denial, ever since Adam and Eve, is finally of *willful* origin (though our fallen selves harbor propensities toward ontological conceit and denial); and a will that wills evil is an evil will. If we learn about the internal relation between the confessing self and its other through reading Augustine's reflections on his life as a confessing self, so too we grasp his understanding of the internal relation of the nonconfessing self to its other through reading Augustine's reflections on his life before confession. Even Augustine's *forgetting* his evil is characterized as *willful.* "I had known it, but I *pretended* not to see it, had *deliberately* looked the other way and let it go from my mind" (*Confessions*, 8.7; my emphasis). Granted that this willful forgetting becomes entwined with enslavement, as lusts conquer the possibilities of reflection, yet at the origin of all such slavery one finds—as with Adam and Eve—a "fault in character," a denial of God in favor of the self. With this conception of will, at the heart of both the pagan and the confessing self, is tied a notion of responsibility equally constitutive of them both.

While Augustine's analysis of the pagan illuminates a dynamic of egoism in a manner very significant for political and social philosophers today (in a world where both conceptually and practically an atomistic individualism has reached extremes exceeding even those Augustine depicted), at the same time, by focusing so exclusively on the self—its will, responsibility, iniquity, slavery—Augustine's writing tends to shift political philosophy away from structural dimensions of power that contribute to the constitution of modes of being. By concealing this dimension of power, Augustine marginalizes an important type of critical reflection and inadvertently contributes to the perpetuation of these structures. Augustine's focus on the self and will, his marginalization of institutional analysis, is linked to power not only through a perpetuating concealment, however. More fundamentally, Augustine—his manner of rendering certain things visible and others invisible—contributes to the development of a form of power whose effects proliferate in the very fabric of his texts. Augustine's particular way of focusing on selves—their gazes, desires, wills—allows him to reach them in their isolate singularity, and it is at this level that the profoundest effects of power operate. The confessing self is fastened to the imperative to discover and embrace God's truths deep within. This imperative means that everything within and outside the self should be revealed in God's light, and what does not shine forth should, one way or another, be transformed or silenced and reduced to the nothing it really is. The "deep-self" focus of Augustine's analysis allows him carefully to isolate and target what does not fit—to locate the will and desire behind the phenomenon, to establish clear responsibility and guilt, to deploy fear and hope in order to correct the "fault."

This power embedded in Augustine's texts aims deep into the souls of those who encounter them. Though Augustine's primary focus is not politics as we tend to understand it today, his texts are political, if by this we mean that which aims to and does effect the ethical comportment and behavior of other human beings. They are persistently engaged in a kind of soulcraft. Not a soulcraft focusing primarily on knowledge of the Good, but rather one addressing the relation between this knowledge and selves characterized by a deeply tenacious recalcitrance. It is a type of soulcraft that persistently focuses on manners of inducing selves into the practice of its own proliferation. We have focused on the proliferation of confession into a self's depth. Yet confession proliferates between selves as well: confession is a relationship within a self and between the self and God, but in its ideal form—as in the *Confessions,* the *publicatio sui,*[22] circles of friends such as the one to which Augustine belonged—it is also *public declaration.* In this sense, it multiplies its effects through a politics of exemplarity. Augustine's *Confessions* provides an exemplary model toward which *others* might strive. This striving is motivated by the hope of eternal life and as good and free a life as one might live on earth,

22. Cf. Foucault, "Christianity and Confession."

as well as the fear of evil self-enslavement and eternal hellfire for non-confessors. Augustine puts his purpose succinctly: "But to whom am I telling this? Not to Thee, O my God, but in Thy presence I am telling it to my own kind . . . to that small part of the human race that may come upon these writings. . . . Simply that I and any other who may read may realize out of what depths we must cry to Thee" (*Confessions*, 2.3). In the present context, it is not simply the recurrent theme of depth that interests us as much as the cry that resounds therefrom. The discovery of God leads to the praise of God, not only deep within, but out into the world. As with the rest of God's creatures, the truth of the self's being is to cry out: "He made me." Humans utter this cry in confession; hence confession's internal mode of proliferation is the exemplary publicization of one's journey in depth as revealed through God's light.

Augustine's portrayal of the confessing self and the pagan self ensures in advance the hegemony—indeed, the ubiquity—of God's light, for both appear only from the perspective of this light: the self attempting to will obedience to God's truth and the evil defier of this truth. An important aim of this chapter has been to show that Augustine's writing was significantly shaped by a concern about the flattening, edge-obliterating imperatives of pagan conceit and a desire to formulate a space for a more polyphonous appreciation of beings as creations of God. The confessing self was a central figure in this project. Yet if God and Christianity are in any sense contestable or at least not the only voices worthy of our ears, then an underside to Augustine's project begins to appear. The will to appreciate God's polyphony becomes at least in part a totalizing Reason/Faith aimed at conquering and silencing *its* others. Between Augustine's confessing self and all he views as non-Christian ontological conceit is a multiplicity of alternatives, a variety of differences whose interminglings might form fertile edges and offer possibilities for existence worthy of our embrace, consideration, tolerance, engagement, awe, encroachment: something more than an assignment to nothingness. Depth becomes not only a space for appreciating mystery beyond the conceited self, a space for God's various voices, but also a space for disqualifying other voices under false pretenses employing false hopes and false fears. (Falseness here is rooted in the Christian narrative's claim to a monopolistic relation to truth.)

I think both of these dynamics are significant aspects of Augustine's writing. On the one hand, there is the Augustine who views the world to

be the infinitely rich incarnation of God's Word. This world is so pregnant with meaning that all we can do—indeed, the highest thing we can
do—is participate in an endless process of deciphering and elaborating
its allegorical being. Each event overflows with significations, and the
church is to be the site of polyphonous interpretation of an inexhaustible
world. Interpreting "increase and multiply and fill the earth" as an injunction to embark on a journey of interpretive profusion, Augustine
writes: "Is not this statement understood in many ways, not by deceit of
error, but by various kinds of true interpretation? Thus do man's off-
spring increase and multiply" (*Confessions*, 13.24). Exemplifying a "fecundity of reason," the church is to be a kind of allegory of allegory: a
community where allegories proliferate whose ultimate meaning is to
deepen our sense of the fundamentally allegorical nature of the world as
God's Word.

At the same time, however, there is the imperialist church. The church
that, like Augustine in *City of God*, is so ungenerous in its reading of most
of what lies beyond a particular vision of Christianity. The church that
views the other as nothingness and others as beings who will either be
brought toward the One True God or suffer eternal hellfire. One might
describe Roman imperialism as one obsessed with unending spatial conquest. Augustine is a penetrating critic of this imperialism, but he is
perhaps implicated in an imperialism of his own. Here I have in mind a
more temporal imperialism, an imperialism narrating the past ultimately
as the work of God in a way that signifies and aims to engender the
increasing and ultimately singular hegemony of his Word in the future.
This is an imperialism that seeks with the weight of a totally Christian
construction of personal and worldly history to constitute a desire—a
futural yearning—for God and his One True City. Finally, for Augustine,
there will be only one city—not on earth but in eternity—and as in
Constantine's Constantinople there will be no pagan temples, no sign of
an other that is not of God. Rome had many gods, but it could not
tolerate what was not Rome. Augustine's One True God is infinitely
polyphonous but does not tolerate God's others. We know what this
meant for the Donatists, Pelagians—and the pagans received a rather
wholesale condemnation. As God's light becomes weaker in the modern
age, the proximity between and meanings of the church allegorical and
the church imperial become problematic in a way that they weren't for

Augustine (but probably were for Augustine's non-Augustinian contemporaries).

As God recedes from the modern world, Foucault and others have argued that man attempts to step to the throne as that being in whom one is promised the discovery of truth and being. With this shift, the confessing self undergoes important changes. While God's voice has an ineliminable and significant dimension of transcendence and mystery, and the experience of this is part of what is sought as one journeys within, the modern confessing self journeys into its depths to discover a truth without excess or mystery, absolute identity. This drive threatens to intensify the dangers already present in Augustine. The nature of the modern journey within and its dangers are the topics of the next chapter. When we turn to Merleau-Ponty in Chapter 4, we will explore a concept of depth that, I believe, seeks to retain what is most admirable in Augustine's thought while avoiding its problems. In the final chapter I return to assess the virtues and dangers of Augustine's project in light of Foucault and Merleau-Ponty.

3 · Foucault

Foucault's Critique of Modernity

In *Discipline and Punish,* Foucault writes: "The man described for us, whom we are invited to free, is already in himself the effect of a subjection much more profound than himself. A 'soul' inhabits him and brings him to existence, which is itself a factor in the mastery that power exercises over the body. The soul is the effect and instrument of a political anatomy; the soul is the prison of the body."[1] Foucault rejects the soul—this "prison"—as well as the belief that it should be the ground and target of our explorations for deep truth and freedom. Instead, he seeks to ask "What is man?" at the boundaries of man's being; at the frequently battered and embattled surfaces where man confronts his others. For Foucault argues that it is the interrogation of man's interiors, the questioning of depths below surfaces of carefully bound and circumscribed realities which so characterizes the operation of power in modernity that he seeks to thwart. Depth, the dimension in which Augustine sought truth, freedom and, increasingly unified subjectivity, is for Foucault the dimension in which human beings are identified, interrogated, constituted: depth is the dimension of subjugation. The constellation of truths, and the freedom that hinges on the progres-

1. Michel Foucault, *Discipline and Punish,* trans. Alan Sheridan (New York: Random House, Vintage Books, 1979), p. 30. Further citations from this edition are given directly in the text.

sive discovery of these truths, is the promise that lurks in depth and draws people deeper and deeper into subjugating examinations of themselves and others—deeper into the prison and its reign of continuous, pure light. The crystalline transparency of Augustinian heaven, where even our internal organs would be visible, is for Foucault a nightmare toward which aspects of modernity press.

In this section I explore Foucault's critique of modernity on two levels. First, I briefly develop the context in which the objectification and subjectification of selves occur in modernity, and highlight some of the disciplines, discourses, and institutions that help make them possible. My purpose here is not to summarize Foucault's project as a whole, but rather to illuminate very selectively dimensions of it that serve as indispensable groundwork for understanding and situating my reading of Foucault in the remainder of this chapter and the ones that follow. In particular, I focus on the way in which the interplay of depth, objectifying and subjectifying illumination, and the will to truth have been central to the constitution and control of groups and individuals in modernity.

Second, I attempt to elucidate Foucault's metatheoretical understanding of this phenomenon as it is elaborated in *The Order of Things*. Although at this level we lose much of the texture found in the genealogical Foucault, we gain a level of generality that offers us insights into the central understandings of modernity governing his work; insights that are quite valuable and less visible in his microanalyses.

In the following section I explore the ethical position animating Foucault's critique of modernity. Foucault's alternative would have us not searching deep within ourselves for truth, but rather creating ourselves at the edges of our being through a dialogical artistic ethos.

Objectification and Subjectification

Let us situate Foucault's discussion of the production of deep subjectivity within his understanding of the broader historical context. Foucault rejects all theories of economic determinism on both historical and theoretical grounds. Yet while he denies that "in the last instance" economic systems are the ultimate subjects of history, he readily affirms that the production of subjects "cannot be studied outside their relation to the mechanisms of exploitation and domination." Rather, subjectification and economic exploitation coexist in "complex and circular relations."[2] Foucault maintains that the proliferation of techniques of subjectification was largely linked to the problems and demands associated with the rise of capitalism. As wealth was accumulated in increasing quantities in workshops, warehouses, and ports, a more systematic and continuous form of policing and punishment of theft was necessary to replace the old system with its dangerous spectacles and tolerated illegalities. It became necessary to make the power to punish "more regular, more effective, more constant and more detailed in its effects; in short [to] increase its effects while diminishing its . . . costs" (*Discipline*, pp. 80–81). Simultaneously, the increasing emphasis on productivity and growth required that the bodies of the workers be rendered disciplined and docile to maximize their utility and to integrate them into relatively rigid mechanized processes.

Foucault refers to the sum of the disciplines, institutions, techniques, and discourses that develop to track, survey, constitute, regulate, and most importantly make more productive both individual bodies and populations as "bio-power."[3] Since the body can be utilized only if it is at once productive and obedient, "micro-powers" that constitute subjects are indispensable to political economies endlessly engaged in enhancing productivity. Although the original context of the development of these forms of power is largely the capitalist system, it has been widely deployed in other societies as well (for example, socialist and fascist).

In discussing these subjectifying practices, I focus first on the ways in which persons are objectified as soul-bearing subjects, and then I turn to Foucault's understanding of how individuals are constituted/constitute themselves as deep subjects in the modern context.

The growing emphasis placed on achieving maximum utilization and control of life was, Foucault maintains, accompanied by the development of "the art of light and the visible" (*Discipline*, p. 171). During the

2. Michel Foucault, "The Subject and Power," in Hubert L. Dreyfus and Paul Rabinow, *Michel Foucault: Beyond Structuralism and Hermeneutics*, 2d ed. (Chicago: University of Chicago Press, 1983), p. 213.

3. In his view, these mechanisms do not all come into being *simply* to meet the demands of a developing global economic system. Rather, they are heterogeneous in origin, developed to meet the requirements of local situations, and are henceforth "invested and annexed by more global phenomena." The relative causality of various historical factors varies widely and is, for Foucault, a question that must be investigated historically case by case.

classical age, military camps, workshops, schools, hospitals, asylums, housing projects, etc., began to be constructed and organized with greater attention to the principle of increasing the visibility of those contained within. Gaps, aisles, openings, walls, the position of tables and beds were designed to optimize surveyability. Groups were divided, organized, and arranged in hierarchies to facilitate inspection, and new groups were formed solely for this purpose. In addition to the profusion of this "general gaze" throughout a myriad of institutions, Foucault argues that the "threshold of visibility" within the gaze was markedly lowered. "For a long time ordinary individuality—the everyday individuality of everybody—remained below the threshold of description. . . . The disciplinary methods reversed this relation, lowered the threshold of describable individuality and made of this description a means of control and a method of domination" (p. 191). In schools, factories, and armies careful attention was given to gestures, punctuality, attitudes, and subtle variations in behavior that had previously gone unnoticed. Regions of the visible were divided and divided again with an ever-intensified focus on details, which became the objects of normalizing judgments.[4]

The function of the normalizing gaze and the penalties that accompany it is to constitute certain actions, attitudes, and abilities and to exclude others. The norm functions to narrow the range of acceptable heterogeneity in a radical fashion as it excludes the abnormal and perverse. Yet within an accepted range, the gaze also identifies, orders, and indeed helps constitute *differences*. Foucault summarizes: "In a sense the power of normalization imposes homogeneity; but it individualizes by making it possible to measure gaps, to determine levels, to fix specialities and to render the differences useful by fitting them one to another" (*Discipline*, p. 184).

Somewhat paradoxically, at the same time that people are abstracted as commodified labor, made exchangeable in highly routinized labor processes, and become formally equal members of political systems, "the individual is carefully fabricated" (*Discipline*, p. 217). Within the limits of

---

4. For example, one of the mechanisms that rendered people increasingly visible was the examination, which allowed for a minutely specified objectification, measuring, grading, and tracking of individual characteristics. As the examination proliferated, persons became objects of a meticulous and relentless will to truth. "Micro-penalties" were introduced at various points to influence behavior according to the normalizing judgments intrinsic to the exam's operation.

the "tolerated," disciplinary power establishes careful hierarchies, and "separations" between those at the same rank. The gaze penetrates bodies not only to exclude differences that do not meet institutional requirements, but in addition to constitute a useful system of differences: "the continuous individualizing pyramid" (p. 220).

Since the normalizing gaze plays a central role in understanding Foucault's view of the functioning of modern power, which frequently "coerces by means of observation" (*Discipline*, p. 170), it is no wonder that Foucault compares these modes of observation with "the telescope, the lens and the light beam" (p. 171). Just as these instruments were central in the development of knowledges that facilitated ordering and utilizing the physical world, so too the "observatories" of human beings made it possible to constitute humans as objects of knowledge—things to be used.

The architectural scheme that most embodied these principles of light and vision was Bentham's plan for the "Panopticon." This structure consisted of a ring of completely illuminated cells surrounding a watch-tower designed to allow the guard to observe the prisoners without their being able to see him. This not only allowed for continuous observation, but more important, gave the prisoner *the sense of* being under continuous observation even though he could not verify this suspicion. This situa-tion—the ever-present possibility of the invisible gaze—compelled the individual continually to watch over his own behavior. The Panopticon manifests "a gaze which each individual under its weight will end by interiorizing to the point that he is his own overseer, each individual thus exercising this surveillance over, and against, himself."[5]

And here we arrive at the heart of disciplinary power: the constitution of subjects that relentlessly subject themselves to self-observation. The aim of the panoptic gaze is not simply to trap and control subjects that would otherwise resist, but ultimately to constitute subjects that will generate their own gazes—gazes that will envelop them with a continuity and thoroughness that the gaze of another could never sustain. The reign of pure light demands finally that the objects under light become *relays and sources* of light. Everything must shine; there must be no shadow; and in this light the otherness of the other is to be dissolved, the difference

---

5. Michel Foucault, *Power/Knowledge*, ed. Colin Gordon (New York: Pantheon, 1980), p. 155. Further citations to this edition are given directly in the text.

where an edge might have formed is to surrender itself to the tightly woven fabric of disciplinary order. The Panopticon was to be auto-catalytic: "the perfection of [this] power should tend to render its actual exercise unnecessary; . . . in short, the inmates should be caught up in a power situation of which they are themselves the bearers" (*Discipline*, p. 201). Hence the creation of an ideal economic situation: maximized control and benefits at a minimal cost.

Yet what is the nature of this disciplinary panoptic gaze and its inter-nalized counterpart? Do they merely judge surfaces, actions, immediately visible behaviors? Certainly these are observed and judged, but conjointly one witnesses a much more profound observation taking place. Foucault argues that with the emergence of disciplinary power it is no longer simply the crime, visible deviation, or error that is judged, but the passions, potentials, drives, instincts, desires beneath the visible as well: "*These shadows lurking behind the case itself*" (*Discipline*, p. 17; my empha-sis).[6] It is this gaze that we internalize and perpetuate. This gaze is *not* to be *equated* with the confessing gaze discussed below, but it is important to note the extent to which at times even this disciplinary gaze has a re-markably subterranean quality.[7]

The correlate of this gaze and these mechanisms of power is the soul, as both the effect of this power and what reproduces it at the level of the self. Just as the body of the king was duplicated and became the un-changing atemporal body maintaining the kingdom in the Middle Ages, Foucault argues that the bodies of those housed in the institutions of

---

6. Perhaps this scrutiny is most obvious in our courts, prisons, and mental institutions, yet it is equally at work in "tracking" children through schools and hiring and promotion processes in which people are often subjected to interviews and exams aimed at discerning not simply relevant capabilities, but the inner nature, character, and "aptitude" of the self as well.

7. Of course, as we look out our windows or walk through the streets we discover very few round, transparent buildings with cornerstones dedicated to Bentham—even if there are many prisons modeled to varying degrees on this architectural form. Yet Foucault's discussions of the Panopticon are not primarily an attempt to persuade us of the per-vasiveness of its literal reality. Rather, Foucault's writing traces the lines of light, the walls, the angles, shapes, patterns, and the intended effects of this structure as he finds it in Bentham's text. It captures his attention as an "ideal form" (*Discipline*, p. 205) of a mechanism of power which has been extremely important during the last two centuries. (The themes articulated in this form have been embodied in a variety of ways, not all of which have been architectural [e.g., the exam], and we can all think of numerous, panoptic devices in our everyday life, from one-way mirrors, to visible and invisible cameras in banks and stores; from intercom systems in schools that allow the principal to listen into classrooms, to urinalysis.)

disciplinary society give rise to their duplicates as well, in the form of the modern soul. Far from being a semisecularized vestige of Christianity or simply an ideological fiction, the soul is a real product of modernity. It is what is constituted by disciplinary power in schools, the workplace, prisons, and psychiatric practices. The soul is the "reality reference" of this power: what is educated, trained, punished, normalized, identified; what is codified and inhabits the body in which it is produced. But perhaps even more importantly, the soul is what surveys and governs man from within, in the name of freedom. The soul is the panopticon each self harbors deep within itself—in a space that itself is a product of the power constituting it.

It is within this context of the production of the modern soul that we can best situate Foucault's discussion of the deep self-deciphering self in Volume 1 of *The History of Sexuality,* for the constitution of this type of self is an additional strategy of subjugation which, though different in important ways, is nevertheless quite consonant with—and often overlaps and is intertwined with—the deployment of the disciplinary gaze.

Both work to generate a self that is related to itself through a colonized, codified, and continuous self-reflection; a self-reflection that tends to normalize as it observes, both by impregnating the self with self-definitions constituted by hegemonic discourses and practices and by engendering certain "desirable" characteristics while reducing those that are "undesirable" or "other." Furthermore, the conception of the self as deep—harboring hidden truths and secret, circuitous causalities—which is tightly bound up with confessional practices, also conveniently serves to multiply the disciplinary holds over the self. It is these similarities that are so conducive to the overlapping deployment of conceptions and practices of the deep self and disciplinary technologies.[8]

Both disciplinary power and the confession of the deep self are characterized by an obsession with minutiae. Yet here, however, we arrive at a

---

8. Foucault argues that we see this overlap in modern treatments of madness as demonstrated by the nineteenth-century "moral methods" that operated through "that psychological inwardness where modern man seeks both his depth and his truth." With the birth of the asylum, guilt was organized to produce deeper, more detailed self-consciousness, responsibility, and unity. Similarly, as we noted above, Foucault argues that our juridical practices have moved toward an examination of the desires, drives, and deep personal tendencies beneath the relevant acts. This is not immediately deep self-reflection, but it is reflection on the depths of selves, a reflection that, when continuous enough, begins to be generated within selves.

central difference between the two as well. For what *drives* the confessing self in endless circles of self-reflection is the attempt to discern the meaning and deep truths buried within and beneath the details of existence. "For the disciplined man . . . [however] no detail is unimportant, but not so much for the meaning that it conceals within it as for the hold it provides for the power that wishes to seize it" (*Discipline*, p. 140). In contrast to the disciplinary gaze, whose direct and primary objective is utilization and control, the gaze of the confessing self is driven by a "hermeneutics of suspicion" that delivers it to infinite depths: meaning behind meaning. If on the one hand the Panopticon ends in *pure light*, the confessing self on the other hand pursues an object that is not susceptible to such an absolute revealing. Sex and all the deep truths humans seek to discover about themselves in the modern episteme are at best a "dark shimmer,"[9] a truth that continually recedes with each approaching gaze, a truth demanding a confession that can never end. If the panoptic gaze is driven by an endless imperative to maximize utility, Foucault argues that the confessing gaze is driven by an imperative stemming from the very being of "man" as he exists in modernity. The most immediate effect of this imperative is the constitution of a hermeneutic subject.

As noted above, the manner in which "Western man" is constituted as a deep, self-examining self is elucidated in Foucault's discussion of sexuality as a locus of modern confession, in which he argues that "we have become a singularly confessing society" (*Sexuality*, p. 59). On his reading, confession has become increasingly important in our institutions, our relations to others—indeed, confession has come to constitute the self's relationship with itself. Inextricable from confession, as both its precondition and its effect, is the understanding of the self as a deep subject. It is this interplay between depth and confession and the role Foucault argues they perform in the constitution of subjectivity that I explore in what follows.

Depth is not, according to Foucault, an essential quality of selves. Rather, it is a dimension that comes into being as an effect of power; a space created as a correlate of a variety of technologies that operate on selves. In conjunction with the production of the "soul," depth is created through the "discursive deployment" of sex as "the secret" that is subtly

9. Foucault, *History of Sexuality*, *Vol. 1*, p. 157. Further citations to this edition are given directly in the text.

and surreptitiously signified by all the actions, thoughts, emotions, and desires of the self. As indicative of "a universal signified" (*Sexuality*, p. 154) to which all things refer, the visible manifestations of selves point beneath themselves to their "true" meaning. Always to be uncovered, sex lies beneath—or better yet, deep within—the visible, which is laden with a depth it simultaneously signifies and conceals.

Yet we become deep selves not only because we are constituted as beings *with* a depth, but moreover because we become beings directed *toward* depth—beings that dwell in and grope through depth. For depth harbors the secret truth that "demands" to surface so that we may obtain our health, freedom, and intelligibility (*Sexuality*, p. 60). Because the promise of liberation lies buried in one's depths, one must delve deep and "tell what one is and what one does, what one recollects and what one has forgotten, what one is thinking and what one thinks he is not thinking" (p. 60). Failure to explore and illuminate our dark interiors will perpetuate our "repression," "inauthenticity," and blindness to our "essential nature."

Foucault argues, however, that these claims that depth is the dimension of truth and freedom are merely the ruse luring people into a form of subjectivity that is a trap. In fact, the space is colonized at its inception and remains a locality that is continually penetrated and invested by a variety of power strategies. Truth is not "the child of protracted solitude" that emerges in purity from deep within. Rather, "truth is a thing of this world, it is produced only by multiple forms of constraint" (*Power/Knowledge*, p. 131). We discover within, the being we have been fabricated to be; and we perpetuate and intensify this form of being when we exalt it as truth. The soul is an effect of a form of power that proliferates in an endless self-discovery of bottomless depth.

Foucault illustrates this dynamic in his discussion of the "latency" that comes to be attributed to sexuality, a latency that conceals the truth of sex from the self. Sex "truly" resides in regions even deeper than those into which we are able to submerge ourselves. We must delve deep, but we are unable to delve deep enough. The last part of the search requires the help of "the other who knows" (*Sexuality*, p. 70). As beings of such profound depth, we often require an other (psychiatrist, psychologist, therapist, counselor, priest, teacher, etc.) to identify the real truths of our soul: a "master of truth" who will decipher what we really are. Through the interpretive voices of these others, a plethora of discourses endlessly develops around the task of deciphering, identifying, and codifying the meanings extracted from the deep. In the scientific discourses, subjects come to be defined and located on a scale stretching from the normal to the pathological. In discourses entwined with power, selves are tracked, attached to imperatives, and ultimately constituted as individuals. In short: "The 'economy' of discourses—their intrinsic technology, the necessities of their operation, the tactics they employ, the effects of power which underlie them and which they transmit—. . . is what determines the essential features of what they have to say. The history of sexuality . . . must be written from the viewpoint of a history of discourses" (pp. 68–69).

Foucault argues that the truth these discourses constitute deep within has a definite bent toward unity. Beneath the ambiguous and shifting surfaces of our flesh and words, signified in multifarious ways, one discovers the "*one* true sex." This insistent quest for unity in depth can be grasped metaphorically in Foucault's presentation of the her-maphrodite Herculine Barbin. The examinations of Barbin are impor-tant for Foucault in part because they exemplify the disciplinary seizure of the body. Read metaphorically, however, they draw attention to the violent and reductive aspects of the search for deep truths. On the surface, Barbin appears to be a most "extreme mixture" of the two "true" sexes. Yet deep below, discovered first by penetrating touch and later by means of the surgeon's blade, one finds the real truth. Barbin is extricated from "the happy limbo of her non-identity"[10] and hurled into the depths beneath her "indeterminate anatomy," where the doctors, lawyers, and judge determine the single truth of her being: "male," before which the truth of Barbin's apparent ambiguous difference as a "hermaphrodite" is evaporated in the prefix "pseudo." Depth is ulti-mately not a dimension into which ambiguity and difference *extend* and *proliferate*, but a dimension of *reduction*. The illusion of richness that depth might conjure—each surface refers to something else—shatters in the "reality" that ultimately they all refer to the same thing. It is not only that Barbin's ambiguous flesh is finally fixed as male, but moreover that "his" *whole being* is fixed as "*male sex.*" Barbin's protean being is crushed, ground, and homogenized by the immense weight of a depth that in the end Barbin cannot bear, an engulfing depth in which "he" drowns.[11]

10. Michel Foucault, "Introduction" in *Herculine Barbin*, trans. Richard McDougall (New York: Pantheon, 1980), p. xiii.
11. Yet if we are simultaneously produced and reduced in depth, we do not all experi-ence depth and sex as did Barbin. Indeed, the task of recovering the truth of our sex has been constituted as something desirable and liberating.

In addition to the effects of depth discussed above, Foucault maintains that the conception of the self as a subject of deep truths functions to disguise the operation of power in which it plays such an important part. Since truth originates in the purity of the inner dimension (the reasons for error are "deep," too . . .), we avoid examining the social, economic, and political practices in which truth and the subject are produced. Instead, to the extent that we examine the effects of the social world on the self at all, it is in the form of the "repressive hypothesis" in which power plays a purely negative role over against the deep self. Hence the constitutive effects of power are disguised, and ironically, people exalt the very effects of power in rather poor attempts to be free. As the deep self—a profound effect of power—becomes the a priori assumption of the analysis of power, power itself becomes increasingly invisible.

One should not read Foucault to be arguing that self-examining, unified deep subjects are produced solely through modern discursive and nondiscursive practices of sexuality. Foucault has chosen sexuality because he understands it to be very important in the production of modern subjectivity, but equally because it functions so well to illuminate the ontological understandings that underlie hegemonic modern ideals of the self, which are by no means limited to sexuality. Foucault sees similar themes embodied in modern "self-absorption,"[12] therapeutic practices, and Sartre's notion of "authenticity" ("Genealogy," p. 237). And though the self-observing self constituted under the eye of disciplinary power is not identical to the hermeneutic subject, we have already noted how a notion of deep truth has made its way into juridical and educational discourses. In short, Foucault believes that the constellation of depth, unity, and self-examination constitutes the epistemic terrain on which most contemporary discussion occurs: it is a central feature of what he calls the "epistemologico-juridical" formation (*Discipline*, p. 23). To gain a clearer understanding of Foucault's analysis of the self as it is constituted within the modern episteme, we must turn to his metatheoretical insights in *The Order of Things*.

Metatheoretical Analysis

In *The Order of Things*, Foucault conducts a metatheoretical analysis of the modern sciences of "man." In this investigation, he does not attempt

---

12. Michel Foucault, "On the Genealogy of Ethics: An Overview of Work in Progress," in Dreyfus and Rabinow, *Foucault*, p. 245. Further citations to this edition are given directly in the text.

to define the various ideas the human sciences have in common or the framework of thought within which they operate. Rather, he is striving to comprehend what he calls the "historical *a priori*"—the conditions of possibility—of modern theories about man. "This *a priori* is what, in a given period, delimits in the totality of experience a field of knowledge, defines the mode of being of the objects that appear in that field, provides man's everyday perception with theoretical powers, and defines the conditions in which he can sustain a discourse about things that is recognized to be true."[13]

Because Foucault contends that man is situated at the heart of the modern "episteme" as the subject and object of knowledge in a way that is very different from previous epistemes, an exploration of the being of man in modern theory is central to his project. In a sense, Foucault is unfolding what we might call a relative ontology of man; an ontology that does not address the being of man's being in any essential or ahistorical sense, but rather addresses "man" as that being which came on the scene at the turn of the nineteenth century, both making possible and governing the human sciences.

Foucault confines himself to archaeological methodology in *The Order of Things*, and hence the connections between knowledge and power which one finds in some of his earlier and later works are absent. Indeed, the appearance of man as that which made the human sciences possible is seen in this work not as a consequence of technologies of power, but instead as "an event in the order of knowledge" (*Order of Things*, p. 345). The methodological shortcomings of this stage of Foucault's thinking have been cogently discussed by Dreyfus and Rabinow and retrospectively by Foucault himself.[14] Nevertheless, one of the things that remains of great value in this work is the sustained analysis of the mode of being of "man" as he appears in a wide variety of modern discourses. We·find here a level of generality that sheds light on some of his later works that tenaciously remain at the level of the particular. I believe that if we read Foucault's archaeologies and his genealogies in light of each other, we can reveal important insights into modernity which are far more illusive when these texts are read separately. Thus far I have summarized Foucault's understanding of the way in which man and the

13. Michel Foucault, *The Order of Things: An Archaeology of the Human Sciences* (New York: Random House, Vintage Books, 1973), p. 158. Further citations to this edition are given directly in the text.

14. Dreyfus and Rabinow, *Foucault*, chap. 4; Foucault, *Power/Knowledge*, p. 113.

sciences of man develop in a society that attempts to bring humans increasingly under observation and control. Knowledge and power "presuppose and constitute" one another: "The subject who knows, the objects to be known and the modalities of knowledge must be regarded as so many effects of these fundamental implications of power-knowledge" (*Discipline*, pp. 27–28).

Yet if knowledge is born in and proliferates operations of power, then we should not only be able to situate and gain a deeper understanding of modern knowledge by studying power, but also be able to learn about power by studying the characteristics of knowledge. If the man that is both an effect of power and a being that extends it is also the man that is the subject and object of the human sciences, then a study of the being of this man that has governed these sciences is likely to give us greater insight into man's relation to power. For this man—his relationship to his life, language, labor, and consciousness, the things he must think and do—is *a thing of this world* of "war by other means." The human sciences attempt to describe a being that exists, and their effort itself, in part, both manifests and constitutes this extant being. And if there are fundamental characteristics defining his being for all of these diverse sciences, we should examine them carefully to discern some of the basic contours of the functioning of power in modernity. The man of finitude and the things he "must" do provide us most profoundly with a general description of man-in-modern-power.

To bring Foucault's discussion of the modern episteme into relief, it is helpful to outline briefly his conception of the classical episteme that preceded it. According to Foucault, the classical age conceived of the world as a great chain of being created by God. Each of the beings lodged within this continuous chain varied only in the slightest manner from its neighbors in the chain. Each being was represented, but its representation was not the creation of another being. Rather, significations and what they signified were transparently and internally connected. In the "Classical Age, the sign is the *representativity* of the representation in so far as it is *representable*" (*Order of Things*, p. 65). "Each [representation] posits itself in its transparency as a sign of what it represents" (p. 66). The place of human beings in this scheme of things was to compare the representations of a world that had been scrambled by time to examine the minute identities and differences between beings, in an effort to construct an order that would resemble as closely as possible the Order that God created.

As is readily apparent, on Foucault's reading, the classical episteme lacked the space in which humans could be originary beings. Representations did not emerge out of the density of man's being; they existed in a completely transparent "strictly binary" relation with the things they represented (*Order of Things*, p. 64); the order that man sought to construct was not the product of a creative effort to make some sense out of a chaotic Godless world, but simply an effort to reconstruct the God-given. The representations given to humans and the things themselves were unproblematically linked in the language people spoke. Hence "man, as a primary reality with his own density, as the difficult object and sovereign subject of all possible knowledge, has no place in [the classical episteme]" (p. 310). The discourse that joined representation and being "provided the link between the 'I think' and the 'I am' of the being undertaking it" (p. 311). And if the being of the "I am" remained unexamined, it was because it could not constitute a "problem" in an episteme where thoughts and beings pressed up against each other so tightly that there was no space to ask a question that would soon become imperative. Man as the object for deep interrogation and analysis did not exist.

Foucault argues that a new epistemic space with new possibilities and new requirements began to emerge at the end of the eighteenth century with the recession of the classical episteme.[15] In the classical age the truth of a thing was defined by its position in the table of representations, which was constructed to mirror God's Order—itself an order of the visible. The thing's visible representative qualities manifested its identity, which could be comprehended in its relation to other representations. Hence, representation—the visible surface of the world—was the locus of beings and their truths. Representation began to be displaced, however, as labor escaped from the table of needs with Smith and became an "irreducible absolute" standard of measurement for analyzing exchange; as character in natural history began to be based on organic structure, "an internal principle not reducible to the reciprocal interactions of representations" (*Order of Things*, p. 227): as the internal principle of inflection usurped the primacy of representation in analyses of language. Foucault argues that these initial changes were further transformed and that they established a complete break with the classical episteme in

15. This is a change Foucault is content to describe as an "archaeological mutation," and makes no attempt to explain until later works.

Ricardo's originary labor, Cuvier's primacy of functions, and Bopp's emphasis on grammatical wholes. Things withdrew beneath their visible surfaces; truth came to reside in their hidden regions. As beings "withdraw into the depths of things" (*Order of Things*, p. 313), "man" emerges in the space left behind—a being at the center of a murky world who *provides himself* with representations. As thought falls outside of its previously transparent relationship to the world, Kant awakens. Restless and uneasy, he begins to ask about the "conditions of its possibility."

Foucault contends that the man emerging in modernity discovers that he is indicated by the positive forms of life, labor, and language in whose midst he finds himself. "Man is designated—more, required—since it is he who speaks, since he is seen to reside among the animals (. . . on extremity of a long series) and since . . . he is necessarily the principle and means of all production" (*Order of Things*, p. 313). Yet as man is indicated at the center of life, labor, and language, he simultaneously finds that his existence is accessible only in these very forms, and that they are older than he is and determine him. Man can be known only as he works, speaks, and lives. Yet only through an ancient language can man speak, only by means of processes older than himself can he work, and he lives only as part of a primordial life that precedes him. Everything indicates man, and everything man can reveal about himself indicates an "irreducible anteriority," gestures toward his ineliminable finitude.

If everything bespeaks man's finitude, however, nothing enables him to "contemplate" it; for everything given in his thought—even his finitude—is itself based on finitude. As man attempts to elucidate the system of words, production, and life that outdates him, what he is attempting to clarify "always already" partially and surreptitiously constitutes his elucidation. Man—what he is and what he is not—is elusive. But that which man is unable to contemplate completely because of its "irreducible anteriority" is at the same time only possible and given to experience on the *basis of man's* finitude. The mode of being of space, life, production, and language is given to man only on the basis of his body, his desire, his work, and his speech. Thus the finite existence that limits his access to things is also what makes all access possible.

It is precisely the evasiveness of finitude—the endless reciprocal referral and deferral of man and things—that harbors finitude's promise. If man is unable to comprehend clearly the precise nature and boundaries of his finitude, it is always possible that there may be a way out: a form of life, labor, and language—soon to be discovered—which would be completely transparent, rational, and unalien. Oddly, man's finitude is accompanied by hope more than by despair. "Heralded in positivity, man's finitude is outlined in the paradoxical form of the endless; rather than the rigour of a limitation, it indicates the monotony of a journey which, though it probably has no end, is nevertheless perhaps not without hope" (*Order of Things*, p. 314). Indeed, this hope and the struggle to realize it are not *possible options* for man to pursue; they are *imperative*. For this finitude originating in man's strange being threatens to cut man off completely from the truth of himself. The ambiguity of finitude that harbors the possibility of escape from an ambiguous existence into a realm of pure truth simultaneously threatens to snuff man out under the tragic weight of error, alienation—the other within. The strategy man employs in his effort to achieve (or at least move toward) transparency and rise beyond his finitude is one that attempts to ground all those things determining him and indicating that he is finite in the positivity of his own being.

Foucault argues that this "analytic of finitude" is "deployed" in three ways: the repetitions of the transcendental and the empirical, the return and retreat of the origin, and the cogito and the unthought. Since the third is most emblematic of the theoretical contours of modern man's relation to himself and to otherness in the context of the objectification and subjectification discussed earlier in this chapter, it is the cogito and the unthought I wish at present to consider. Foucault argues that within the modern episteme, man is unable to infer a total, immediate, and transparent "I am" from "I think." The "I think" is able to think what it thinks only on the basis of what it does not think. As we have seen, man's thought is carried along by a language, a life, and a labor that are older than man and not completely intelligible to him. As such a being, man is the "locus of misunderstanding . . . that constantly exposes his thought to the risk of being swamped by his own being, and also enables him to recover his integrity on the basis of what eludes him" (*Order of Things*, p. 323). Being neither a dead object nor an absolute subject, man is "always open, never finally delimited, yet constantly (but always only partially) traversed" (p. 322) by a gaze, a thought driven by fear and hope.

The unthought that haunts man does not have the character of an external limitation. Rather, what man does not think—his other—is born with man: it is the "shadow" he casts with each thought. Thus the "I think" that led Descartes to truth and certainty must be for modernity a project that is never completed and ceaselessly renewed. And if Kant stepped to the threshold of modernity when he began to question the conditions of possibility of truth, fully modern man is obsessed with the possibility and actuality of "what eludes him." Hence man "*must* traverse, duplicate and reactivate in an explicit form the articulation of thought on everything within it, around it, and beneath it which is not thought . . . a *constantly renewed interrogation*" (*Order of Things*, p. 324; my emphasis). Everything that, in the depths of man and surrounding him, evades man's thought now threatens man's entire existence with error, alienation, and madness. The shadows that man casts with each thought have been cast by all men during all of time, and the darkness of this collective shadow carries him forth as a grain of sand on the crest of a turbulent wave. Better yet, as an inept god thrashing uneasily in a murky ocean of his own creation. The ocean roars to man's horror "I am other," yet without it he would be desiccated and succumb to an unlivable gravity, for the other is the necessary condition of man's being: a life, labor, and language to which he is not identical nourishes and sustains him.

In his effort to recover his position as the pure origin and certain sovereign of thought, man penetrates into the region of the other. This constant obsession with and interrogation of the unthought does not culminate in the dissolution of opacity, however. Rather than completing his project, man establishes himself in the endless "*illumination* of the *element of darkness* that cuts man off from himself" (*Order of Things*, p. 328; my emphasis).

Hence Foucault argues that "for modern thought no morality is possible" (*Order of Things*, p. 328), for it is always in movement *toward*, but never arrives with certainty at, a secure self-identical thought no longer plagued by an unthought residue which might enable us to grasp the laws of the world's ethical order previously grounding Western morality. Indeed, the only "imperative" this thought-that-never-arrives can generate—an imperative of no small importance—is that of its own movement: continuously expanded reflection-illumination of its atramentous depths.

Yet if thought must ceaselessly shed reflective light, this is not to say that thought is simply bound up with itself and, because of its uncertainty, unable to act. On the contrary, Foucault maintains that "modern thought, from its inception and in its very density, is a certain mode of action" (*Order of Things*, p. 328). In modernity, thought has always "left itself"; it has never stayed within the domain of the theoretical. Modern thought has always been compelled to move beyond itself to what is not thought—to what is "unthought." And where contact has been made, there has been disturbance. For thought does not simply "reveal," but rather is "a modification of what it knows" (p. 327). Thought exercises power not merely because of its content and its bases in societal struggles. Moreover, modern thought is linked to power because of its *fundamental trajectory*, because it is always "advancing towards that region where man's Other must become the Same as himself" (p. 328). Modern thought moves to make all that is other identical to its concept, and in so doing, it enslaves and obliterates the other's difference. It constitutes a new thing that is the same. Before *prescribing* action, thought in modernity *is* action. More concretely, we can think of the ceaseless efforts to ensnare the untamed protean world within truths which reduce it to the terms of hegemonic discourses—terms of "the same"—the reduction of dreams to Oedipus, of homosexuals to medical categories, of dissidents to psychological classifications, of nature and people to the discourses of utility, of the self to deep truths, lest the True, Normal, Healthy, Useful, Deep man be forever cut off from himself.

There are few places in *The Order of Things* where Foucault comes as close to leaping out of the archaeological dimension as he does in the passage above. In what is more than simply a discussion of thought and unthought as archaeological contemporaries, Foucault offers us the broad contours of his understanding of how modern thought in its very being manifests a type of power. In this analysis of the episteme he recognizes characteristics of modernity—the restless, unending illumination, identification, and transformation of otherness in an effort to constitute the same in its purity—which he studies on a microlevel in his more genealogical works. Though there are many very important differences between Foucault's archaeological and genealogical periods, the broad insights in the former and the particular analytics in the latter both belong to a "structure of perception" that remained remarkably constant in important ways.

Foucault's critical perception of the trajectory of modern thought is brought into sharper focus when it is contrasted with his understanding of the trajectory of thought in the classical age. The classical episteme, as we have seen, was based on an ontology of continuity. The world was perceived as a great chain of beings that varied only in the slightest manner from their neighbors in the chain. It is easy to see how thought that identified reality with the well-ordered table would be likely to distort and subjugate reality violently under the guise of transparent and innocent representations. This order of things could be—and, as Foucault shows in other works, was—implicated in a very problematic set of practices. The exclusion of madness in the classical age illustrates the extent to which this form of reason could be involved in the obliteration of otherness. Foucault never indicates that the classical age was a "good time" or a period we should return to. Yet on the perceived ontological continuity of being, classical theory was concerned with distinguishing *difference:* among "the secretly varied monotony of the like." The trajectory of classical thought was toward "the never-completed formation of Difference" (*Order of Things,* p. 339).

Modern thought, in contrast, moves in the opposite direction. In the attempt to secure man from the erosive forces threatening his precarious being as it is given in the analytic of finitude, man must ceaselessly show that he is the complete foundation of what can be a stable truth; that the unthought can always be thought; that he can seize his origin. Man must attempt to squeeze shut the gaps where the other might arise.

Foucault summarizes: in modernity "we have moved from a reflection upon the order of Differences . . . to a thought of the Same, still to be conquered in its contradiction." "It is always concerned with showing how the Other, the Distant, is also the Near and the Same" (*Order of Things,* p. 339). The ultimate consequence is that modernity harbors within itself a most compulsive imperative to obliterate difference. All that is other threatens "man's" inherently unstable position and must succumb to the same. If the classical age closed out the other at the level of its ontology, modernity is founded on an ontology in which the other is continually reborn in the depth of being—not simply exterior to but within the very flesh of man—and must be ceaselessly transformed, identified, made the same. The same is no longer the *ground* for activity; it is now what the trajectory of activity aims to achieve. And it seems that Foucault perceives the activity of revealing the same to be even more dangerous than the ground of the same. If in the latter the other might avoid recognition and exist simply as a nonbeing, in the former there is absolutely no place for the other to hide. The other is ceaselessly present, as an absence recognized as the danger of Death and Madness, and must be the target of continuous, detailed, deep illumination and intervention.

Precisely at the point where thought has become a restless activity that must ceaselessly reflect on the question of man, however, Foucault maintains that thought is "falling asleep" (*Order of Things*, p. 341). The point at which modernity perceives the awakening of philosophy—the point at which man kills God and dissolves the visible surface of his classical order into depth—is for Foucault only an instant of consciousness that is engulfed once again by Morpheus. But this time Morpheus rules as a God not from without, but from within—as man in the analytic of finitude.

Rather than overcoming premodern dogmatism, the analytic of man merely "consists in doubling over dogmatism" (*Order of Things*, p. 341). The positive and the fundamental are made to refer to one another endlessly in an effort to render the foggy depths a place fit for sovereignty.

> In this Fold, the transcendental function is doubled over so that it covers with its dominating network the inert grey space of empiricity; inversely, empirical contents are given life, gradually pull themselves upright, and are immediately subsumed in a discourse which carries their transcendental presumption into the distance. . . . All empirical knowledge, provided it concerns man, can serve as a possible philosophical field in which the foundation of knowledge, the definition of its limits, and in the end, the *truth of all truth* must be discoverable. (p. 341; my emphasis)

Yet the ideals governing man's being—transparency, identity, sameness—are precisely those that were shattered when man killed God. They can be for man only an impossible promise. As man steps to the vacated throne, he finds that God's world has deserted him. The dim, Godless world resists the principles that rendered God's sovereignty so unquestionable. The order crumbles; being sinks beneath the reach of his gaze. In man's attempt to be the ground of the same, he merely situates "his language, his thought, his laughter in the space of that already dead God" (p. 385); and hence man's death is simultaneous with his murderous birth.

Man is born in the effort to see man—not God—as the self-present, self-knowing origin of his own being. With the death of God, however, there is no ontology that will enable man to attain the presence God had before man dethroned him. Man cannot be the God he killed; he is somnambular in his efforts (to use a word Nietzsche enjoyed). Morpheus is the only god man can be. The anthropological sleep is restless, dangerous—modern Morpheus snores toward nightmares.

Foucault ends *The Order of Things* with the ambiguous prophecy that man may soon be "erased, like a face drawn in sand at the edge of the sea" (p. 387). What Foucault hopes might emerge, we discuss in the next section. What is clear thus far, however, is that for Foucault, man—and the attempt to discover the "truth of all truth" in himself which defines him—leads power and knowledge in a direction that makes freedom and thought increasingly impossible. "The man whom we are invited to free, is already in himself the effect of a subjection much more profound than himself" (*Discipline*, p. 30).

We have seen the sense of this statement in light of the practices of power that define the truths of human beings and fasten them to these truths. So, too, this sense emerges in the practices in which selves fasten themselves to both the truths that are deployed and the deployment of truth. The studies of man in the analytic of finitude are deeply entwined with this project, for they perpetuate an ontology and a specific understanding of "liberation" central to the operation of power in modernity. Correlatively, they necessitate a will to truth and a will to light that are also fundamental to these forms of power. The archaeology of these sciences reveals dimensions of our modernity which illuminate our situation in ways that may help us transform it.

But if Foucault rejects deep man and the search for the "truth of all truth," does he then simply revel in the pit of irrationality? Does this abandon leave him in the existentially crippled condition of absolute relativism? Is he unable to affirm one set of practices over another? No.

The arguments to support such bluntness lie in the next chapter, but the "no" whispers in the final pages of the "Man and His Doubles" chapter we have been discussing. Here Foucault celebrates the death of man not as the end of thought, but rather as thought's *dawn:* "The end of man . . . is the return to the beginning of philosophy. It is no longer possible to think in our day other than in the void left by man's disappearance. For this void does not create a deficiency; it does not constitute a lacuna that must be filled. It is nothing more, and nothing less, than the unfolding of a space in which it is once more possible to think" (*Order of Things*, p. 342).

And lest one think that by "thinking" Foucault has in mind something that originates only in Foucault's skeptical laughter—and it does find a home there—we might note that he speaks of awakening modern thought "in order to recall it to the possibilities of its earliest dawning" (*Order of Things*, p. 341). These passages should caution us against quickly leaping to the conclusions that many have seized to dismiss Foucault. A space. Nothing more, nothing less. A space of possibility. In the following section, I argue that the emerging space in which it is once again possible to think arises from Foucault's understandings of the human body which erode the assumptions and positions of Western metaphysics broadly construed. What emerges is nothing short of a radical transformation of Enlightenment, but a transformation that Foucault nevertheless places within the tradition it transforms. It is a transformation explicitly attuned to the possibilities of Enlightenment's earliest dawnings.

The Affirmative Trajectory of Foucault's Thought

Foucault's critical insights have spawned debates that vary widely in their acuity and value. Yet this is not the terrain on which he faces his most serious challenges. Even among those who acknowledge that Foucault's studies illuminate dimensions of our modernity, we hear the incessant charge that Foucault is essentially nihilistic and unable to tell us why he criticizes some things and not others, let alone provide us with a positive vision or affirmative ethic. Thus Habermas has claimed that Foucault rejects the Enlightenment, is a "young conservative," and lacks "normative yardsticks"; Charles Taylor refers to Foucault's "monolithic relativism" and his inability to affirm one set of practices over another; Michael Walzer charges him with "infantile leftism" and "anarchism/nihilism"; Richard Wolin accuses him of an "aesthetic decisionism" within which he is forced to take "irrationalist leaps" to affirm anything.[16] The list of these dismissive labels is a long one.

16. Jürgen Habermas, "Modernity v. Postmodernity," *New German Critique* 22 (Winter 1981), 13 (a more textured analysis with a few sympathetic dimensions is Jürgen Habermas, *The Philosophical Discourse of Modernity*, trans. Frederick G. Lawrence [Cambridge: MIT Press, 1987], chaps. 9 and 10); Jürgen Habermas, "Taking Aim at the Heart of the Present," in *Foucault: A Critical Reader*, ed. D. C. Hoy (Oxford: Blackwell, 1986), p. 108; Charles Taylor, "Foucault on Freedom and Truth," in Hoy, *Reader*, pp. 69–102; Michael Walzer, "The Politics of Michel Foucault," in Hoy, *Reader*, pp. 51–68; Richard Wolin, "Foucault's Aesthetic Decisionism," *Telos*, no. 67 (Spring 1986), 71–86.

In spite of Foucault's frequently conspicuous silence regarding the affirmative dimensions of his thought, however, I believe that a strong argument can be made that his criticism wells forth from an ontological position (emphasizing difference and the agonistically dialogical character of being) that not only plays a central role in determining the domains, focus, character, and style of his work, but is entwined with a positive "ethos" (emphasizing artistic self-creation in a dialogical context) that provides the general outlines of an alternative vision of selves and social relations as well. Moreover, I maintain that the ontological and ethical dimensions of Foucault's thought—missed all too often by many of his interpreters—are among the most important aspects of his work. Foucault's ethics provides a general framework for postmetaphysical criticism and supplies us with a loosely defined vision of the human world which affirms diversity, dialogical artistic existence, and a transfigured sense of "belonging" with different others. I begin with a discussion of his ontology and follow with an interpretation of his ethics.

Ontology of Difference

Guarding the entrance—and seeming to prohibit entry—to an understanding of Foucault which seeks to place an ontology of the body at the center of his thought is the following: "Nothing in man—not even his body—is sufficiently stable to serve as the basis for self-recognition or for understanding other men."[17] This passage might be interpreted to mean that we are hopelessly cut off from "the truth" of ourselves because there is nothing in our being "sufficiently stable" for us to seize and interrogate in an effort to understand who we are. Indeed, the "who" at any moment is merely the "current episode in a series of subjugations" ("Nietzsche," p. 148). The effort to essentialize the "who" is an important strategy in this episode. Certainly if the body is infinitely malleable and there is no basis for self-recognition, talk of an ontology of the body seems absurd?!

It seems to me that this interpretation of the passage, though it starts

17. Michel Foucault, "Nietzsche, Genealogy, History," in *Language, Counter-Memory, Practice*, ed. Donald Bouchard (Ithaca, N.Y.: Cornell University Press, 1977), p. 153. Further citations to this edition are given directly in the text.

on the right track, largely misses Foucault's point; and that rather than being a *barrier* to an ontology of the body, this passage leads directly *toward* such an ontology—even though it is one that radically opposes the unitary, essentialist, and teleological theories that have nearly defined ontology in the Western metaphysical tradition. In fact, it is these theories that are the most formidable barriers to the ontology Foucault seeks to develop. Hence the first movement toward a new ontology of the body involves shattering these barriers, and this is precisely one of the functions of the passage in question. The "self-recognition" that the body cannot provide—indeed, defies—is that of a "rediscovery of ourselves" ("Nietzsche," p. 154) which would demonstrate the metaphysical truth of our being in an origin. Yet in "shattering the unity of man's being" (p. 153), Foucault's genealogies do not leave nonontology, but rather provide us with a *different* ontology: that "introduces discontinuity into our very being" (p. 154). Instead of perceiving discontinuity as the surface beneath which one can discover the truly unified character of being, genealogy perceives the continuities and unities that metaphysical thinking takes to be truth as constructions frequently obfuscating, mastering, and enslaving beings that are often multiple, heterogeneous, and recalcitrant. As we shall see, Foucault is arguing not that we should become disintegrating selves, but rather that "truths" and "unities" of a metaphysical character are bound up with constraints that have an a priori unquestionable appearance, eclipse our differences, and are undesirable to the extent that they prevent the artistic fashioning of ourselves in dialogical engagement with the differences within ourselves and between ourselves and others.

Foucault discovers a plurality of pleasures, thoughts, possibilities that do not fit neatly in the carefully fabricated hegemonic identities, "a complex system of distinct and multiple elements, unable to be mastered by the powers of synthesis" ("Nietzsche," p. 161). But the genealogist does not simply *discover* that man is not the original unity he claims to be. As essentially engaged knowledge, genealogy instigates and enhances some of the dissonance it discovers and is "capable of liberating divergence and marginal elements" (p. 153). We might think here of cacophonous erotica in an age of heterosexuality, true sexuality; insubordinate dimensions of the self which resist for other possibilities surveillance, order, and utilization in an age of hierarchies and disciplines aimed at increasing productivity; friendship in an age of insidiously possessive love; noncodified distinction and abnormality in an age governed by the norm.

Perhaps Foucault would have been better understood if he had said, "Nothing in man—*especially* not his body" can ground metaphysical self-recognition; for the body is a rather recalcitrant and unstable target for such unities. In a rhetoric aimed both to disclose and to incite, he refers to it as a "volume in perpetual disintegration" ("Nietzsche," p. 148). Foucault frequently appeals to the body in his attempt to unseat the perpetual rediscovery of the self-as-origin. It is to "bodies and pleasures" "*in their multiplicity*" that Foucault gestures in *The History of Sexuality*, Volume 1, as a possible locus of opposition to the unifying deployment of sex (*Sexuality*, p. 157). With this he aims not at the end of all self-recognition, but at a recognition of the distinct and often multipicitous dimensions of the self which do not fit comfortably within and are not reducible to the hegemonic categories that now appear as contingent rather than essential.

The notion of difference with which Foucault works needs clarification, for it is remarkably divergent from those most often expressed in Western thought. It is in "Theatrum Philosophicum," a very favorable review of Gilles Deleuze's *Différence et répétition* and *Logique de sens*, that Foucault most explicitly discusses difference as it appears in these texts.[18] Given his expressed agreement and the concordance between this essay and other of Foucault's works, I discuss the notion of difference in this review as one that Foucault largely affirms at the ontological level even though the ethical implications he draws in other works are *not* Deleuzian.

Characteristic of Western thinking, and its "first form of subjection," is that "difference is transformed into that which must be specified within a concept, without overstepping its bounds" ("Theatrum Philosophicum," p. 182). As specified and without excess, difference is made equivalent to the concept(s) that identifies it—the same as the thought that thinks it. The unmastered singularity of events is obliterated as thought makes them identical with its own categories. Yet this oblitera-

---

18. Foucault's admiration for Deleuzian philosophy echoes throughout this essay, in which he says that with Deleuze "thought is again possible" and "perhaps one day this century will be known as Deleuzian." "Theatrum Philosophicum," in Bouchard, *Language*, p. 165 (hereafter cited directly in the text).

tion of otherness, which occurs the instant that thought specifies in order totally to seize, is merely the first stroke of a long, grinding process. As specified, difference is specie-fied; made to appear on the basis of differentiations within commonalities that are considered to be more fundamental. "For the concept to master difference, perception must apprehend global resemblances . . . at the root of what we call diversity" (p. 183). Herculine Barbin is identified and seized as "male hermaphrodite": a species of sexuality. The genus defines the species, and both define Barbin. What is this peculiar body-event called Herculine Barbin? It is a type of male hermaphrodite. What is a hermaphrodite? A type of sexuality. Herculine Barbin's difference assumes significance for hegemonic nineteenth-century French society *only* when it is essentialized and made to appear within the categories of the same. Barbin's raw difference is eclipsed as Barbin appears in hegemonic society only as essentially male-sexed. The individual differences of Barbin's body are examined, measured, compared with those of other members of this species, and located within an organized spectrum of variation. It is the assumed underlying identities that *call forth* examinations, make possible comparisons, and provide the framework within which the pseudorecognition of differences occurs.

The Deleuzian/Foucaultian alternative to the tradition of Western metaphysics is difference conceived "differentially": difference as "a pure event," not completely reducible to conceptual generalities ("Theatrum Philosophicum," p. 182). The "freeing of difference" demands "thought that accepts divergence; affirmative thought whose instrument is disjunction; thought of the multiple—of nomadic and dispersed multiplicity that is not limited or confined by the constraints of similarity" (p. 185).

Central to Foucault's project is the attempt to make us more aware of the difference and particularities of events and others and, further, to lodge a sense of difference between the self and the world. In "The Order of Discourse," written at about the same time as the review of Deleuze, Foucault cautions us against imagining that we have a "primordial complicity with the world" which would allow us perfectly to know and identify it with our thoughts. "The world is not the accomplice of our knowledge; there is no prediscursive providence which predisposes the world in our favour. We must conceive discourse as a violence which we do to things, or in any case as a practice which we impose upon them."[19]

The status of an ontology arising from this understanding of the world obviously cannot be that of an objectively apprehended truth. Rather, Foucault draws on genealogy itself to secure his theoretical perspective. He substantiates this perspective as he repeatedly shows what is eclipsed and obliterated in our established identities and understandings. In light of Foucaultian genealogies, difference appears everywhere, unstable, elusive—emblematic of the ineliminable excess through which beings escape from the clutches of identifying thought. The world around us is always partially other. Far from leading toward some form of relativism or nihilism, however, in Foucault's view this ontology constitutes the space in which it is "once again possible to think" (*Order of Things*, p. 342). Or better still, as we shall see, this ontology opens the opening—shut by Western metaphysics—in which it is possible to reformulate the *practice of freedom*. For difference conceived differentially is ultimately not simply a new way of thinking, but more profoundly a new mode of being.

For Foucault, difference signifies a new attitude toward and engagement with otherness. It calls us to act with an eye toward normally eclipsed specificities rather than in the light of preconceived identities. This does not mean that existence is to become a blind deconstructive rampage that smashes and shatters everything within reach in order to maximize "difference" and worship atoms. If this is where Foucault's thought led, the charges that it is infantile and empty would be warranted. Instead, it indicates that the differences within our own being and between ourselves and what is other should be acknowledged and moreover reckoned with in our efforts to create our existences, rather than insidiously denied, obliterated, ignored, or dealt with through absolutely fixed moral categories of metaphysical origin. Foucaultian ontology calls us to throw the metaphysical veils off of ourselves and others, and dwell with more "maturity" in the midst of the living, multipicitous particularity of ourselves, others, our social practices, and our history.

A delight in difference clearly radiates from many of Foucault's texts. Yet it should not be understood as an overall plea simply to "let difference be," for such a plea is itself laden with metaphysical residues that

19. Michel Foucault, "The Order of Discourse," in *Untying the Text*, ed. Robert Young (New York: Methuen, 1981), pp. 65, 67.

are no longer tenable in light of Foucault's ontology. The injunction simply to "let difference be" assumes that there is some sort of preordinated harmony in the world which makes life livable and worth living without human praxis and intervention. Equally important, it assumes that the self would cohere as something interesting without any imposition of form, content, commitment, etc. Yet the human world revealed by the genealogist is far too discordant for any of these fantasies to remain standing. Even at the level of the body: what sense does "let difference be" make as an overall prescription when the body is a "volume in perpetual disintegration"? Not much sense at all; and hence it appears that while Foucault undermines metaphysical unities that obfuscate difference, he simultaneously undermines what is perhaps the last gasp of metaphysics: "Let it be."

But then what prescription for action might follow from this ontology of difference? What does dwelling with maturity in the midst of bodies, pleasures, and others who are different from the given hegemonic identities and harbor no deep truths mean? Foucault writes: "From the idea that the self is not given to us, I think there is only one practical consequence: we have to create ourselves as a work of art" ("Genealogy," p. 237).

Foucault's ontology of the body and his aesthetic understandings of existence draw significantly from Nietzsche. Yet his notion of the self as a work of art differs in crucial ways from a theme that finds frequent expression in Nietzsche: the "monological artist."[20] While Nietzsche's monological artist escapes the normalizing gaze, in his particular manner of doing so he risks creating in a very substantial *oblivion* to the multiplicity that must be confronted as the ontological context for freedom. In other words, the notion of the monological artist risks obliterating some of the most important insights of Nietzsche's ontology.

In contrast, Foucault's understanding of artistic existence in which we seek to give ourselves form takes place at the limits of our being in *dialogue with* what is different from us or what within us finds no place within the reigning identities. Giving form to one's life involves accentuating and developing certain dimensions, placing others in the background, foregoing certain possibilities: fashioning our lives in the midst

20. Friedrich Nietzsche, *The Gay Science*, trans. Walter Kaufmann (New York: Vintage Books, 1974), p. 324.

of and with a sharper ear to the multiple and differing voices within and around us.

Yet is not this injunction that we create ourselves still rather empty and unable to inform our creativity in any way? Does Foucault leave us with anything more than an absolutely relativistic sense of creativity that is not much help at all? It seems to me that his notion of artistic existence both avoids relativism and is able to inform our creative activity in an important manner that avoids nihilism and indifference at the same time as it avoids the metaphysical solutions to these very problems. For Foucault's notion of the artistic ethos provides us with a loosely articulated conception of the social context conducive to artistic existence, which, in a very broad sense, might guide our activity. In its creativity, artistic existence seeks in part to work toward and enhance conditions in which an artistic ethos might become a more general and *vital* possibility. If human life should be a thing of art, then the artistic practice of caring for life should be linked to the creation of *situations and forms* of existence in which life can flourish as art. It is toward this end that Foucault's corpus—in many ways exemplary of the artistic activity he describes—strives. The artist in part seeks to contribute to a world in which one could answer the question, "Couldn't everyone's life become a work of art?" with a resounding yes ("Genealogy," p. 236). Let us explore what this seems to entail.

"What Is Enlightenment?": The Dialogical Artistic Ethos

Shocking as it may be to some of his readers, in his later essays on Kant and the Enlightenment, Foucault places himself in a certain fundamental respect squarely within the Enlightenment form of reflection. Yet this should not come as a surprise, nor should it be read as a dramatic change in his position. For already in *The Order of Things*, as we have seen, Foucault urges us beyond the analytic of truth not in order to usher in nihilism, but in order to reawaken modern thought "to the possibilities of its earliest dawning" (*Order of Things*, p. 341). The nature of these "possibilities" remains unclarified, however, until his later essays, where it receives important elaboration.

Foucault understands his discrepant positions on enlightenment to arise from discrepancies within enlightenment itself and particularly within Kant. On the one hand, Kant of the *Critiques* begins a tradition of philosophical reflection aimed at discovering the truth of truth in man conceived as a transcendental subject. Foucault has consistently opposed this tradition and shown ways in which it is closely aligned with modern forms of power and subjugation. On the other hand, however, Foucault sees in Kant's essays on enlightenment and the French Revolution the beginning of a radically different sort of reflection, one that characterizes the dimension of enlightenment within which he situates himself. "Here it is not a question of an analytic of truth, but what one might call an ontology of the present, an ontology of ourselves." Most succinctly, this philosophical tradition consists in "problematising its own discursive present-ness."[21]

In asking the question "Was ist Aufklärung?" Kant takes up the project of inquiring about the historical moment to which his own voice belongs. Kant defines enlightenment as an "exit," a "way out" of human's immaturity—that is, a release from our "self-incurred tutelage"[22] toward the autonomous and critical use of our reason. Yet if the Kant of the *Critiques* sought to know the definitive limits of knowledge—beyond which we must not go—Foucault, inspired by "Was ist Aufklärung?," seeks to release himself (and us) from the authoritarian tutelage of transcendental limits and use critique to explore both the contingency in these limits and the possibility of thinking and acting differently. In other words, the Kant of the Enlightenment essay, inquiring about the contingent historical location of his own thought, spurs Foucault to critique the *Critiques* and that dimension of modernity seeking to impose transcendental, unquestionable truths and practices. Here it is a matter not of discovering a transhistorical set of truths, but of having the "courage" to use one's critical capacities to reveal contingent constraints and expand the scope of creative freedom. Let us explore this more thoroughly.

It is the "attitude" of "problematizing our own discursive present-ness," rather than any specific doctrine or legacy, within which Foucault places himself. Central to this modern relationship with the present is what he identifies as a "*belonging*" and a "*task*."[23] With respect to the

21. Michel Foucault, "Kant on Enlightenment and Revolution," trans. Colin Gordon, *Economy and Society* 15 (Feb. 1986): 96, 89. Further citations are given directly in the text.
22. Immanuel Kant, "What Is Enlightenment?" in *On History*, ed. L. W. Beck (Indiana: Bobbs-Merrill, 1963), p. 3.
23. Michel Foucault, "What Is Enlightenment?" in *The Foucault Reader*, ed. Paul Rabinow (New York: Pantheon, 1984), p. 39. Further citations to this edition are given directly in the text.

first, the philosopher questions the knowledge and practices of the present as those to which he or she belongs, and as those that are necessary to comprehend in order to understand the constituting context of his or her own being. Indeed, it is in problematizing and understanding this present—and the fact that one belongs to it—that one "is to elicit at once [one's] own 'raison d'être' and the foundation of what one is to say" ("Kant," p. 89). It is through understanding the present of which one is that one determines what one is to do, say, and become.[24] It is because philosophers belong to "a certain 'we,' a we corresponding to a cultural ensemble characteristic of [their] own contemporaneity" (p. 89), that their self-understanding, self-direction, and self-creation are inextricable from an inquiry into their social present. The question regarding what one should say and do concerns the "we"; the ontology of the present is an "ontology of *our*selves"—not of one self in isolation.

Here we arrive at a more profound understanding of the "belonging" of modernity. For insofar as we recognize that self-creation demands an interrogation of the "we," as moderns, we belong to this ceaseless inquiry. The modernity Foucault describes in "What Is Enlightenment?" is characterized by the *belonging to the questioning of that to which we belong.* As moderns, we create ourselves by ceaselessly taking up the question of our present. This is the "task" to which we belong, a task we share as moderns. In short, part of modernity's unity lies in this question, in a shared being *as questioners* entwined in dialogical agonisms rather than as transcendental subjects. It is both the particular humility and the audacity of living in an interrogative mode that contribute to this sense of belonging. (As we have frequently heard from Foucault, this is very much at odds with significant dimensions of modernity that seek to impose administrated answers. Foucault's comments above, as we shall see, are "ironic.")

Foucault understands this task as "a critique and permanent creation of ourselves in our autonomy: that is, a principle that is at the heart of the enlightenment itself" ("Enlightenment," p. 44). Consistent with his genealogical efforts and his emphasis on local inquiry, Foucault's notion of critique and creation—the artistic ethos—revolves around what he calls

24. Thus in Kant's case, it is his understanding of the present, the fact that his answer to the question "Was ist Aufklärung?" is "man's release from his self-incurred tutelage" and the free use of his reason, which calls for and guides the work of his critical efforts to determine the conditions of possibility of truth and the legitimate uses of reason.

a "limit-attitude," which would continually direct us to the limits of our being, to that edge where we face the other. In this sense, Kant's monological notion of autonomy undergoes a dialogical transfiguration. Foucault is advocating not a blind rejection of all limits, but instead, a careful analysis of the boundaries of our being. This analysis of limits would attempt to illuminate "in what is given to us as universal, necessary, obligatory, what place is occupied by whatever is singular, contingent and the product of arbitrary constraints" (p. 45). In contrast to the Kantian project of determining the boundaries of the legitimate use of reason, Foucault advocates a critique of established boundaries to determine areas of "possible transgression." Rather than determining why we must remain the same given the "truth" of who we "are," the task is to determine in what ways it might be *possible and desirable* to become different and "to determine the precise form this change should take" (p. 46; my emphasis).

Foucault is careful to stress that this critical ontology of ourselves is not a doctrine—which would insidiously reestablish a Truth—but rather an "ethos." Here what is involved is a general manner of living. This ethos is elaborated in the notion of the "self as a work of art," which is most developed in Foucault's later essays and interviews, and is rooted in Baudelaire, Nietzsche, and the ancient Greeks. As a work of art, "one take[s] oneself as [an] object of a complex and difficult elaboration" in an effort to create one's existence ("Enlightenment," p. 41). As we have seen, this effort takes place at the limits of our being and involves a questioning attitude within which one seeks to define the shape of one's being and contribute to the creation of the social world.

Even considered most narrowly, this task—though it aims at creating an existence intended to be established not as a universalized norm, but rather as a shape only for a particular self—is not an isolated, self-enclosed project. Indeed, this self-enclosed selfhood-ness is characteristic of those projects that seek to "liberate" and realize "the truth" of oneself, to become what one "really is." But this is diametrically opposed to Foucault's notion of the self as a work of art. In the latter, the task is to create the shape of one's life through a careful experimentation with limits. And dwelling at the boundaries of one's being essentially entails a continual dialogical encounter with *otherness* and *others*. Hence the self as a work of art entails the exploration and transformation of more than just the self.

In an effort to gain a clearer understanding of this relationship between the notion of the self as a work of art and the encounter with otherness, let us take Foucault himself as quite exemplary of these notions. Foucault's life, as much as any other, was a life aimed at self-understanding and self-creation; understanding and creation that, as we have shown, are inextricably connected to understanding and showing possibilities for creating the "we" to which the self belongs. (Already we have gone beyond the boundaries of the self, but the self does not dissolve into the we, for each person, as "different," will have a particular understanding, particular practices he or she embraces, and a uniquely shaped life on these bases.) His life was, to reflect back on himself words he uttered in another context, "a philosophical life in which the critique of what we are is at one and the same time the historical analysis of the limits that are imposed on us and an experiment with the possibilities of going beyond them" ("Enlightenment," p. 50). It seems to me that his work persistently engaged with otherness in some ways that were central to his life as artistic self-creation.

To begin with, Foucault continually sought to elicit the "insurrection of subjugated knowledges" (*Power/Knowledge*, p. 81)—knowledges disqualified and silenced by hegemonic discourses and practices. The purpose of this attempt to make these other knowledges audible was twofold. First, Foucault sought to amplify these knowledges in an effort to establish a historical memory of the struggles through which hegemonic forms of power and discourse established themselves. By doing this, he illuminated some of "the *contingency* that has made us what we are" ("Enlightenment," p. 46). He attempted to show that the practices and understandings we perceive to be necessary are (at least in part) products of conflicts for power in which the hegemonic powers have sought not only to produce certain utilizable forms of being and eliminate others, but to reduce the expression of conflict with the others to silence as well.[25] By bringing the contingency of our thoughts and practices to

25. For example, in *Madness and Civilization*, Foucault records a history of "that other form of madness, by which men, in an act of sovereign reason, confine their neighbors, and communicate and recognize each other through the merciless language of non-madness" (p. ix), rather than a history that assumes the unchallenged superiority of "reason." He shows reason to be in part the outcome of its struggle with an other— "madness"—rather than a teleological development of its own pure essence. In short, to quote *Madness and Civilization* (and I think this indicates the continuity of Foucault's project), "What is in question is the limits rather than the identity of a culture" (p. xi).

light, Foucault seeks to loosen our identity with them, an identity that is most complete when the terms of the present appear so ubiquitous and necessary as to allow neither the possibility nor the desirability of criticism and change. It is only when our identity with the same is slackened that we can consider possibilities of creating existences other than those that are "given."

The second reason for amplifying the "insurrection of subjugated knowledges" is to provide a different perspective on the truths, norms, unquestioned identities, imperatives, and practices of a period. The objective here is to question the hegemony of certain discourses from the perspective of the others they exclude: "To entertain the claims to attention of local, discontinuous, disqualified illegitimate knowledges against the claims of a unitary body of theory which would filter, hierarchise and order them in the name of some true science" (*Power/Knowledge*, p. 83). Hence Foucault seeks to rediscover the knowledges of mental patients, prisoners, students, "hermaphrodites," etc., in an effort to make audible the voice of the other in a world where it is rarely heard. Through these other claims, Foucault seeks to shed critical light on features of the present which aspire to the status of universals; and he seeks to help different voices enter into the discussion about what the order of things is and how it should be.

A further way in which encountering otherness was central to Foucault's life-as-art has less to do with how otherness explicitly and directly confronts dominant knowledges and practices, within a given period, but concerns instead the value of the experiences and practices of other periods of history in illuminating possibilities of living differently. His analyses of the relationship of the early Renaissance to madness and of ancient techniques of the self are precisely such efforts to think about how we might formulate different social practices. But not merely "social practices." Equally at issue is the shaping and transformation of Foucault's own thought and existence.

The connection between philosophical-historical understanding of otherness and the creation of self is perhaps most explicit in *The Use of Pleasure*. Reflecting in the introduction on the motivation for his work, Foucault says:

Michel Foucault, *Madness and Civilization*, trans. Richard Howard (New York: Random House, Vintage Books, 1973).

It was curiosity . . . not the curiosity that seeks to assimilate what it is proper for one to know, but that which enables one to get free of oneself. . . . There are times in life when the question of knowing if one can think differently than one thinks, and perceive differently than one sees, is absolutely necessary if one is to go on looking and reflecting at all. People will say, perhaps, that these games with oneself would better be left backstage. . . . But, then, what is . . . philosophical activity . . . if it is not the critical work that thought brings to bear on itself? In what does it consist if not in the endeavor to know how and to what extent it might be possible to think differently, instead of legitimating what is already known? . . . The 'essay'—which should be understood as the assay or test by which, in the game of truth one undergoes changes, and not the simplistic appropriation of others for the purpose of communication—is the living substance of philosophy.[26]

The understanding of otherness is part of the "critical work" that enables "one to get free of oneself."[27] Since we are beings essentially embodied in the social world, artistic self-creation implies critically understanding and creating this world. The dichotomy between the creation of the self and the creation of the social world breaks down in their internal relation. But the dissolution of this *dichotomy* does not lead to the obliteration of *differences* between the self and this world. Just as it is the discovery of otherness and of the contingent limits of the present which is an essential aspect of creating the self, so too it is to a large extent in becoming *different* that the self partakes in the creation of the social world. The form the self takes as a particular being is aimed in part at transforming the social world toward enabling greater possibilities of different expressions of artistic existence.

For Foucault, though encounters with otherness may gesture in helpful ways in certain directions and away from others, what is most important in the encounters is that they reveal the *possibility* of being different. In the light of difference, thoughts and practices previously considered necessary begin to be seen as contingent; and in recognizing the contingency of being, we return to the possibility of creating alternative practices that might enhance the artistic ethos—we return to the pos-

26. Michel Foucault, *The History of Sexuality, Vol. 2: The Use of Pleasure,* trans. Robert Hurley (New York: Pantheon, 1985), pp. 8–9.
27. Of course, Foucault is perfectly aware of the *limits* of getting free of oneself, which is exactly why the labor of freedom always takes place at the *limits* of our being. We cannot simply leap over our limits.

sibility of freedom. It is partly because his work is governed by this end that Foucault is so evasive when Dreyfus and Rabinow repeatedly question him about whether or not the Greeks offer an "attractive and plausible alternative" ("Genealogy," p. 231). Indeed, as he notes, the Greeks subjugated women, had slaves, subject-object dichotomized sexuality; it is only the notions of "art of life" and "self as a work of art" that Foucault offers as specific helpful insights we can gain from the Greeks. And these are in the realm of "ethos"—an ethos of creative activity—rather than specific concrete practices partially rooted in a naturalist teleology.

In light of this, one should be wary of attempting to read Volumes 2 and 3 of the *History of Sexuality* as containing the specific contours of the ethos toward which Foucault strives. He finds interesting suggestions in the ancients yet seeks to elaborate these elements on a radically different conceptual and historical terrain. "This does not mean that contact with . . . a philosopher cannot produce something, but we would have to understand that this thing is new."[28] More than in Foucault's discussion of the ancients, we find his notion of self as a work of art elaborated in his philosophical reflections and exemplified in his philosophical activity.

Yet I think this conception, elaborated, that Foucault repeatedly engaged himself with different modes of being *in order to* reveal the possibility of creating himself/ourselves, or even *in order to* gain insights for his/our creative task, obfuscates a dimension of this engagement at the same time that it clarifies certain others. For there is an important sense in which the ends-means separation that lingers in this formulation fails to do sufficient justice to the "ethos" toward which Foucault gestures. Inherent in this artistic ethos is a vision of *exemplary metastyle.* And this metastyle is precisely that of *dwelling dialogically* with what is and those who are different at the limits of our being. (I call it "metastyle" to emphasize the great diversity of dialogical styles within this more encompassing notion.) This dialogical engagement with what is other is for Foucault the stylistic essence of the artistic life; it is through this engagement that we create ourselves. This conversation within which one gives shape to one's life as a specific voice *is* creative activity. Hence while the content aim of the artistic ethos can be defined very broadly as the enhancement of conditions that make possible the "permanent creation

28. Michel Foucault, "The Ethic of Care for the Self as a Practice of Freedom," in *The Final Foucault,* ed. James Bernauer and David Rasmussen (Cambridge, Mass.: MIT Press, 1988), p. 15.

of ourselves in our autonomy"—and central to this are more dialogical and less disciplinary social discourses and practices—the exemplary metastyle is achieved to the extent to which we fashion ourselves into dialogical beings. Such beings dwell in the difference of being and shape their lives there rather than blindly accepting hegemonic identities and dwelling in complacent *indifference* in the home of the same, the norm, the truth. In this sense, Foucault's dialogical engagement with difference, while *in part* a means to another end, is also in part an end in itself: the embodiment of the metastylistic ideal of the artistic ethos. This is further exemplified in the way Foucault's work develops and is portrayed. Is there any other philosopher in modern times who has so persistently used the conversation/interview format to express and develop his ideas—and also to gesture toward a particular way of being?

The importance of the dialogical essence of both the style and the content of the artistic life must not be underestimated, for it is at the heart of Foucault's understanding (sometimes explicit, more often the "unthought thought" Heidegger refers to) and is what links the affirmation of the self's distinction inextricably to the distinction and difference of others. In a late interview with Rabinow, Foucault stresses not only that the "dialogue situation" was essential to his "way of doing things," but moreover that "a whole morality was at stake" in the difference between dialogical versus polemical styles of existence—a morality concerning "the relation to the other."[29]

By sketching a vision in which the notion of self as art is intrinsically related to encountering otherness, Foucault is able to suggest a way in which the affirmation and enhancement of the self's creative activity,

29. Michel Foucault, "Polemics, Politics and Problematizations," in Rabinow, *Foucault Reader*, p. 381. This dialogue situation was clearly not at the heart of the ancient Greeks' "techniques of self." For them—on Foucault's reading—it is much more the case that "the relationship to self takes ontological precedence" over the care for others (*Final Foucault*, p. 7). Proper relations with others emerged out of a proper relation to oneself. This entailed knowing "ontologically what you are" as well as what is suitable to you in various roles as head of the household, citizen, etc., and acting accordingly (*Final Foucault*, p. 8). Yet the teleological framework that housed this ontology and these roles and enabled the self's relation to itself to be primary in these senses is, Foucault maintains, unavailable to us and at any rate undesirable. In a postmetaphysical world, the ontological framework for an aesthetic existence must be rooted in a critical engagement with the historical contingency that penetrates us and a keenly developed sense of the intertwining of diverse freedoms. Hence a "whole morality is at stake in the dialogue situation." Hence the creation of oneself demands confrontation with the various others Foucault sought out. Hence the persistent critique and attempt to transform needlessly nondialogical situations.

difference, and autonomy would occur not in atomistic oblivion to others, or through obliteration of others as is the case when difference is conceived of on the basis of equivalence, but instead through the dialogical engagement with others who are different. A primary virtue of this philosophy of the self is its increased appreciation of otherness. Foucault points toward a philosophy in which *dialogue* plays a central role in determining what *one* will say, in which dialogue is essential to self-creation. *It is the budging, blurring, tossing, glaring, shifting nature of our encounter with otherness and others which opens the opening of freedom.* And it is within this dialogical situation with others that our freedom acquires the form and content of a carefully shaped existence.[30]

It seems to me that Foucault's understanding of the relationship between the encounter with otherness and freedom offers us a fundamental reworking of the latter concept as it has often been formulated. For Foucault, freedom does not arise out of some sort of access to "the truth"; it is not to act according to self-generated transcendental laws of reason; it is not most profoundly opened as we face the possibility of our death and return from the anonymity of the "they" (*das man*) to the particular "there" of our Being; nor does it arise out of an "authentic" relationship to our "true self." Rather, we are returned to the contingency of the world and our relationship with it, as well as to our being as the

30. There are clearly some affinities between my reading of Foucault and Hans-Georg Gadamer's discussion in *Truth and Method* (2d ed., trans. Joel Weinsheimer and D. G. Marshall [New York: Crossroad, 1989]) of Thou-ness, the priority of the question, the disjunction of worlds as one participates in play, etc. For both, the other is central to one's life. Although the affinities are significant and should not be underplayed, there are substantial differences. Gadamer views the dialogical nature of hermeneutical experience primarily as the historical elaboration of truths understood as the participatory expression of being and beings. In Foucault's texts, there is a greater accent on divergence, contingency, transgression, and power in thinking and history, and these greatly tame the insistent and expansive consensualism one finds in Gadamer's writings. Further, they engender a greater dimension of exteriority in dialogue: that is, the effort to contextualize voices (other's, our own) as partial effects of historical contingencies and power relations in order to consider their meaning from "outside" and hence to problematize them in a way that is different from what is available to dialogue in a more strictly immanent sense. For all this, Foucault says that while we must not be insistent consensualists, we "must be *against* nonconsensuality" (*Foucault Reader*, p. 379), and the dialogical stance toward the other doesn't simply abandon immanence, but rather seeks to sustain an enlightening agonistic tension between interiority and exteriority. I think this argument distances him substantially from later Derrida's position, but it resonates with some of Derrida's earlier writings (cf. "Violence and Metaphysics: An Essay on the Thought of Emmanuel Levinas," in *Writing and Difference*, trans. Alan Bass [Chicago: University of Chicago Press, 1978]).

possibility of self-creation, through dialogical encounters with otherness. We are exposed to the radical contingency of our practices—and more generally, that of the world we experience and partake in—through our agonistic encounters with others with different thoughts, practices, and experiences, and the other experiences within our own being. In our engagements with others, we simultaneously have the possibility of giving them the gift of freedom we receive. Hence our own freedom is inextricable from—and thus in part should be guided toward creating—a social world that, to a greater extent, provides space for others who are different and difference within the self. When we close this space, we simultaneously drain our world of the (always limited) possibility of divergent self-fashioning through dialogue. Our divergent freedoms are intertwined, and an increasingly disciplined, normalized world increasingly closes off freedom not only at the level of the constitution and exclusion of selves, but equally important, because it withdraws the experience of otherness which both opens the possibility of our freedom to begin with and provides us with multiple points for creative engagement. The more we approach otherness within the terms of the same, the less we encounter otherness. In this light, the Foucaultian position seeks to discover the extent to which we can eliminate such practices. (This project, as I argue below, is not without its structure and hence is not a project that reduces to abstract "openness.") Of course, we never *completely* encounter otherness. Rather, our experience of otherness begins when we sense the surplus of the other—that which is different. The encounter with otherness is in this sense always in a state of beginning. Normalizing practices attempt to disguise the surplus and thwart this beginning.

No doubt, important questions arise concerning the possibility of social and political coherence within this philosophy of distinction. The central concept through which Foucault's position is able to address these questions is that of "belonging." Before we further develop this concept, let us briefly, and somewhat simply, summarize three notions of belonging that one can draw out of Foucault's thought as we have discussed it thus far. First, we are essentially beings whose existence is inextricably intertwined with our social milieu. Hence our self-understanding and self-creation must refer in part to the society to which we belong. Second, as moderns, we belong to the questioning of that to which we belong. In spite of radical differences in style and content, this questioning is something we do—or should—share; it should bind us to some extent and lend us a degree of solidarity, even if very loosely. Third, since our freedom emerges from and develops within our dialogical encounters with others who are different, each of us should belong to the task of creating a society and politics that enhance the possibilities for the expression of difference (differences that are not constituted around the obliteration of different others) and the dialogical engagements among these differences. At least in this very broad sense, the freedom of others is entwined with our own: our creative freedoms—with all their agonistic tensions—belong together if they are to be at all.

But one gets to the end of this list wondering if there is any relation we can take to the present—*to who we are at present*—which is anything other than genealogical criticism and "possible transgression." Can we belong to our present in any way that transcends questioning? Is our freedom in any way entwined with the present day or does it simply lie beyond it? To the extent that societies have ever "held together" in a nonauthoritarian manner, they have done so in part out of some sense of shared belonging to a set of values and practices which guides life in the present and helps generate the dreams for the future. Albeit that these traditions have always involved the exercise of power and subjugation, they have for better or worse been the foundations of the order of their day. Although we want to move in a direction away from these subjugative practices, we cannot move away from *some* sense of shared practices and values. It is a very *textured* identity that makes social life possible. As fundamental and illuminating as Foucault's vision based on the artistic ethos may be, it is difficult to believe that what we have discussed thus far would be sufficient for the existence of a social order. There has to be a way to belong to the present which is *not merely* that of getting free of it.

It seems to me that the notion of "ironic heroization," developed in the context of his discussion of Baudelaire, points in this direction. For Baudelaire, in Foucault's words, one of the central characteristics of modernity is "the will to 'heroize' the present" ("Enlightenment," p. 40). Heroizing the present involves an attitude of recapturing "something eternal" that lies within the fleeting present. It is the attempt to "extract" the "poetry" from within modernity. Yet this heroization is ironic in that while seeking the eternal in the present, it does not seek to *eternalize* the present. Instead, the eternal that is made manifest is itself a "transfiguration [that] does not entail an annulling of reality, but a difficult interplay between the truth of what is real and the exercise of freedom" (p. 41). In this transfiguring, "beautiful" things become "more than beautiful" (p. 41). One stretches reality toward what one dreams it could be, by grasping and developing what within reality most closely embodies this dream. Foucault writes: "For the attitude of modernity, the high value of the present is indissociable from a desperate eagerness to imagine it otherwise than it is, and to transform it not by destroying it but by grasping it in what it is" (p. 41).

Perhaps as illuminating as Foucault's attempts explicitly to describe "ironic heroization" is the essay "What Is Enlightenment?" itself when considered as an exemplary manifestation of this endeavor. What is his characterization of modernity as the "ethos" of critically examining our boundaries and exploring the possibilities of going beyond them if not ironic? Has not the great bulk of his work aimed at showing us how modernity insidiously *disguises* itself and drives toward an organization of being that posits the same as fundamental and the other as what must be made the same? In the essay "Kant on Enlightenment and Revolution," Foucault includes Hegel as an early representative of "a form of reflection within which I have tried to work" ("Kant," p. 96). But there are few essays where Foucault has not in some way strongly criticized Hegelian dialectics or at least hurled a sarcastic remark in that direction simply to distinguish his own project. Can a Foucaultian heroization of Hegel be anything but ironic?

Nevertheless, it is still a heroization. And in this notion of ironic heroization of the present lie the germ cells of a theory of "belonging" quite different from the theories of identity that have dominated Western metaphysics. In that tradition, identity has been thought primarily in terms of equivalence.[31] The goal with respect to the self has been to discover the truth of what one *is* and govern one's thoughts and actions in accordance with this identity, to the extent that it is humanly possible to do so. To identify with a community—worldly or spiritual—has been to thoroughly embrace its fundamental faith, truths, and the practices that follow. For Foucault, however, the "who" to which we belong is not a truth to be apprehended in its essence. Rather, the determination of the

---

31. For an account of identity in Western thought, see Martin Heidegger, *Identity and Difference*, trans. Joan Stambaugh (New York: Harper and Row, 1969), or Max Horkheimer and Theodor Adorno, *Dialectic of Enlightenment*, trans. John Cumming (New York: Seabury Press, 1972).

"who" to which we acknowledge our belonging is always a partially transformative activity in which we selectively *illuminate our being in the light of who we long to be.* We do not choose our identities out of nothing, but neither are they objectively given for us simply to acknowledge as true. The belonging of ironic heroization is "an exercise in which extreme attention to what is real is confronted with the practice of a liberty that simultaneously respects this reality and violates it" ("Enlightenment," p. 41).

But *why* would Foucault seek to acknowledge a "belonging" and affirm a "respect" for the present? Why would he ironically heroize Hegel? I think that his affirmation of "belonging" is rooted in his ontology just as deeply as is his notion of freedom as artistic transfiguration. Foucault reads the world to be a contingent, often discordant interplay of differences. His statement, "My point is not that everything is bad, but that everything is dangerous" ("Genealogy," p. 231), is based on this reading, and most of his work attempted to illuminate dangers, violence, and subjugation that modernity has disguised in the name of truth, virtue, and humanism. In accordance with his ontology and understanding of subjugation, his vision of the future has been guided toward a world that would affirm far more space for difference. Yet this ontology that demands critique and transformation also issues forth a *warning of caution.* For if everything is dangerous, transformation is dangerous—requiring "patient labor." And in the ubiquity of danger, we must not simply dismiss all of the present world, but rather carefully search for the *possibilities* it presents which may be worthy of our affirmation. Since the possibilities for freedom are as tenuous as they are, those thoughts and practices that make it possible in the present should not be cast aside in a reckless fashion. Those thoughts and practices that encourage dialogical engagements with otherness and artistic existences (or those within which this ethos can be encouraged) are too rare to be taken lightly. By belonging to them, we place ourselves in the opening they provide, to refuse closure with our own being—or, in more positive terms, to *affirm a situation* that enhances artistic existence. In a world that continually attempts to suture shut the openings, belonging is crucial to our freedom. The possibilities of the present should be carefully held in an artist's hands, transformed "not by destroying [these dimensions] but by grasping [them] in what [they are] ("Enlightenment," p. 41). The artist carefully works on the present in part through the openings it provides, to increase their scope and create others in a way that will avoid collapsing what is beneficial in the present. These favorable dimensions of the present which call us to make explicit our belonging serve as focal points around which we might coalesce and develop a greater sense of how we belong together as diverse beings affirming certain shared practices.

In this manner, Foucault heroizes Hegel and enlightenment. Having criticized Hegel in a variety of ways, he nevertheless sees in Hegel a project—an ontology of the present—worthy of affirming and belonging to, albeit in a different form. We heroize that which offers us the possibility of freedom. But our heroization is rarely rid of irony. Our belonging is always constituted in tension with who we long to be.

Questions for the Genealogical Artist

It seems to me that this is where Foucault jumps off the boat of theory and onto the shifting sands of the shores of the modern world. Here, continually at the edge of our existence, he has taken up the task of meticulously combing through who we are. Beyond (or out of) the themes discussed above, what Foucault offers us, I believe, is an acute awareness of the limits of these themes—of the way in which questions of ontology, ethics, belonging, and freedom, and the concrete individual and social practices that embody the dialogical artistic ethos, demand profoundly historical inquiry and articulation. It is when the philosophical task of creating ourselves becomes historical that it commences the activity of freedom.

I have argued that Foucault's dialogical artistic ethos arises from his ontological insights into the discordance and violence that accompany all modes of being, social practices, and discourses. Yet if Foucault's ethics appear to have developed in the context of his ontology, it is not at all clear that his ontology would be sufficient to *sustain* this ethos, either theoretically or practically. Granted that "discourse is a violence we do to the world." Granted that this is an insight most discourses go to great lengths to hide and Foucault's focus on violence must be read in this context. Nevertheless, if our perceptions, thoughts, and practices are construed *simply* as violence, imposition, discordance, what would draw one toward being an artist? Could a person sustain an artistic relationship to life in light of a basic philosophy that construed all its thoughts and practices as violent? Why would and how could a self who viewed the world only in this way somehow express a sense of respect for, affirmation of, and commitment to other selves? Why care? What could "belonging" mean in light of a *thoroughly* discordant philosophy? And to what extent is such a philosophy able to make sense of the full range of human experience?

As insightful as much of Foucault's ontological work is, if we take what may be his rhetorical exaggerations (designed to disturb) literally, we are left with a view of things that provides far too little support for anything as heroic as the artistic ethos. Foucault did not intend that his ontological statements be read in a way that was at once literal and totalizing. And we should be wary of reading him this way. Yet even if we avoid this error, it is still the case that some very important ontological issues remain unaddressed, and they are not without ethical and political consequences. I don't think Foucault has convincing responses to the questions posed above. One does not find them adequately discussed in his writings.

It seems to me that Foucault's thoughts on ethics tacitly rest on and require an ontology that acknowledges that although discord is an ineliminable dimension of our relations to the world, these relations offer us the possibility of more than simply discord and transgression. Indeed, this possibility is implicit in almost all his ethical writing. Yet this brings us to an interesting problem. Are we to revise an ontology because it is not in line with an ethics? Why not the other way around? Moreover, once we move beyond transcendental ontology, what do we draw on to support one ontological or ethical understanding in favor of another? We return to these questions with respect to Foucault in the final chapter. Before that, however, I wish to begin to explore them in the work of Maurice Merleau-Ponty.

Merleau-Ponty's ontology, ethics, and political theory all emerge from his strong sense of the discordant dimension of existence. Yet intertwined with this insight is a sense of an expressive dimension of existence that is not simply violence. Interestingly, "depth" is a central term in Merleau-Ponty's philosophy. It is a dimension that calls attention to the "transgressive," "eclipsing" nature of our existence, which various philosophies and political practices deny, yet at the same time it is a dimension of profundity, mystery, reverence. As it was for Augustine, the acknowledgment of the depth of being is for Merleau-Ponty vital for

4 · Merleau-Ponty

Merleau-Ponty's Philosophy of Depth

Augustine sought depth as a dimension of refuge and Truth. Foucault's studies reveal depth as a "dimension of reduction," and "truth" as the dazzling lure with which we are led into depth in order to cleanse ourselves of "the other." For Augustine, depth is the dimension of salvation. For Foucault, depth is the dimension of subjugation. If one of Augustine's most central yearnings is to return humans to depth, one of Foucault's most important tasks is to expose depth as a myth and thereby free us from it: depth is a dimension constructed in disciplinary society through which to wage "war by other means" on selves.

It appears perhaps that these alternatives cleave our conceptual universe regarding depth right down the middle in an exhaustive manner. We must struggle for our freedom within either one or the other. At best we can allow the thesis we ultimately reject to inform us of the underside of our most basic convictions, and possibly we can use it to tame partially the imperatives generated by our own position. Perhaps.

A dialogue between these two positions is indeed worthwhile and is part of the project at hand. But before the discussion takes place, it is helpful to consider the work of Merleau-Ponty. Though his position is sympathetic to certain dimensions of both Augustine and Foucault, his writing also contests the very terrain on which they oppose each other.

Merleau-Ponty explicitly rejects the notion that philosophy and life should assume the Augustinian project of turning inward to seek deep truths. He does not believe that "truth dwells in the inner man." Yet he is equally opposed to any position that would deny that depth is "the most 'existential' of all dimensions."[1] If he can simultaneously oppose both the Augustinian and Foucaultian positions on depth—while offering us a position capable of appreciating important aspects of each effort—it is primarily because he has reformulated depth in a manner that partially escapes the excessively constricting universe unwittingly appropriated and perpetuated by the Christian and the Nietzschean. It is the implicit thesis of this chapter (though his relation to the other two theorists is explicitly developed in the conclusion) that Merleau-Ponty's understanding of depth is an important contribution to our discussion because it alerts us to dangers inherent in each of the other two positions (dangers that might otherwise go unrecognized) and, simultaneously, allows us to fortify some of their most valuable contributions. Merleau-Ponty sketches an understanding of being in the world which gestures toward an ethics and politics with which to move away from nihilism, resist disciplinary power, and affirm human identity and difference (though this ethics and politics do not lie fully formulated in Merleau-Ponty's work and require a not insignificant degree of elaboration).

The Trajectory Away from Husserlian "Augustinism"

Although I wish to forgo a careful analysis of the relationship among Augustine, Foucault, and Merleau-Ponty until the final chapter, it is helpful to introduce Merleau-Ponty's philosophy of depth by situating it within the context of some of the themes that have arisen in earlier chapters. Perhaps the best place to begin is with a brief discussion of Merleau-Ponty's understanding of his relation to Husserl, since the early Husserl—as Merleau-Ponty interprets him—elaborated a philosophy that illustrated some of the worst developments one might try to trace to the Cartesian transformation of Augustine's thought and exemplified

1. Maurice Merleau-Ponty, *Phenomenology of Perception*, trans. Colin Smith (London: Routledge and Kegan Paul, 1962), p. 256. Original: *Phénoménologie de la perception* (Paris: Gallimard, 1945). Further citations to the English edition are given directly in the text.

some of what Foucault considered to be the most dangerous and insidious characteristics of philosophy in the modern episteme.

Merleau-Ponty's relationship to Husserl is a curious one. Although Husserl is the philosopher to whom he believed he had the greatest debt, Merleau-Ponty appropriated key Husserlian concepts such as "phenomenological reduction," "cogito," "intentionality" in a way that radically transformed the meaning they had for the early transcendental Husserl and, even in Merleau-Ponty's words, "pushed" the later Husserl of the *Lebenswelt* "further than he wished to go himself."[2] There can be no doubt that Husserl's later formulations in *The Crisis of the European Sciences, Ideas II and III,* and *Cartesian Meditations* were vitally important for Merleau-Ponty, no matter how much one wants to argue that he "coherently deformed" much of what he found there. One misses what most fascinated Merleau-Ponty about Husserl, however, if one reduces it to the theses that can be selectively appropriated from the latter's late and unfinished works, for what most enthralled Merleau-Ponty with Husserl was "instead of his theses, the very *movement of his thought.*"[3] What he discerned in Husserl's work was a trajectory, a path of projection whose course and value emerged as much in the impossibilities, shortcomings, and dangers illuminated in the early steps as in the later, more sophisticated formulations. Even more important was the "unthought thought" that Merleau-Ponty perceived to be implicit in the partial successes and failures of Husserl's thought-as-movement. Husserl's thought was, in Merleau-Ponty's view, a gesture, and as such its meaning was not to be found so much in its specific statements as in what was beyond itself toward which it moved. Merleau-Ponty was interested not in producing an accurate repetition of Husserl's formulations, but rather in resuming the movement of his thought, in formulating the "unthought-of element in his works which is wholly his and yet opens out on something else"

2. Maurice Merleau-Ponty, *The Primacy of Perception and Other Essays,* ed. James Edie (Evanston, Ill.: Northwestern University Press, 1964), p. 72 (further citations to this edition are given directly in the text). Some maintain more bluntly that Merleau-Ponty attributed his own ideas to Husserl. Cf. H. L. Dreyfus and Paul Rabinow, *Michel Foucault: Beyond Structuralism and Hermeneutics,* 2d ed. (Chicago: University of Chicago Press, 1983), pp. 35–36; James Schmidt, *Maurice Merleau-Ponty: Between Phenomenology and Structuralism* (New York: St. Martin's Press, 1985), chap. 2.

3. Maurice Merleau-Ponty, *Signs,* trans. R. C. McCleary (Evanston, Ill.: Northwestern University Press, 1964), p. 84. Original: *Signes* (Paris: Gallimard, 1960). Further citations to the English edition are given directly in the text.

(*Signs,* p. 160). For the purposes of the present work, it matters little whether or to what extent Merleau-Ponty correctly interpreted Husserl. Since I am interested in Merleau-Ponty's discussion only insofar as it illuminates Merleau-Ponty, I make no attempt to discover the "real" Husserl but simply pursue Merleau-Ponty's reading.

So let us briefly explore his understanding of Husserl's "movement." Merleau-Ponty summarizes this movement most revealingly in the following:

> Originally a project to gain intellectual possession of the world, constitution becomes increasingly, as Husserl's thought matures, the means of unveiling a *back side of things* that we have not constituted. This senseless effort to submit everything to the properties of "consciousness" (to the limpid play of its attitudes, intentions, and impositions of meaning) was necessary—the picture of a well-behaved world left to us by classical philosophy had to be pushed to the limit—in order to reveal *all that was left over:* these *beings beneath* our idealizations and objectifications which secretly nourish them and in which we have difficulty recognizing noema. (*Signs,* p. 180; my emphasis)

On Merleau-Ponty's account, Husserl's early phenomenological efforts exemplify classical philosophy's most extreme attempt to flatten being. They are an effort to "arrive at an evidence concerning [reflective consciousness] which is absolutely final," in which "what appears and what is are not distinct" (*Primacy,* p. 64). Husserl went through remarkable contortions to formulate this absolutely transparent certainty, yet as he does, the project itself begins to change and grow "more profound." Still, the flattening project had its persistence, and in spite of all the dazzling openings one glimpses in a work like *Cartesian Meditations,* Husserl still is able to close the text with: "I must lose the world by epoché, in order to regain it by a universal self-examination," followed by Augustine's famous line in *De Vera Religione,* "*Noli foras ire, in te redi, interiore homine habitat veritas.* (Do not wish to go out; go back into yourself. Truth dwells in the inner man.)"[4]

----

4. Edmund Husserl, *Cartesian Meditations,* trans. Dorion Cairns (The Hague: Martinus Nijhoff, 1977), p. 157. For a provocative reading of Husserl's project which illuminates some of the brilliance of this text and others by Husserl, see Derrida, "Violence and Metaphysics," in *Writing and Difference.* See also *Husserl: Intentionality and Cognitive Science,* ed. Hubert Dreyfus and Harrison Hall (Cambridge, Mass.: MIT Press, 1982), for some different interpretations.

Merleau-Ponty seems to think that these lines capture the spirit of earlier Husserl, not the Husserl of the text they close. Yet they are illuminating in the context of the project at hand since they explicitly illustrate one possible modern appropriation of Augustine.[5] Augustine's search for the transcendent God within was transformed by early Husserl into the search within for the transcendental ego as the source of the world's intelligibility. In the depths of the ego, Husserl sought a flattened world and a flattened empirical self.

As the passage quoted above at length indicates, however, Merleau-Ponty thought Husserl increasingly came up against "the back side of things," an intransigent world that resisted his scheme. Husserl pushed classical thought as far as it could go only to discover an endless horizon beyond his well-behaved world. The relentless attempt to objectify inadvertently led him to reveal the essentially inexhaustible dimensions of being which in part nourished, but also resisted, his objectifications. Merleau-Ponty claims that in Husserl's late works his project fundamentally changed with his heightened recognition of the *Lebenswelt* (the life-world the self discovers herself always already in the midst of) as the inexhaustible ground out of which reflection arises and to which it must return. Husserl's attempt to possess the world was short-circuited and moved toward becoming a project that revealed the impossibility of complete possession. "Willy-nilly, against his plans and according to his essential audacity, Husserl awakens a wild world and a wild mind."[6] (*Sauvage*, which I have translated as "wild," also means untamed, uncivilized, savage, rude.) Husserl discovers the depths of being.[7]

According to Merleau-Ponty, Husserl's uncovering of depth transformed his project from one aimed at "possession" of otherness to one aimed at revealing the surplus of being beyond our objectifications in order to challenge our possessive comportment toward the world and open us to a relation that is more genuinely dialogical. "Making explicit" becomes largely a task of revealing the forgotten "dehiscence" of Being,

5. On my reading, the *Cartesian Meditations* is an effort to explore the paradox that while "the world 'transcends' consciousness," at the same time "it is conscious life alone, wherein everything transcendent becomes constituted" (p. 62). Sometimes this exploration is flattening; sometimes it takes us to the edge of conceiving of the world as depth.

6. *Signes*, p. 228; *Signs*, pp. 180–181.

7. That the "wild" is "depth" becomes intelligible, of course, only after the discussion of Merleau-Ponty's conception of being as depth, which comes later in this chapter.

so well concealed by objectifying thought. In short, "phenomenology's task was to reveal the mystery of the world and reason" (*Phenomenology*, p. xxi). Of course, phenomenology was not *simply* to lead us to an open-mouthed awe in the face of being, but this awe was to be the strange foundation of its more constructive efforts at self-understanding, ethics, and politics.

Gone is the notion of an "inner man" to which we should strive to return in our quest for truth. In the preface of the *Phenomenology of Perception*, Merleau-Ponty repeats the phrase from Augustine's *Of True Religion* which closed the *Cartesian Meditations*—without even mentioning Husserl's appropriation of the passage—to define what phenomenology is *not*. "There is no inner man, man is in the world, and only in the world does he know himself" (*Phenomenology*, p. xi). Humans are thrown into the depths of being, and the task is not to eradicate this and recover an original, flat, self-possessing being in the depths of the self, but instead to inform and guide our lives in *recognition* of and a dialogue with being as depth.

It is this notion to which we now turn, beginning with Merleau-Ponty's critique of rationalism and empiricism, and followed by his development of his philosophy of depth.

Beyond Classical Thought and toward Depth

The starting point for Merleau-Ponty's development of his philosophy of being in *Phenomenology of Perception* consists of a careful critical analysis of rationalist and empiricist theories of our knowledge of the world. Rejecting the notion that the two radically contest one another, Merleau-Ponty argues that in fact both approaches are situated on "the same terrain."[8] Both posit and relate us to a completely determinate, unambiguous objective world as the ground of their investigations, empiricism through a process of causal relations, rationalism by way of consciously constituted relations.[9] Merleau-Ponty subjects these theories to ex-

8. *Phenomenology*, p. 26; *Phénoménologie*, p. 34.
9. Empiricist theories attempt to explain experience in terms of atomistic "sensations" conducted from the entirely determinate world to our brain by our sensory apparatus. Our brain then discerns a world of things by connecting the array of sense-data atoms (which correspond to the world itself) through "association," which is supposed to result from

tended, thoroughgoing, and persuasive criticism, which I wish to summarize selectively in the briefest of ways.[10] To begin with, Merleau-
Ponty finds that neither theory can account for the way we go about
learning of the world—an important criticism, given that this is the
stated goal of both approaches. Empiricism, which admits only of knowledge "produced" by the world, "cannot see that we need to know what
we are looking for, otherwise we would not be looking for it," while
intellectualism, which conceives of a world completely constituted by
consciousness, "fails to see that we need to be ignorant of what we are
looking for or equally again we should not be searching" (*Phenomenology*,
p. 28). At the root of this problem is that, whether as an effect of the
world on a passive consciousness or as a result of a consciousness that
constitutes the world, both theories can conceive only of a *completely
determinate* knowledge and a completely determinate world, and hence
are unable to grasp the "circumscribed ignorance" both motivating our
relation to the world and necessitating that there be something to be
learned.

   This argument leads us to the heart of Merleau-Ponty's criticism. In
positing our presence to a world of objects, each of which is completely
determinate "in itself," rationalism and empiricism falsify our experience
of the world and indeed make experience itself impossible. Examining
our experience more carefully (following Gestalt theory), Merleau-Ponty
finds that there are no objects given purely in identity with themselves
and that the most basic unit of experience emerges from difference: that
between a figure and a background. Pure identity—the homogeneous
sensation "in itself"—cannot be experienced; rather, it is this difference
that gives birth to our perceptions of the world. Thus, rather than being a

---

their de facto contiguity. The outcome, of course, is the possibility of a perfectly objective
experience of a perfectly objective world. Rationalist, or "intellectualist," theories of
knowledge likewise presuppose the objective world as the basis of their analyses. While
empiricism treats this world as "in itself," however, rationalism treats the world as the
product of a constituting consciousness "which eternally possesses the intelligible structure of all its objects" (*Phenomenology*, p. 28). Subjects are related to this world through
"attention," which illuminates and elucidates objects like an unconditioned searchlight,
with the strange power of bringing to consciousness what consciousness itself constituted
and already included. Although rationalism explicitly rejects the empiricist's notion of
sensation—arguing that sensations are themselves imperceptible—and replaces it with
"judgment," in fact, judgment is ultimately dependent on sensation at "the boundary of
our consciousness" (p. 32) as that which it interprets in a logical fashion.
   10. See especially chaps. 1–3 in *Phenomenology*.

composite of given sense atoms, the perceived world comes into being through a structuration of differences in which a figure emerges from an indeterminate background, which is itself prior to and the condition for sensing identifiable things within the perceptual field. The identity of an individual thing is perceptible to the extent that it stands out from its background.

Yet the figure-ground structure of the perceived world does more than indicate the extreme inadequacies of sense-data atomism. More fundamentally, it calls into question the rationalist and empiricist notions that the "objective world" is the stuff of experience. For it is obvious that the figure-ground structure in which the world always appears does not present us with a completely given and determinate experience of things, but instead shows the experienced world to be something that has a degree of ambiguity and is partially contingent and variable, depending on the specificities of the relationship between self and world. On Merleau-Ponty's reading at the most basic level, the world we experience is a world essentially open to diverse "structurings"—diverse determinations—through which it is simultaneously revealed and concealed. The world always retains an inexhaustible reserve of otherness (in the simplest sense, background), which exceeds, harbors, permeates, and constitutes the perceptions that emerge from our contact with it. This quality of the perceived world as structured-yet-open is what both motivates and makes possible our living experience of the world. Our new perceptions always emerge from and are motivated by our past experiences (rather than being determined by them or arising from nowhere, as with classical epistemology), and are possible precisely because the past did not offer us the world in completion.

This essentially ambiguous world that Merleau-Ponty begins to unveil no longer rests within the objectivity of the "in itself." Along with the perceived world's essential *transcendence* (its openness and elusive otherness), Merleau-Ponty discovers an essential *immanence:* an ineliminable relation between self and world. The phenomenological world is always revealed as "perceived by" an incarnate self, a being embodied within it from whence it is witnessed. The appearance of the world is always bound up with my spatial and temporal position (as well as the positions I can possibly inhabit) in it, as well as my incarnate history in a social, cultural, economic, and political world. The intersection of each social incarnate self and the world gives rise to perceptions that are always rooted in a particular existence. The self and the world refer endlessly to one another in a process of cocreation. If the phenomenal world is always in part sustained by an incarnate self, this is not for Merleau-Ponty a return to subjectivism, for the self is in turn its relationships with a world that, to a large extent, is not of its choosing. The self and world are reciprocally intertwined, and as one Merleau-Ponty scholar has put it, "the edge of [this] dialectic moves too quickly to be caught at rest."[11]

Hence in contrast to the "objective" world, Merleau-Ponty seeks to explore the world as it is given to us in our primitive experiential contact with being in order to reformulate our conceptions of self and world, and conjointly, to develop an ontology that is radically different from that of classical thought. He seeks to unveil the world as we experience it before our familiar acceptance of "things" and before our theoretical grasp of it. In other words, he aims at "return[ing] to that world which precedes knowledge, of which knowledge always *speaks*" (*Phenomenology*, p. ix). This forgoing of our everyday acceptance of the world is what Merleau-Ponty (following Husserl) calls "phenomenological reduction." It is the

11. Charles Fox, "The Existential Phenomenological Alternative to Dichotomous Thought," *Western Political Quarterly* 33 (Sept. 1980), 375. In this brief and most basic sketch of some of Merleau-Ponty's philosophical ideas, what we begin to see is a world far different than that of classical thought; a world that most fundamentally appears not as simply "in itself" but through our intersection and communion with it. Merleau-Ponty notes, however, that this world—both immanent and transcendent—is not the world that we generally recognize in our everyday life. In our everyday attitudes, we tend unreflectively to take the world as simply and completely "there." We generally lose sight of the way it is rooted in our living relations with it and the extent to which it maintains itself as partially other than and resistant to our sense of it. In short, Merleau-Ponty argues that in our everyday unreflective attitude, we usually accept the world as an objective thing—something closer to the world of classical thought than the phenomenological world Merleau-Ponty seeks to bring forth.

Nevertheless, he claims that this "objective world" always rests on the world of our primary experience, which emerges from our brute intersection with the world. Humans perpetually lose sight of this, he argues, because it is the essence of perception to forget itself, to lose itself in the things that appear in the perceived world. Indeed, its ability to lose itself is precisely what allows there to be "things" for us. "Obsessed with being and forgetful of the perspectivism of my experience, I henceforth treat it as an object." For all the manipulative capabilities to which this attitude gives rise, however—including scientific thought, which Merleau-Ponty wants not to disregard, but to limit—he contends that it conceals the fundamental being of the world on which it rests. This forgetfulness obfuscates the nature of both selves and the world, and has dangerous methodological, ethical, and political manifestations that Merleau-Ponty finds accentuated in various aspects of the modern world.

attempt to grasp the world as it emerges into being for us, not to reveal it as the correlate of a transcendental ego as early Husserl did, but "to reveal the mystery of the world and of reason" (p. xxi) which is concealed by classical thought. Merleau-Ponty's philosophical explorations of the phenomenological world are to provide us with understandings of the world which heighten our awareness of its paradoxical and ambiguous nature and illustrate that the mystery of the lived world is not its weakness, but precisely what lets it be "there." Of rationalism and empiricism, Merleau-Ponty remarks, "They levelled out experience" (p. 56). In opposition to this flattened world, Merleau-Ponty seeks to disclose being as depth.

Yet the disclosures of the phenomenological reduction never coincide with immediate experience, for they themselves are a form of reflection and as such present us never with brute experience but, instead, with unreflected experience as it is understood and worked over by reflection. While returning to the lived world provides Merleau-Ponty with a vantage point from which to critique decisively forms of objectifying knowledge based on identity, nevertheless the lived world does not signify a privileged domain capable of providing the existential phenomenologist with a complete knowledge. Rather, by pointing to the lived world, Merleau-Ponty gestures to that mysterious region that calls us to a continual questioning engagement. Living experience, in its depth, always transcends our reflection on it and ushers forth a dialogical relation with being which we must continuously renew. Hence while the phenomenological reduction is central to Merleau-Ponty's philosophical strategy, he cautions from the beginning that the "most important lesson which the reduction teaches us is the impossibility of complete reduction" (*Phenomenology*, p. xiv). The wondrousness of the world rests in part on its ability to exceed even our attempts to grasp its wonder.

An important dimension of this paradox is that for Merleau-Ponty, both the experienced world and philosophical reflection are in a perpetual process of cocreation:

> The phenomenological world is not the bringing to explicit expression of a pre-existing being, but the laying down of being. Philosophy is not the reflection of a pre-existing truth, but, like art, the act of bringing truth into being. (*Phenomenology*, p. xx).

There is no pure and absolutely unexpressed life in man; the unre-flected [*irréfléchi*] comes into existence for us only through reflection. (*Primacy*, p. 30)

In these passages, we glimpse the circularity that is a central theme in Merleau-Ponty's ontology and manifests itself in almost all of his work. On the one hand, reflection always refers back to a layer of unre-flective life out of which it emerges. On the other hand, however, this unreflective life does not exist for us unless we return to it and bring it forth through reflection. Yet unreflective life is neither everything (ac-cording to a superficial reading of "the one hand") nor nothing (accord-ing to a superficial reading of "the other hand"). Instead, it should be conceived of as not fully determinate existence that is open to a variety of appropriations and resistant in varying degrees to all appropriations as well.

As noted, philosophical reflection *transforms* being in its attempt to express it. Indeed, "without reflection life would probably dissipate itself in ignorance of itself or in chaos" (*Primacy*, p. 19). Recalling Marx's eleventh thesis on Feuerbach that "philosophers have only *interpreted* the world, in various ways; the point, however, is to *change* it,"[12] one should note that for Merleau-Ponty, the philosophical act of understanding the world is already a transformation of this world. This is not in any way to assert that Merleau-Ponty advocated a praxis of inner life; much of his writing on politics and religion is aimed at refuting this notion. Neverthe-less, if praxis does not end with philosophy, it takes an essential first step with it. Emphasizing the seriousness of the philosophical project, he writes: "We take our fate in our hands, we become responsible for our history, through reflection, but equally by a decision on which we stake our life, and in both cases what is involved is a violent act which is validated by being performed" (*Phenomenology*, p. xx). To understand the transformative aspects of Merleau-Ponty's reflections, we must explore his philosophy of depth.

12. Karl Marx and Friedrich Engels, *The Marx-Engels Reader*, ed. R. C. Tucker, 2d ed. (New York: Norton, 1972), p. 145.

Philosophy of Depth

The centrality of "depth" (*profondeur*) in the work of Merleau-Ponty
has generally been overlooked or underestimated by his interpreters.[13]
Many of his texts contain discussions of depth, however, and he uses the
word repeatedly in *The Visible and the Invisible* in his attempts to distinguish his philosophy from Kant, Bergson, Sartre, Husserl, and others.
In the *Phenomenology of Perception*, Merleau-Ponty states that depth is
"the most existential of all dimensions" (p. 256). In a working note in *The
Visible and the Invisible*, he says that without depth, "there would not be a
world or Being."[14] While these passages taken alone are obviously insufficient to illustrate the claim that Merleau-Ponty is most profoundly a
philosopher of depth, they do indicate that it is an important notion for
him and one that needs to be carefully explored in order to understand
his philosophy. They are especially provocative for the present inquiry,
given his explicit rejection on more than one occasion of a "deep self" or
"deep truth." If there would be no Being without depth, and yet depth is
not—nor harbors—objective truth, we are led to ask, How must we
understand this depth so essential to Being that Being would not Be if
not as depth? Let us look more closely.

Merleau-Ponty's first discussion of depth occurs in *Phenomenology of
Perception*, where as usual, he launches his own analysis from a careful
critique of empiricist and intellectualist approaches. Both theories, he
argues, are alike "in denying that depth is visible" (*Phenemenology*, p.
254). For classical thought, which assumes that depth is simply "breadth

13. For example, there is little or no discussion of depth in the following works on
Merleau-Ponty: Sonia Kruks, *The Political Philosophy of Merleau-Ponty* (Brighton, U.K.:
Harvester Press, 1985); Gary Brent Madison, *The Phenomenology of Merleau-Ponty: A
Search for the Limits of Consciousness* (Athens: University of Ohio Press, 1981); Albert
Rabil, Jr., *Merleau-Ponty: Existentialist of the Social World* (New York: Columbia University
Press, 1967); Schmidt, *Merleau-Ponty*. Samuel B. Mallin, *Merleau-Ponty's Philosophy* (New
Haven, Conn.: Yale University Press, 1979), addresses certain aspects of depth. This is
not to dismiss the aforementioned works, for I have benefited in important ways from
some of them (and other works on Merleau-Ponty that have overlooked "depth" as well),
and often issues of "depth" are addressed using other terms from Merleau-Ponty's
lexicon. Nevertheless, it is interesting to find such a consistent silence in spite of the
multiplicity of concerns the texts above represent.
14. Maurice Merleau-Ponty, *The Visible and the Invisible*, trans. Alphonso Lingis (Evanston, Ill.: Northwestern University Press, 1968), p. 219. Original: *Le visible et l'invisible*
(Paris: Gallimard, 1964). Further citations to the English edition are given directly in the
text.

seen *from the side*" (p. 255), depth cannot be seen because the seer is in
no position to see it. It is either concealed by the first surface in sight,
which blocks our vision of all that is in the depths behind it; or in the case
of the distance between our eyes and the first surface, there is no way of
actually *seeing* this depth itself, since "this distance is compressed into a
point" in our flat visual field (p. 255). Classical depth can be seen only if
the observer conceptually moves to the side, in which case it becomes
breadth, and hence classical thought argues that we experience depth not
by seeing it, but rather by intellectually *interpreting* it in terms of breadth
from facts such as the apparent size of the object in our visual field and
the angle of convergence between our eyes.[15]

Merleau-Ponty finds serious problems in this objectivist rendering of
depth. He argues that these approaches "do not give us any account of
the human experience of the world; they tell us what a God might think
about it"—a being at once everywhere and no particular place (*Phenomenology*, p. 255). Yet we are clearly not such beings, and the essence of
our experience of depth is precisely that of an incarnate being specifically
located in the lived world. For this being, for human experience, depth is
not equivalent to breadth and height, dimensions that are laid out in
plain view before us. Far from indicating a world given "in itself," the
appearance of depth, more than the other two dimensions, speaks of its
inherence in a *relation*, a primordial communication between a self and
the world which is at the origin of spatial experience. By collapsing depth
into breadth and then conceiving of a "cerebral alchemy" that facilitates
this conversion, classical thought jumps over this difference between
depth and the other dimensions and assumes a thorough knowledge of
an entirely uniform objective space as the *basis* of our experience. This
assumption begs the question, however, which is precisely to ask how we
come to experience space—and depth in particular—to begin with. Our
experience of depth must be prior to and cannot be founded on sophisticated calculations based on a space to which depth itself gives rise.

In contrast to these abstract approaches, Merleau-Ponty contends that
we must seek to disclose the way in which depth comes into being for us
as depth. To do justice to this "most existential dimension," we must
explore the existential *relations* between the self and the world, since it is

15. In other words, the experience of depth is here understood as a cognitive activity in
which we judge the objective breadth we would discover between ourselves and things if
we were to see this distance from the side.

through these relations that our experience of depth and the world originates. (These relations cannot be comprehended "objectively" lest we
assume as "given" what on this account "gives.") Before taking for
granted the world in which science has "levelled down the individual
perspective," we must rediscover "the *originality of depth*" (*Phenomenology*,
p. 256).

Taking depth's gesture toward the relation between the self and the
world as his starting point, Merleau-Ponty states that the experience of
depth is fundamentally "a possibility of a subject involved in the world"
(*Phenomenology*, p. 267). The self ceaselessly finds itself thrown into
thickets of being of which it is not the creator, and it responds to this
thrownness through a continual effort to get a grip on this wild and quite
indeterminate world that surrounds it. Yet the self's partial ability to get a
hold on being—to sense *something*, rather than be condemned to thrash
aimlessly forever amid an entirely foreign world—is not simply a result of
its own will, but rather emerges from the fact that it belongs to a more
primordial and "general existence," from which it originates as divergence, separation (*écart*). While this general existence is referred to in
the *Phenomenology of Perception* (cf. p. 216) and often implicitly underlies
his discussions even where it is not mentioned, Merleau-Ponty does not
submit it to a more careful and developed analysis until his later treatment of the "flesh." Without fully developing this notion until later, I
wish to begin with a brief and simplified discussion of flesh, since it
sheds a certain light on Merleau-Ponty's earlier experiential discussions
of the self-world relation with respect to depth which will allow us to
explore them while avoiding some of their obscurity.

Among other things, we find in his notion of flesh the ontological
possibility of the "self," the "world," and the relations between them.
Merleau-Ponty calls not only my carnal existence but also that of the
world "flesh" in order to indicate a "kinship" between them which
makes possible the sensible world that emerges through their communion. Indeed, the communication between the self and the world is
possible only because, in a general sense, they share similar flesh. Expressing his theory of embodiment in its more developed form as "flesh
among flesh," Merleau-Ponty writes: "If [the body] touches [things] and
sees them, this is only because, being of their family, itself visible and
tangible, it uses its own being as a means to participate in
theirs . . . because the body belongs to the order of the things as the

world is universal flesh" (*Visible*, p. 137). My flesh can be present to that of the world because at a certain level they are similar stuff. My body lends itself to the world and the world inscribes my body because they "belong together" as differentiations of a common flesh. Without this commonality, nothing would be "there."[16] Merleau-Ponty uses the term "flesh" in part to indicate this commonality and in addition to distinguish his philosophy from any materialistic philosophy that would reduce the "coiling over" of flesh on flesh to a relation among mere "things in themselves." Flesh is (as we shall see) "a general manner of being" (p. 147), inexhaustible, and not to be subjugated to our experiences of it as object.

As humans, we thus find ourselves tossed into the jungle of flesh, and our existence is at a most fundamental perceptual level a constantly renewed attempt to establish and maintain a hold on the world. It is not the easygoing hold of a subject and a world that are rationally designed for one another. No, Merleau-Ponty's "world ceaselessly assails and beleaguers subjectivity as waves wash around a wreck on the shore" (*Phenomenology*, p. 207). The commonality of the self's flesh and that of the world does not ensure a harmony, merely the possibility of something rather than nothing. In the midst of this condition, existence is the primordial attempt to make being determinate for oneself, the effort to experience a world with distinctions, significance, references, and poten-tials—a world with a degree of familiarity in which we can find and guide ourselves.

Because my sensual field belongs to the finitude of a historical bodily being submerged deep in the world, in the most basic sense I cannot be everywhere at once or present all at once to everything. Nor even can I be present simultaneously to everything that most immediately surrounds me. The finitude of my being, which precludes ubiquitous presence to everything, behooves that my perceptual contact with the world be through *something*. Hence my perceptual bond with the world must be essentially directional, proceeding to and fro between myself and some-thing in the world. It is through this directional attempt to grasp the world so as to further direct my existence within it that depth comes into being for us. "Depth is born beneath my gaze when the latter tries to see

16. Just as I can touch my own body by applying flesh to flesh, so too can I sense the rest of the world because I am thick, as it is; and when I palpate it with my touch or my gaze, it resists me, forming at the interface a surface of sensibility.

something" (*Phenomenology,* p. 262; Merleau-Ponty's emphasis). At a most basic level, the perception of anything is (as we have already seen) the accomplishment of a depth organization of the perceptual field into figure and ground. To perceive something, it must "stand out," a trope already indicating the essentiality of depth to perception. The emergence of a distinct something implies the submergence of the rest of the world into the depths of varying degrees of indeterminacy.[17]

Thus when Merleau-Ponty refers to "the originality of depth," clearly the figure-ground structure of all perception which brings things forth in our sensual field is part of what he has in mind. This depth founds a world with distinctions and texture that allow us partially to grasp it. Yet what is the essence of things brought forth in this field? (I use the word "essence" as Merleau-Ponty does, not to indicate a static nature, but thinking instead of *Wesen* and *ester*—active verbal essence.[18]) Are they flat entities laid out completely before us? Merleau-Ponty's response to this question is a definitive no. Things are "things" not only through the depth of their distinction from their surroundings, but because they themselves have depth. Indeed, this quality is intertwined with their distinction. "Depth is the means the things have to remain distinct, to remain things, while not being what I look at present" (*Visible,* p. 219). Without their own depth, things would be indistinct from their sur-

17. Yet it should be emphasized that our grasp on the world is not at all the free act of a constituting subject. The phenomenological world emerges through the carnal intercourse between the flesh of my body and the flesh of the world. Depth emerges as I "try" to see something, yet "the act of focusing . . . is equally a response to a question put by the data [*les données*] and this response is contained in the question" (*Phenomenology,* p. 262; *Phénoménologie,* p. 303) If, as Merleau-Ponty says, it is impossible "to see the spaces between the trees as things and the trees themselves as background" (*Phenomenology,* p. 263), it is because the world demands that the incarnate self perceive it within particular limits. My body cannot climb the space between the trees just as it cannot pass through the trees as if they were space. As my body moves, it intersects the world in ever-new ways; and its movement is in a relation of circularity with its perceptual grasp of the world in depth, insofar as it simultaneously presupposes and ceaselessly forms and transforms this field. As the world seduces, yields, and resists us in multitudinous ways, our perceptual world is called forth. Even these formulations, however, are abstract moments of my body's *relation* to the world—a relation in which flesh "coils over" on flesh—which is more primary than either of the moments. The body and the world it is submerged in ceaselessly interpenetrate one another through reciprocal carnal "motivations." The field of depth emerges through this intertwining, and ultimately "it is the *field itself* which is moving towards the most perfect possible symmetry, and depth is merely a moment in arriving at a perceptual faith in one single thing" (*Phenomenology,* p. 262; *Phénoménologie,* p. 303; my emphasis).

18. Cf. *Visible and the Invisible,* pp. 203, 206–7.

roundings and indistinct from me as well, since I would totally possess them; they would not *be.* Hence contemporaneous with the birth of something in my perceptual field is the rendering of the *thing* in depth, and this depth implies the spatiality of the world as well.

Merleau-Ponty pursues this genesis of the experience of depth in his discussion of our perception of a cube sketched on paper. I see a three-dimensional figure—rather than nothing or a mere incoherent juxtaposition of lines—by inhabiting it and animating it with my gaze in ways the lines themselves call forth. This depth perception brings forth a "thing," a "locality," which gathers together the lines on the page so thoroughly that their appearance is governed by their mutual implications. Angles that are acute or obtuse when viewed in terms of the flat objective juxtaposition of lines appear immediately in depth as right angles, and the lateral faces (objectively diamond-shaped) appear as "squares seen askew." Depth is precisely this bringing forth, this gathering together, this instantaneous crystallization of a significant perception in which something and a "there" appears—that is, a being, volume, locality, the multiple parts of which "belong together" through their reciprocal implications. Before this there is nothing, and no "there," only vague indeterminacy.[19]

In addition to this indication of both the structure of all perception as figure and ground and the originary depth of things, another aspect of depth is crucial for Merleau-Ponty. Depth inheres in the perspective of our perceptual field. As my grasp on the world, the world's grasp on me, the depth in and through which things appear always expresses the stretch between them and me. Things appear not only as distinct from a background, but as distinct from myself as well. Each thing is "being at a

19. Merleau-Ponty elaborates this point with a discussion of our perception of a sketched cube, because the sketch is sufficiently ambiguous partially to disclose the manner in which the depth rendering brings the field into being and holds sway over the aspects of the field, endowing angles and shapes with a significance they acquire through their relations with other parts, pulling forth some lines, repelling others back, separating the figure of the cube from the background of the page; in short, giving birth to the "there." What Merleau-Ponty says of the sketched cube applies to all perception, however (except, of course, with the obvious difference that a real three-dimensional cube is rendered in a depth with a tactile thickness that accords with its visibility). When I perceive a real cube, say the sugar cube on the kitchen table, its being springs forth from the background as a thick, angular thing whose angles, shadows, and faces cohere together in an originating spatial depth. All perceived things appear as things through this experiential pulling forth and pushing back, which generally occur instantaneously, distributing their parts in a depth that sustains their significance and calls forth the "there."

distance" (*Signs*, p. 167), and it appears as a significant thing only by cohering in a depth that reveals the various distances of its different parts from me. Without this implicit stipulation, no thing can be; not even a flat juxtaposition of lines on a flat surface, for "there are forms and definite planes only if it is stipulated how far from me their different parts are" (*Primacy*, p. 180). This "stipulating" is not one of an objective thought that would measure the distance, but more fundamentally the depth that emerges with the perceptual field as soon as it is perceptually grasped as "there," as soon as there is anything to measure.

Hence we see not only that our experience of things originates in depth, but that in giving birth to "being at a distance," depth *renders open the "clearing"* in the midst of which we always find ourselves. It is the depth of the perceptual field which clears being, which holds the field open, instead of smothering us in the absolute proximity of an indeterminacy from which we can distinguish neither ourselves nor a world. Here we begin to see the specificity and uniqueness of depth, the reason Merleau-Ponty calls us to think it. Depth as the essence of the clearing is not the "third dimension" of the world, which, like the other two dimensions, can be measured. Rather, Merleau-Ponty speaks of depth as that through which our experience of the world and the three dimensions *originates*. "Depth thus understood is, rather, the experience of . . . a global 'locality'—everything in the same place at the same time, a locality from which height, width and depth are abstracted, of a voluminosity we express in a word when we say that a thing is *there*" (*Primacy*, p. 180). The "there" emerges in depth as the visual field "pulls forward," "pushes back," implicates, reveals, and conceals to present the space of the world. A volume of experience is given to which we belong.

Merleau-Ponty's inquiry into depth calls attention to the paradoxical nature of the world's presence, in which the depth of each being is grasped on the basis of distinctions allowing it to "stand out" from and eclipse what it is not, while in turn these distinctions and this envelopment appear on the basis of each being's depth. "The enigma [of depth] consists in the fact that I see things, each one in its place, precisely because they eclipse one another and that they are rivals before my sight precisely because each one is in its own place. Their exteriority is known in their envelopment and their mutual dependence in their autonomy" (*Primacy*, p. 180). Indeed, things are only "there" through a sort of self-eclipse, in which their present surface of visibility is indebted to and indicative of a latent invisibility harbored in the depths of their being. Emerging from the depths of things through the coiling over of flesh on flesh, "the look does not overcome depth, it goes round it" (*Visible*, p. 219). The world and the things that appear within it are this *transcendence* as depth, this presence of the *inexhaustible*.[20]

Yet if we have established that depth renders open the clearing of the lived world and that it is the dimension of transcendence, a crucial question looms large concerning the relationship between this experience of things and the flesh of the world. Does our experience "correspond" to the world's flesh? Does it "express" this flesh? It is "attuned" to this flesh? After all, have we not asserted an ontological collusion between the self and the world by calling them both "flesh?"

I wish first to develop Merleau-Ponty's response to these questions by further elaborating his discussion of our experience of the world, and then to explore the "indirect ontology" that grows out of this discussion and remains in progress in his final works. There he addresses the relation between our experience and the Being of things.

As we have begun to see, the depth organization of the perceived world simultaneously reveals and conceals the beings that appear therein. Merleau-Ponty also employs metaphors such as "express" and "transgress" however, which are far less neutral and far more illuminating for the discussion at hand.[21] To have the world partially in our grasp, to have it in the depth of a perceptual field, is to "express" it in a manner that brings it into being in ever-new ways emerging from our intersection with it. But it is also essentially to render the world partially invisible—hidden in the backsides, the insides, the horizons of our perceptual field—and to elevate and subordinate its qualities and dimensions in ways that

---

20. This discussion of depth has drawn substantial support from illustrations that are visual in nature. However, Merleau-Ponty's contention that the perceived world originates through a depth rendering in which things find both their cohesion and their distinction from other things applies to the perceived world as such, not just visual perception. As my fingers run through the warm sand on a beach, at least for an instant the rest of the tactile world surrounding me is partially eclipsed and driven back by the thick being of the resistant sand. As I am captivated by Coltrane's saxophone, it bubbles out of the depths of an irreverently noisy bookstore, pressing the chatter, the jingle of coins falling into a cash register, the squeaky door, the sliding of books into the deep reaches of its shadow, eclipsing them so thoroughly that they are almost driven from the room. And his wild improvisation is able to do this only because it is *there*—a thickness of inexhaustible sound that both appears through and demands its distinction.

21. "Transgress" is found especially in *Visible and the Invisible*.

transform, bend, and transgress its polyphonous and often cacophonous being.

One particularly apt word Merleau-Ponty uses to describe originating perception is *jaillir*—to shoot forth, to gush, to flash.[22] To perceive is to experience the figure of perception shooting forth in a flash that captures my attention and blinds me—at least for an instant—to the rest of the world. For Merleau-Ponty, there is a sense in which all perception is dramatic. If we are usually unaware of this drama, Merleau-Ponty argues that it is because we tend to lose ourselves and the profundity of each instant in the world that is revealed through continuous experience. We take this world as simply there, yet it always originates in the perceptual field that gushes like a spring out of our communion with things.

Summarizing the turbulence and transcendence of things, Merleau-Ponty writes:

> [Visible things] are always behind what I see of them, as horizons, and what we call visibility is this very transcendence. No thing, no side of a thing shows itself except by actively hiding others, denouncing them in the act of concealing [*masquer*] them. To see is as a matter of principle to see farther than one sees, to reach a latent existence. The invisible is the outline and the depth of the visible.[23]

The perceived world is *"wild Being"* (*L'être sauvage*)[24] and depth vacillates like the surface of a raging ocean, as figures emerge and submerge in the flow of experience. Things coexist as "rivals" in my perceptual field, ceaselessly upsetting its balance, imparting perpetual life to perception rather than subsuming themselves neatly in a vision that is "once and for all." "Things dispute for my gaze; and anchored in one of them, I feel in it the solicitation of the others which makes them coexist with the first—the demands of a horizon and its claim to exist."[25]

Nevertheless, the world Merleau-Ponty describes is not one of *incoherence* in which the surface transience of experience is its greatest depth. He does not describe a world that is predominantly discon-

22. *Phénoménologie*, p. 30; *Phenomenology*, p. 22.
23. *Signs*, pp. 20–21; *Signes*, p. 29.
24. *Visible and the Invisible*, p. 170; *Visible et l'invisible*, p. 223.
25. *Signs*, p. 49, changed to present tense.

tinuous—completely made and remade—from one instant to the next. Rather, the depth of our experience of the world which renders things both "there" and open to new and different perceptions also ensures that there can be some degree of continuity to our experience, that it can cohere and elaborate rather than be ontologically doomed to proceed as a succession of utterly discontinuous differences.[26] The figure that currently dominates my perceptual field harbors in the depths of its background horizons the other things surrounding it and hence tacitly implies them. It is this mutual implication of other things and other experiences in the depths of each thing and experience which maintains the possibility of some continuity in our experience of the world.[27]

If Merleau-Ponty depicts "a world of teeming exclusive things which could only be taken in by means of a temporal cycle in which each gain is at the same time a loss" (*Signs*, p. 49), this is not to establish a philosophy that affirms all perceptions as "equally valid." As I shall develop more fully below, some perceptions express the world better and transgress it less harmfully than others. Those that close us off from different others and close us to the possibility of different experiences in the future transgress the world in a way that fundamentally violates depth itself. Transgressions—"coherent deformations"—that bring forth a dialogical encounter with the world and maintain an openness to the future are in contrast (as we shall see) the essence of depth itself. The world continually participates in the clarification of the relative values of our perceptions as it "crosses out" those perceptions that prove to be unsustainable on further contact. Yet even sustainable perceptions contain an ineliminable transgressive quality. To render the world into the depth of the clearing is not just to "deliver" it into the open, but to "rend"—in the sense of to tear it open. One of Merleau-Ponty's most important insights,

26. As we shall see, the depth and hence the worldliness of our experience can break down and consequently either freeze our experience or release it to utter discontinuity. At this point we cease to experience the world in some very fundamental ways. For the moment, my discussion is confined to the world as depth.

27. The importance of this basic coherence and continuity of the clearing should be emphasized. It is what allows that our different experiences, no matter how discordant, might speak in the conversation of our existence and offer us the possibility of developing a greater understanding of ourselves, others, and things in the world. Without this basic belonging-together-in-the-same-"there" of our experience, existence could be nothing but a gauntlet in which it would be impossible to "rise to our feet." Depth vacillates like a raging ocean, but as inhabitants of this sea we simultaneously experience the marked cohesion of this massive fluid.

it seems to me, is that perception is unavoidably a "violent act" (*Phenomenology*, pp. xx and 361).[28]

Nevertheless, the depth of the "there," which always violates things as it expresses them, is equally what maintains the *openness* of our experience and provides the possibility of new perceptions that reveal dimensions hitherto disregarded. The backsides, the backgrounds, the horizons of my perceptual field absorb my senses into the thickness of a fertile and protean soil capable of nurturing new visions that transcend old closures. Through the *temporal elaboration* of experience, I can become aware of differences and otherness to which I had previously been oblivious. But the will to eliminate transgression from each and every perception, to be present all at once to all differences, is unwittingly the will to express nothing—to let no difference figure on a ground.

This discussion has thus far taken place at the experiential level. Yet we are already closer than we may think to an ontology of "depth Being." If I have put forth a lengthy portrayal of Merleau-Ponty's discussion of experiential depth, it is not simply because of its intrinsic value—although there is a great deal—but also because it is in keeping with Merleau-Ponty's contention that "one cannot make a direct ontology" (*Visible*, p. 179). "For how would we speak of Being, since those beings and shapes of Being, which open to us the only conceivable access to it, at the same time hide it from us by their mass."[29] Instead, we must proceed through a careful examination of beings and experience in order to "advance obliquely" toward an ontology of this elusive Being (*Signs*, p. 83). Understood in this light, Merleau-Ponty's writing, at least from the *Phenomenology of Perception* on, can be seen in retrospect as part of his working out of an "indirect ontology" that supports his later work but also requires the final, unfinished writing to show that the earlier effort "is in fact ontology" (*Visible*, p. 176). The task at hand is to discern the

28. "Transgression" is, one might argue, a strong and upsetting term. Yet it has the advantage of calling our attention to the way in which, even at a perceptual level, our existence encroaches on the world. An awareness of this encroachment should not incapacitate our ability to act in the world, yet it should call us to question many of our actions. Violence becomes especially dangerous when it is denied or unrecognized. Further discussion of how we might think about what constitutes desirable versus undesirable transgression is left until the next chapter, where I develop the ethical and political implications of Merleau-Ponty's philosophy of experience and ontology.

29. Maurice Merleau-Ponty, *Themes from the Lectures at the Collège de France, 1952–1960*, trans. John O'Neill (Evanston, Ill.: Northwestern University Press, 1970), p. 111.

trajectory of his final work in an effort to illustrate how he gathers his earlier insights into an ontological development that significantly deepens them.

In a "working note" entitled "the 'senses'—dimensionality—Being," Merleau-Ponty ponders the relation between "the sensible" and Being in a way that is extremely insightful and opens the door to a discussion of his ontology. He writes: "What is proper to the sensible (as to language) is to be representative of the whole, not by a sign-signification relation, or by the immanence of the parts in one another and in the whole, but because each part is *torn up* [*arrachée*] from the whole, comes with its roots, encroaches upon the whole, transgresses the frontiers of the others."[30] This is a passage of great fecundity, for in it Merleau-Ponty begins to illuminate the relation between "the sensible" and "the whole" (Being) it represents, in a manner that sheds a great deal of light on his understanding of the active essence of Being itself. In stating that the sensible is "torn up" from the whole, he indicates a profound yet discordant kinship between the sensible and Being, which is central to his ontology. The sensible is not a phenomenal fabrication of a noumenal being that is completely other than what we sense; nor is it *simply* a violence we do to things. Instead, the sensible is a "part" of Being, and hence it speaks to us—if only indirectly through "the voices of silence"—of Being itself. The task of Merleau-Ponty's "indirect ontology" is to "rediscover this world of silence" that speaks through the beings we perceive; to disclose the Being of beings in such a way as to gain insight into both our experience of things and their transcendence—our experience of beings *as* transcendent.

Our exploration of the "wild Being" of the perceived world revealed a primordial layer of experience that is ceaselessly transformed and deformed as it becomes present in diverse depths. But what sort of nature is open to such diverse renderings? These are the questions to which Merleau-Ponty's interrogation of "brute" experience gives rise, for it illustrates not only the untenability of past ontologies, but the pressing need for ontological reformulation as well.

We must approach his ontology carefully, for even the question "What is Being?" can lead us astray if we take it to gesture toward some sort of "in itself." If Merleau-Ponty responds to this question—and he does—it

30. *Visible and the Invisible*, p. 218; *Visible et l'invisible*, p. 271.

is precisely by changing the meaning of each of the terms; for "what," "is," and "Being" each harbors a thickness and inertia stemming from its employment in traditional philosophy, which powerfully implies ontological conceptions that he explicitly rejects. To inhabit the question without transforming it is to be carried along in a blindness that renders the interrogation called forth by the question mark meaningless from the start. Hence it is crucial to note that the governing idea of Merleau-Ponty's ontology is that Being "is not only *what it is*" (*Visible*, p. 181). Let us explore this assertion.

In his interrogation of this elusive Being, Merleau-Ponty uses a cluster of terms; by far the most important concept, however, is "flesh," which I briefly elaborated earlier. "Flesh is what 'lines' the visibles, 'sustains them, nourishes them' " (*Visible*, p. 132). Flesh is that out of which the sensible is "torn up." It is what the visible transgressively presents. Yet it is not itself a "thing." Rather, flesh is "a *pregnancy* of possibles" (p. 250), "polymorphism," a "latency," "openness"—most profoundly "depth" and "nowise a layer of flat entities or the in itself" (p. 252). It is in this notion of "pregnancy of possibles" that we begin to see the way in which Being is not only what it is.

Earlier I indicated that one reason Merleau-Ponty calls being "flesh" is to emphasize the commonality between the pulp of my body and that of the world. He deepens this insight significantly, however, when he argues that the commonality is one not just of "similar stuff," but of "similar style" as well. Merleau-Ponty calls Being "flesh" because my bodily flesh "is to the greatest extent what every thing is" (*Visible*, p. 260). Being is called "flesh" in an effort to evoke a quality—an essential activity—that is most proximally experienced in my own flesh; a quality of which my flesh is the most profound amplification. What characterizes my flesh, Merleau-Ponty maintains, is its "reversibility," the fact that it is both sentient and sensible. My flesh is both a being that perceives and a perceived being; both a field or clearing and part of what appears in the clearing. This flesh "is a relation of the visible with itself that traverses me and constitutes me as a seer, this circle which I do not form, which forms me, this coiling over of the visible upon the visible" (p. 140). I am this essential activity (*Wesen, ester*), which is the visible's relation to itself such that a dimension is cleared in which it appears. *This*, finally, is the openness, latency, pregnancy, depth of flesh—not just the flesh of my immediate body, but (in a way that is very similar yet very different) the flesh of the world as well.

Yet one will protest that rather than being what characterizes the similarity between my flesh and the world, the quality we have just described is precisely what *distinguishes* the two. Is not to argue otherwise to return to a strange philosophical position resembling early Greek hylozoism? In response to this imaginary interlocutor, Merleau-Ponty explicitly asserts that "this is not hylozoism" (*Visible*, p. 250). "The flesh of the world is not *self-sensing [se sentir]* as is my flesh—It is sensible and not sentient" (p. 250). In spite of this crucial distinction, however, Merleau-Ponty nevertheless argues that all flesh is a mode of reversibility: all flesh both appears in the clearing and participates in clearing the clearing. In another working note, we find: "My body is to the greatest extent *what everything is:* a *dimensional this.* It is the universal thing—But, while *the things become dimensions only insofar as they are received in a field,* my body is this field itself, i.e., a sensible that is dimensional *of itself*" (p. 260; my emphasis and his). Hence this dimensionality of things—their mode of reversibility—comes into being only when things are presented in the sensual field of my body. But this is not to say that in the last instance the dimensionality of things is simply a quality that I impart to things, a quality that does not belong to them as well. If we recall our earlier discussion, we note that our perception of things—their appearance within a perceptual field—is neither our creation nor a quality of things in themselves, but rather what emerges through the intercourse between the flesh of my body and that of the world. This intercourse *brings forth aspects of being* that were only latent possibilities beforehand. Yet along with any thing's appearance in the clearing, we simultaneously elicit another essential possibility of the thing: its dimensionality. This dimensionality is a dependent dimensionality, but it belongs as essentially to anything that appears as its very appearance itself.

Hence the essence of the flesh of things is not simply to appear to us as inert beings within a perceptual field, but to participate in clearing the field as well: to "represent," to make present (and thereby partly conceal and thereby transgress) the Being of which they are a part. Things and parts of things interact not just as "things," but by being "dimensions" through which other beings (and other parts of themselves) are expressed, brought into being, presented. Depicting this mode of reversibility, Merleau-Ponty writes: "There is dimensionality of every fact and facticity of every dimension—This is in virtue of the 'ontological difference'" (*Visible*, p. 270). It is this ontological difference that is the depth of Being.

Let us explore this a bit more carefully. The dimensionality of the world is perhaps most simply revealed in Merleau-Ponty's discussion of color in the working note with which we began our discussion of the indirect ontology of *The Visible and the Invisible*. Yellow, he argues, is not merely a sensible color but "surpasses itself of itself: as soon as it becomes the color of the illumination, the dominant color of the field, it ceases to be such or such a color, it has therefore of itself an *ontological function*, it becomes apt to *represent* all things" (*Visible*, p. 217; my emphases). Yellow is a dimension in the sense that it is not simply the presence of a particularity, but a sensible that opens—presents—the world as well: "It . . . gives itself as a *certain* being and as a *dimension*, the expression *of every possible being*" (p. 218). As the illuminating color, yellow presents the rest of the world, expressing and transgressing it in the process. However, dimensionality is not just a quality of sensible beings which so clearly radiate throughout the rest of the world. *All* sensibles are dimensional (to varying degrees) in that they partake in opening the perceptual field as a whole. "Perception is not first a perception of *things*, but a perception of *elements* . . . of *rays of the world*, of things which are dimensions . . . I slide (*glisse*) on these 'elements' and here I am in the *world*" (p. 218). When I perceive the room around me, it is not present completely and all at once, but rather present through various fragments that reveal it to me. It may appear through my absorption in my mother's painting on the far wall or through the close proximity of the page I am absorbed in as I write. In each case the sensible that is torn out of Being and "figures" in the perceptual field presents the room as a whole: for example, I see "room through my mother's painting." I "*glisse*" on the canvas and enter the world through it—a room that is highlighted and shadowed, amplified and muted, and in general appears with a certain significance endowed largely by the painting. Hence the "dimensionality of every fact"; a dimensionality that, along with the facticity of the sensible, is "torn out" of Being and expresses everything it presents and everything it claims to be through encroachment and transgression.

As I have noted, this "reversibility" of being—the simultaneous facticity and dimensionality of the sensible—is central to Merleau-Ponty's

understanding of Being as "pregnancy of possibilities," latency, openness, and depth. If beings were not this reversibility, one might argue that
Being was infinite and never subject to complete experience, but not that
it was a pregnant openness. Descartes, Leibniz, and Spinoza all took this
approach to Being, conceiving of it as a "positive infinity" that is effectively more than we will ever be able to know. As infinite, the world is
conceived as a determinate endlessness (*Unendlichkeit*) of which we
ceaselessly uncover small fragments which leave so much remaining in
the dark. The invisible, the unknown, is conceived as "a positive only
absent" (*Visible*, p. 251). Given this understanding of being, there may be
endless cross-sections of each thing, but in each of these views, everything would stay put in its own proper place; everything would be present
in the stillness and "in itself" proportionateness of the Renaissance perspective. Each view—at least when cleansed of prejudice—would express perfectly a fragment of the infinite. But this is not at all the infinity
of which Merleau-Ponty speaks. His infinity is an "operative infinity":
"the infinity of *Offenheit* [openness] and not *Unendlichkeit* [endlessness]"
(p. 169). It is an infinity that ceaselessly *proliferates* not simply because
there is an endless number of cross-sections we can make of any thing,
but because *each sensible*, as a dimension, *brings forth* into the visible the
thing and world from which it is torn in a new way (partially transgressive). It thereby establishes, within each being and among beings,
relations that are not simply those belonging to things "in themselves"
(which at most could be endless), but relations of re-*presentation* which
multiply by ceaselessly giving birth to both the visible and an ever-
replenished pregnant reserve in the depths of the invisible. This reserve
is not just a hidden thing that can be revealed, but a being that, when
made determinate, will itself represent the world anew—coherently
transforming and deforming the world. These relations of "clearing"
within being make possible and necessary an expressive-transgressive
activity within Being which is utterly other than the "in itself."
    In this light, Merleau-Ponty's contention that Being is depth begins to
be comprehensible. The intercourse of our historical bodily flesh and
that of the world brings forth a field in which each part partakes in
relations of depth with other parts: pulling things forth and pushing
things back in the depth of the clearing. Facticity and dimensionality are
abstract moments of the reversibility that characterizes the thingness of a
thing—that is, the depth, the "there is" of things which is never that of a

neutral visible. In its intersection with our body, the sensible *presents* things, but it does so in a depth that maintains them at a distance; repels things as it brings them forth. "Depth is the means the things have to remain distinct, to remain things, while not being what I look at present. It is preeminently the dimension of the simultaneous. Without it there would not be a world or Being" (*Visible,* p. 219). We might add that with it the world that emerges is "wild Being," a Being with an operative depth that proliferates everywhere we look and maintains the ineliminable otherness of things. In marked contrast to the conquering world of objectifying thought, Merleau-Ponty argues that otherness is the very Being of things and the world. "The look does not overcome depth, it goes round it" (p. 219).

Yet Merleau-Ponty does not posit a complete and total otherness in the place of a complete and total identity. If things remain distinct in depth, so too they are *presented* in depth, though never in the purity of an expression without transgression. There is a certain complicity between the historical body and the world, but one in which expression and transgression, like Hobbes and fear, are "born twins." It is a complicity that enables there to be a dialogue between the self and the world, but one that gives rise to the possibility of extreme contestation as well as agreement.[31]

Depth: The Dimension of Being *with* Others

Thus far we have explored depth as what most characterizes beings and the clearing that emerges through the intercourse between the body and the world. Depth is the Being of flesh that continuously coils over on

---

31. It must be emphasized that all we have said about the self's relation to the world extends to the self's relation to its self as well. "I who see have my own depth." As an "exemplar sensible," I am not self-present simply and all at once, but rather I am continually rendered present in and as a depth that violates dimensions of my being just as it brings others toward creative fruition. I never coincide with myself in a complete self-presence, and it is precisely this invisibility and absence—characterizing even my most inward experience of myself—that allows me to open out on and experience a world that inheres in its otherness. A flat, self-possessing cogito could never allow a wild, mysterious world to seep into its hermetically sealed experience of certainty. On the other hand, the deep, noncoinciding self is thrown into the depths of the world. As nonidentical, it is confronted with the task of creating itself in contact with its own and the world's otherness.

itself, giving birth to the visible pregnant with the invisible. Yet if our words were to break off here, we would perhaps obfuscate depth more than illuminate it; we would be far more Cartesian and far less deep than we imagine. For the experience of depth is essentially intercorporeal: it springs forth through our contact with others who are different. According to Merleau-Ponty, in total absence of these others, there is no experience of depth, no "there." Hence to speak of the experienced world as deep only or even primarily in terms of a single self's communion with the flesh of the world is, once again, to ignore the originary intercorporeality toward which depth gestures and deny depth by assuming that we can speak of a self, a world, and their relations in absence of others. It is to perpetuate that flat "I" that Virginia Woolf sees materializing across the pages of a proliferating literature written mostly by men.[32] When Merleau-Ponty writes that those who attempt to construct phenomena starting from the "solipsist layer" "ignore the profoundest things Husserl is saying to us" (*Signs*, p. 175), he is speaking as usual not only or perhaps even primarily of what is important in Husserl's philosophy, but of what is central to his own. For Merleau-Ponty, the isolated self, the "solipsist layer," is not at all primary, but rather a "thought experiment intended more to reveal than to break the links of the intentional web" (p. 173). Thus far we have discussed depth without explicitly addressing others, in an effort to disclose some of the primordial characteristics of our relationship with the world. Equally primordial is our relationship with others. In approaching "the profoundest things" Merleau-Ponty is saying to us, we must elaborate the circularity in which depth renders possible our experience of others, and others give birth to a central dimension of our experience of depth. Only then will we kick the habits of the flattened "I": its flat ontology, ethics, and politics.

We have shed light above on Merleau-Ponty's comment that without depth there would not be a world or Being. He could equally have written that without others who are different there would be no experience of this "*être profond.*" For Merleau-Ponty argues that before "intersubjective life" there is no "there," but only anonymity in which "there is neither individuation nor distinction" (*Signs*, p. 174): no experience of differentiation, transcendence, and depth. It is only after the self is dis-

32. Virginia Woolf, *A Room of One's Own* (London: Harcourt Brace Jovanovich, 1957), p. 103.

tinct for itself—something (as we shall see) that emerges simultaneously with its grasp of others who are different—that the world emerges in its transcendent depths. Before this there is only a "primordial generality" (p. 174) lacking the depth through which things appear "at a distance." This is not to say that without others who are different our senses would cease to open out on the world. For example, I would still see the yellow mass that is my bicycle helmet. Yet I would not see it as a thing distinct from me and hence it would not exist for me in the depth that separates it from me and allows it to be "there" in its own right. As I have argued, depth and distinction are co-originary. What is crucial to note is that the *primordial distinction* with which the depth of the "there" fully emerges— the primordial difference that releases beings from "primordial generality" and into the depth of the clearing—is that between the self and all that it is not, which springs forth as the self confronts different others.

This is an insight of no small importance and calls for further careful elaboration. To understand more clearly Merleau-Ponty's circular comment that "the fully objective thing is based upon the experience of others, and the latter upon the experience of the body, which in a way is a thing itself" (*Signs*, p. 176), we need to address several issues. First, I very briefly summarize his discussions of what it is about the nature of our bodily being that opens us to the experience of an "other." Second, I discuss the importance of the "difference" between selves as essential to the perception of both others and the self. Finally, I discuss the way in which our existence as beings among different others confers objectivity and depth on the clearing to which we belong.

The modern "problem of the other" stems from Descartes's formulation of the cogito, in which the fact that "I think" is taken as the first, absolute, and most fundamental ground of my certainty. He argues that all other knowledge is rooted in this transparent fact and has the status of being the cogito's mental judgment of its representations. Descartes himself avoids the solipsism suggested by this position through his "proof" that there exists an undeceiving God, one who guarantees that my most rigorous representations of the world and others are not merely illusory, but representations of beings that do exist in fact. For those lacking Descartes's certainty in God, however, the existence of others and otherness becomes a Problem. If transparency and pure self-presence are the ground that ensures my certainty of a being's existence (namely, that of my own *res cogitans*), then how can I possibly be certain of the existence of another "for itself," a being defined by its *absence* from me insofar as I can never coincide with it? How can the other be for me anything but my representation (and hence not truly an other)? Our presence to others as such is an unsolvable problem for the philosophy of consciousness, and this problem is perhaps the greatest testimony of its poverty. Nevertheless, it is a pervasive poverty, one that dominated the intellectual milieu from which Merleau-Ponty emerged and hence one that he felt compelled to address.[33]

He does not, of course, address the problem on its own terms. Indeed, his approach to the problem demands a radical transcendence of the philosophy of the cogito from which it emerges. Merleau-Ponty writes, "What is interesting is not . . . to solve the problem of the other" but rather to effect "a transformation of the problem" (*Visible*, p. 169). The essence of this transformation is to ask not how my constituting consciousness can come to know of another constituting consciousness, but rather how my bodily being experiences another bodily being. The secret to the latter question, he argues, can be partially illuminated by reexamining how my body perceives itself, for the perception of others "presents us with but an amplification of the same paradox" (p. 9).

Unlike the Cartesian cogito, which is completely present to itself at each instant of its thought—able to perceive itself perceiving—the self-perception of Merleau-Ponty's incarnate self is characterized by a certain absence. As my right hand attempts to touch the actual touch of my left hand, the latter retreats into the depths of my being just as my right hand is about to succeed. My body is never completely present to itself in the act of perception, because perception is an "ek-stase" in which the self is thrown outside of itself and into the world ("world" in this instance meaning this visible body of self-perception). Perception must in part lose itself to gain access to the world. In this perpetual thrownness, the self-as-sensing recedes into the depths of the figure of the self-as-sensed. My left hand is given as an animate sensing thing, but one to whose sensing my right hand cannot be completely present. Hence Merleau-Ponty writes that "the reflection of the body upon itself always miscarries at the last moment" (*Visible*, p. 9).

This remark goes a long way, for it forces us to abandon Cartesian

---

33. Cf. Schmidt, *Merleau-Ponty*, chap. 3.

self-presence and resituate our sense of self in the depths of the world to which we belong. The body's presence to itself has no absolute privilege over its sense of the rest of the world, for I am given to myself, as a part of the world and "I who see have my own depths" (*Visible*, p. 135). Because all that is present including myself is "there" in a depth that presents an absence as well, the fact that I am unable to coincide with the perceiving being of an other no more threatens her existence for me than my lack of coincidence with my own perceiving being threatens my existence for myself. And if I sense myself as part of the sensible world—as an animate being presented with a living grip on the world—then why, when I see other similar animate beings, would I not recognize them as "others"? Indeed, it is because I sense myself as a "perceiving thing" in the world that I am able to sense corporeally that there are "other myselves." Merleau-Ponty writes: "My right hand was present at the advent of the left hand's active sense of touch. It is in no different fashion that the other's body becomes animate before me when I shake another man's hand or just look at him" (*Signs*, p. 168). My body is able to recognize an other when it witnesses the latter livingly and transcendently engaged with the world, intertwined with the visible in a manner that bears an undeniable human style.

But what sparks this sudden recognition of an other living human being? Though Merleau-Ponty never gives this question as extended an analysis as one would like, he addresses it briefly in various texts in ways that are both consistent and highly illuminating. The central notion that runs through these discussions is that the other is revealed as an "other" when I encounter her difference from myself and my expectations. Before the unexpected, the strange, the shocking encounter with another, the *other as such* does not really appear. In *The Visible and the Invisible*, Merleau-Ponty writes:

> Here is this *well-known* countenance, this smile, these modulations of voice, whose style is as familiar to me as myself. Perhaps in many moments of my life the other is for me *reduced* to this *spectacle*, which can be a charm. But should the voice alter, should the *unwonted appear* in the score of the dialogue, or, on the contrary, should a response *respond too well* to what I thought without having really said it—and suddenly there breaks forth the evidence that yonder also, minute by minute, life is being lived: . . . *another private world shows through*, through the fabric of my own and for a moment I live in it. (Pp. 10–11; my emphases)

It is, then, the unusual—something that transcends the same—that kindles our sense of the other, whether it be a direct difference of content or style, or an uncanny proximity ("responding too well") that upsets established "proper distances." Merleau-Ponty makes a similar argument in the chapter entitled "Dialogue and the Perception of the Other" in *The Prose of the World:* "If the other person is *really another,* at a certain stage I must be surprised, disoriented"[34] (my emphasis). In *The Primacy of Perception,* he emphasizes the discrepancy that gives birth to our experience of the other: "The body of the other . . . *tears* itself away from being one of my phenomena, offers me the task of a true communication" (p. 18; my emphasis). What is crucial to note here is that we do not fundamentally recognize others in realizing that they are human beings who are "the same" as we expect them to be. It is through this sameness that the other slides into the status of "one of my phenomena" and hence ceases to be "other" for us. It is precisely in others' *difference*[35] that we recognize them as "other" beings who, like us, participate in being human. Emphasizing the importance of difference in giving birth to a mode of coexistence that is distinctly "there" in depth, Merleau-Ponty speculates in *Sense and Nonsense* that "one might even say that what Heidegger lacks is . . . an affirmation of the individual: he does not mention that struggle of consciousnesses and that opposition of freedoms without which coexistence sinks into anonymity and everyday banality."[36] With Hegel, Merleau-Ponty contends that the recognition of self and other emerges simultaneously in the surprises and tensions between others who are different.[37]

34. Maurice Merleau-Ponty, *The Prose of the World,* trans. John O'Neill (Evanston, Ill.: Northwestern University Press, 1973), p. 142. Further citations to this edition are given directly in the text.

35. Here I include their *shocking* concordance with us as well as their more straightforward differences.

36. Maurice Merleau-Ponty, *Sense and Non-Sense,* trans. H. L. Dreyfus and P. A. Dreyfus (Evanston, Ill.: Northwestern University Press, 1964), p. 69. Original: *Sens et non-sens* (Paris: Gallimard, 1948). Further citations to the English edition are given directly in the text.

37. Unlike Hegel, however, Merleau-Ponty ultimately seeks not to overcome all difference (here we speak of what is unpredictable and not entirely comprehensible—not the domesticated difference that remains in *Philosophy of Right*), but rather to search for ways in which society can allow differences to exist in both mutual recognition and contestation. To flatten out all difference is, as we shall see, to destroy the depth of the intercorporeal world—to sink out of a "there" that is alive with distinction and pregnancy, and back into anonymity.

Being with different others who transcend our grasp pulls us out of anonymity and hurls us into an intercorporeal world with depth and distinction. And at the instant that I become aware of an other perceiving being, so too, for the first time, I become aware of myself. As I perceive the other, "for the first time, the seeing that I am is for me really visible; for the first time I appear to myself completely turned inside out under my own eyes" (*Visible*, p. 143). As I realize that I "figure" in the perceptual field of an other, I become distinct for myself as well. The perception of self and other spring forth together. Indeed, the notion of *my* self has meaning only in contrast with other selves from which I am distinct. Hence (following Lacan's analysis of the "mirror stage")[38] Merleau-Ponty completely leaves the terrain of the cogito and asserts that it emerges only through contact with others who transcend our grasp and tacit expectations. Thus, though my body is such that it prepares me to experience the other insofar as its own self-presence can only be in depth, its depth should not be thought of as a "prior *reality*" on which the rest of our experience is based. The body as depth being is realized only with different others: "The constitution of others does not come after that of my body; others and my body are born together from the original ecstasy" (*Signs*, p. 174)—that which occurs when they are thrown together.

This original ecstasy that gives birth to the distinction between self and other simultaneously gives birth to the distinction between self and world and is the primordial distinction on which the depth of the "there" arises. As the self emerges in its own right, so too does the world, as a distinct "there" at a distance. At the same time that our experience of others inaugurates the difference releasing us from "primordial generality," however, the presence of their perceptual opening on the world we share brings forth a clearing with a far more textured, distinct "visible" and an "invisible" of which we are far more aware—in short, a clearing with a far greater experience of depth—than we could experience in absolute solitude (supposing that the latter itself was possible). Indeed, the presence of the perceiving other "confers on my objects the new dimension of intersubjective being or, in other words, of objectivity" (*Primacy*, p. 18).

Merleau-Ponty's elaboration of this insight is perhaps sharpest in an

---

38. *Primacy*, p. 136; Maurice Merleau-Ponty, *Consciousness and the Acquisition of Language*, trans. H. J. Silverman (Evanston, Ill.: Northwestern University Press, 1973), p. 55.

early section of *The Visible and the Invisible,* which presents us, I think, with some of his most fascinating writing. Here he describes the inter-corporeal world through an analogy with the world that springs forth in binocular vision. The visual images that each eye alone is able to render, deliver us to a relatively flat realm of "phantasms," lacking both the distinct presence and the latency emerging with the depth world that appears as both eyes focus together. In the latter instance, the different images of each eye synergistically combine to produce a world that is "there" in a far more protean manner. Similarly, the different perceptions of others combine in communication to bring forth a world that is "there" far more profoundly—deeply—than the "private world" pre-sented to a single self: "Communication makes us witness to one sole world, as the synergy of our eyes suspends them on one unique thing" (*Visible,* p. 11).[39] "Yet, just as above the monocular phantasms could not compete with the thing [seen by both eyes], so also now one could describe the private worlds as divergence with respect to the *world itself*" (p. 10). As two persons are present to each other in and through the world that is before them, each of the "private worlds" that appears in their respective perceptual fields "is given to its incumbent as a variant of one common world" (p. 11). Though each person becomes present to this common world through the synergy among others, no one possesses it completely, for each field is only a "divergence."

The depth through which we come to witness a common world does not homogenize our different perspectives any more than the depth that emerges as we train both eyes on a thing demands that each eye have an identical vision. Instead, in both cases, depth emerges as the being of things which both makes possible divergent views and is called forth as divergences are brought together or "suspended" on one thing. Depth is the dimension in which differences join in a thing, not to be squashed and extinguished, but to communicate and give birth to a sense of the richness and wildness of the world which qualitatively surpasses what the differences are able to present in isolation. Our experience of depth emerges most profoundly not when two or more persons realize that they see the same world in the same way, but in the tension that arises as they recognize that they see the same world differently. It is in the attempt to

39. It should be recalled that communication is fundamentally "gestural" for Merleau-Ponty; hence he is referring to nonverbal communication as well as verbal.

elaborate and communicate these differences that my private world must open to the experience of depth in order to harbor what belongs to the things I see while not having been (or perhaps not even being) present immediately before me. As I attempt to recognize the otherness of the other's perceptions of the world to which we both belong, my world attains a texture and latency that it did not have before. I realize that the world I am present to is much more than I see, far more "there" than my singular vision attests.

If the monocular-binocular analogy is extremely revealing in certain respects, however, we must be careful not to let it mislead us. The depth that emerges through the synergy of our two eyes gives birth to a world that is so convincing that we are almost never aware of our single eyes as divergent visions. Yet the intercorporeal world that emerges among different others is different, for here the sense of discrepancy that gives birth to the world as such is not subsumed so *harmoniously* within it. Rather, the social world is what "envelops the individual, simultaneously soliciting him and menacing him . . . each consciousness both finds and loses itself in its relationship with other consciousnesses . . . the social is not *collective consciousness* but intersubjectivity, a living relationship and tension among individuals."[40] Nevertheless, this tension should not be thought of in terms of differences each of which exist completely in their pure self-same identity and henceforth partake in discussion. Our selves—our divergent worlds—are variants of this intersubjective world that partially envelops us, and it is *as variants* that we are different. We are with others as variants of an "anonymous visibility" that "inhabits us both"; as different positions in a conversation of which we are not so much the constituting agents, but rather beings borne along by this lively being-in-tension with respect to which we are formed as we attempt to specify our differences. When Merleau-Ponty writes that my body and others are born together in an "original ecstasy," he conceives of our *being thrown* into the world itself as an *intercorporeal structure:* "The other's words, or mine in him, do not limit themselves to vibrating like chords the listener's machinery of acquired significations. . . . Their flow must have the power of *throwing me* in turn toward a signification that neither he nor I possessed before" (*Prose*, p. 142; my emphasis).

It is perhaps here, in rediscovering the depth of the clearing that

40. *Sense,* p. 90; *Sens,* p. 157.

emerges in the intercorporeal world, that we can most appreciate Merleau-Ponty's Husserl and the meaning of his comment that "Husserl awakens a wild world and mind." For Merleau-Ponty, it is the *dialogical* relation with different others which continually confers on the world a distinctness and specificity it would never have if I were a being completely alone. As *we* stare at the sunrise, our conversation brings forth a world with more and more texture: the greens near the horizon, the rays of light flashing above the clouds I had not seen before spring out of our dialogue and throw me into a world I cannot quit. The agreements that are achieved among different others combine in the world to multiply the density, complexity, and fertility of the figures that appear before us, as well as our sense of reality. But also, the things the other sees there, which I cannot quite accomplish in my own vision, reveal the horizons, the backsides of my own immediate perceptual field. My field harbors an invisibility in its horizons which makes it even more "there" than it immediately appears to me. I am struck by the world's transcendence, its capacity to outstrip and resist my attempts to grasp it. I am called before a depth that opens up the possibility of an endless dialogue with the natural world which is present most profoundly as question and exclamation.

Let us not sound so optimistic, however. For this intercorporeal world that brings forth depth also menaces the depth of selves and the world as it does so. We are so often flattened, torn up, obfuscated in our lives with others. Yet this assertion ostensibly has an odd ring within the philosophy we have just elaborated. Have we not argued that the world is essentially *être profond?* What does it mean to speak of "flattening" in this context? I address this question in two parts, first by identifying some places where Merleau-Ponty seems to indicate an awareness of the danger of some sort of flattening, and second by elaborating a possible phenomenology of flattened being.

Dangers of Flat Being

For the most part, if one wants to understand why objectifying and subjectifying thoughts and practices that flatten being intensify, diversify, and proliferate with such ubiquity in modernity, the works of Hegel, Marx, Nietzsche, Weber, Lukács, Heidegger, Adorno, and Foucault are far more fecund than those of Merleau-Ponty. Other than occasional echoes of Hegel, Marx, Lukács, and Weber, and vague statements such as "Certain ideas have a pre-established affinity with certain politics or interests because each of them presupposes the same conception of man,"[41] we gain little historical insight into the increasing hegemony of these thoughts and practices. Indeed, Merleau-Ponty's apparent belief that perception's propensity to lose sight of itself is an origin of objective thought, though insightful in some ways, lends itself to hopelessly uninsightful and ahistorical understandings of contemporary discourses and practices. But if he did not delve deeply into the causes of reified thought, he did have a profound sense of the dangers it harbored, and, I believe, much of his philosophical writing grew out of these concerns.

That depth itself appears at some level—as yet unspecified—to have an aspect of contingency is hinted at in a passage we have already quoted, in which Merleau-Ponty emphasizes the importance of different others and recalls "that struggle of consciousnesses and that opposition of freedoms without which coexistence sinks into anonymity and everyday banality" (*Sense*, p. 69). Were the agonistic tensions and bizarre proximities of our lives with others to begin to wither away in some sense, the depth that is born in this realm would begin to disappear as well. Coexistence would move away from the distinction and latency characterizing the depth of the "there," toward "anonymity." If our distinctive individualities were to be increasingly normalized, rather than illuminating a world of depth, our intercorporeal existence might increasingly present an anonymous, flattened view of the world—a view perpetuated in a continual exchange of flat agreement. For Merleau-Ponty, this is not simply an imagined danger but a menace that is steadily at work in modernity's persistent attempt (in a variety of forms) to flatten the wildness of Being with objectivist understandings of humans and the world.

In a brilliantly blunt footnote in *The Visible and the Invisible*, Merleau-Ponty writes: "Every attempt to reinstate the illusion of the 'thing itself' is in fact an attempt to return to my imperialism and the value of *my* thing" (p. 10). To posit the thing itself in this sense is to assert its determinate existence, of which I am witness, as independent of its relations with me. To sever the threads that connect us with things and things with us is to posit a world lacking both immanence and transcendence. This world and these things are flattened to my view of them insofar as I deny

41. Maurice Merleau-Ponty, *Humanism and Terror*, trans. John O'Neill (Boston: Beacon Press, 1969), p. xli. Original: *Humanisme et terreur* (Paris: Gallimard, 1947). Further citations to the English edition are given directly in the text.

entirely the perspectival and carnal character of my vision and lay absolute and exhaustive claims to the "in itself" from a position of "high
altitude thought" in which I perceive a world entirely spread out before
me. Rather than the "truth" that it claims to possess, however, this
thinking actually inaugurates an "imperialism" because it flatly denies
both "other" aspects of the thing and all perceptions others may have of
the thing which are not its own. Devoid of otherness, devoid of its
intrinsic claims, devoid of the claims of others, this world awaits manip-
ulation. In further attempting to define the thing in terms of objective
thought and the "prior possibility of thinking it," this thought "impose[s]
upon the world in advance the conditions for our control over it" (*Visible*,
p. 39).

These conceptualizations tend to reduce humans to a subset of
things—to a set of transparent operations that eradicate the otherness in
others and ourselves and substitute for it a thorough "intelligibility." Yet
it is not simply a "misconception" that Merleau-Ponty is concerned with,
it is an erasure of Being. Expressing this prospect, he writes that the
danger of increasingly

> set[ting] out to construct man and history on the basis of *a few abstract*
> *indices* (as a decadent psychoanalysis and a decadent culturalism have done
> in the United States) [is that], since man really becomes the *manipulandum*
> he takes himself to be, we enter into a cultural regimen where there is
> neither truth nor falsity concerning man and history, into a sleep, or a
> nightmare, from which there is no awakening. (*Primacy*, p. 160)

This is a strongly worded statement, and it is strange to read this
philosopher of contingency speak of what seems like the contingency of
radical contingency itself: a closed regimen "from which there is no
awakening." Undoubtedly, this is an exaggerated rhetoric deployed to
shock us into an awareness of a great danger. Almost everywhere else
Merleau-Ponty has argued that the contingency that threatens us equally
prevents the evil in the present from attaining the status of absolute
finality. Whatever the case may be with regard to the possibility of an
"ultimate flattening," however, what seems quite clear with respect to the
quoted passage is that Merleau-Ponty sees in modern objectivist constructions of human being a certain flattening of being that at least works
toward a kind of closure as it proceeds. By taking ourselves to be—and

increasingly becoming—the "manipulandum," we increasingly close
ourselves to the polyphonous character of our being and simultaneously
close ourselves to the experience of different others. In short, we become
increasingly severed from the depth of the clearing.

But what could this possibly mean? What might Merleau-Ponty have
in mind when he speaks of sinking toward an anonymous coexistence, a
nightmare from which there is no awakening? He does not pursue these
questions rigorously with respect to the passages above, so we can only
formulate what he *might* have said in light of what he writes in other
contexts and his philosophy as we have explored it thus far.

The only place Merleau-Ponty attempts a phenomenology of flat being
is in his discussion of hallucinations in the *Phenomenology of Perception*.
Although the flatness we are concerned with will obviously be different
from the individual hallucination in important ways, nevertheless I think
one can argue that objectifying and normalizing theories and practices
flatten being in several ways hauntingly analogous to that of the hallucination.[42]

What distinguishes the hallucinatory thing from a real thing in the
world is that the former, unlike the latter, is not a "depth being" (*être
profond*).[43] While the thing in the world is distinctly present in a depth
that prevents us from ever completely possessing it, the hallucination
lacks a certain transcendence and is "an artificial world answering to the
total intention of [the hallucinator's] being" (*Phenomenology*, p. 341). This
lack of depth has several important manifestations. To begin with,
whereas the real thing is open to endless, inexhaustible, and detailed
exploration as our senses move around its depth, in contrast, the "hallucinatory thing is not . . . packed with small perceptions which sustain its
existence. It is an implicit and inarticulate significance" (p. 339). It lacks
the "consummate fullness" of the thing in the world which presents itself
with textures, details, and other sides implicit in the horizons of my
present perception though not explicitly before me. The imaginary thing
is "there" as *complete* without reserves, a pure correlate of our intentional
being that "has no depth and does not respond to our effort to vary our

---

42. My interest in Merleau-Ponty's discussion of hallucinations was stimulated in some
discussions with Anthony Steinbock while he was working on the issue of hallucinations
and depth. Cf. Anthony Steinbock, "Merleau-Ponty's Conception of Depth," *Philosophy
Today* 31 (Winter 1987), 336–51.
43. *Phenomenology*, p. 339; *Phénoménologie*, p. 391.

points of view" (p. 323). Because its being is absolutely complete and lacking horizons, Merleau-Ponty argues that it is "played out on a different stage from that of the perceived world" (p. 339). It is simply there, superimposed on the world but not existing within it. The hallucinator can find no paths to connect the hallucination with the rest of his experience and that of others; it is wholly outside the intercorporeal realm.

On Merleau-Ponty's reading, the hallucination is a "running wild" (*l'affolement*) of the body's perceptual power to the extent that fragments of the world are unrecognizably distorted, or in even more extreme instances, the world is lost altogether. The clearing emerges no longer "through dealings with a harsh, resistant and intractable world which has no knowledge of us," but rather in the "fabrication of an isolated fictitious setting" (*Phenomenology*, p. 342). It is a setting that, in the complete flatness of its presence, is unsusceptible to interrogation by the self or others, and hermetically sealed from the expressive force of the world.

In what sense can the anonymity of objectified and normalized coexistence be compared with the hallucination? Clearly, they are quite different insofar as the hallucination is a private experience, while the anonymity to which we refer is a collective phenomenon. The flattening in which we are interested concerns the perceived world—not a "different stage"—and the perceptual field does not lose the depth of its figure-ground structure. As our perception becomes increasingly normalized, however, this structure becomes increasingly "frozen." The latency of the perceptual world, which once solicited our senses and provided ever-new perceptions of things, is more and more locked out of the foreground. For example, for many men, women may "figure" in the perceptual world only according to normalized objectified indices of femininity and sexual figure. The rest of women's cacophonous being is frozen in a background that, for all practical purposes, may be inaccessible to these men. Similarly, as nature is reduced to the status of "object," all those dimensions that do not fit within this general fixed figure are increasingly frozen out of our experienced world. The multiplicity of selves and the world is increasingly closed out by normalized perceptions that intensify as they circulate among people in institutions, discourses, and practices.

We saw that central to Merleau-Ponty's understanding of the depth emerging in the perceptual field was the notion of being as a "perpetual pregnancy." Yet it is precisely this that withers as our figures freeze. The normalized world increasingly loses its powers of wild solicitation. At the heart of the normalizing gaze is a denial of the possibility of a background that might be surprising, disruptive, desirable. This gaze parades in a flat completeness parallel to that of a hallucination, a completeness in which we cannot vary our points of view. As we approach the world and others through this conceptual and perceptual scheme and as the world of flesh itself is coerced to "snap into position," it becomes for us a being increasingly lacking transcendence. Yet as we have seen, transcendence is the essence of the world for Merleau-Ponty. Hence we become present to something that less and less has the character of "world" in the deepest sense, and more and more begins to acquire qualities of the hallucination. Beings increasingly appear as correlates of the subject—in this case collective—and in this mode of presence, interrogative relations that might upset this basic misperception are less likely to arise.[44]

If I go to such lengths to illustrate the similarities between the hallucination and operationalized coexistence, it is to underscore that what is at stake in taking this path concerns important aspects of the depth of the experienced world. If the "unwonted" is, in Merleau-Ponty's view, essential to the depth of the clearing, it is equally important to realize that the objectifying norm takes aim at this very depth.

What begins to emerge in Merleau-Ponty's discussion of Being as depth and the possibilities of flattening is, I think, quite profound. Implicit in this discussion are gestures beyond modernity's nihilistic inability to affirm and sustain ethical values. For *the world's depth,* far from being devoid of value, implies *a recognition and reaffirmation of the value of different others* (who are willing to make a similar affirmation) and, more generally, the otherness of the world. For the singular self or the collective subject that denies all difference, the world is increasingly flattened and supplanted by a complete depth-denying presence. The *expression of beings,* that they appear in the openness of the clearing, is entwined with an affirmative valuation of otherness. This expression implies transgression; but it is a transgression that brings forth *something* into our field of perception with a latency in which the temporal elaboration of experience

---

44. Of course, Merleau-Ponty was not a theorist of "one-dimensionality." As much as he was aware of the dangers of flattening, in which what is other than and in the background of the established visible is "locked out," nevertheless, what appears always does in fact appear with a latency that *though effectively locked out is not nothing.* Hence even as the world is flattened, it harbors the possibility—which can be reduced but not extinguished—of resisting flattening modes of perception.

may bring forth previously transgressed elements. The objectifying gaze sinks toward *no-thing*, a hallucinatory image beneath which the world is held in a transgression that denies its own violence and seeks to eternalize itself.

In pursuing the phenomenological project of exploring the origin of the world's wondrous presence to us, Merleau-Ponty discovers that "principle of an ethics" that he adumbrates at the end of his prospectus for the Collège de France. As an ethic of the world as such, it provides us with an important step in "revaluating values" and frees us of the nihilism that necessarily accompanies objectivist understandings of the world as simply and completely there (i.e., not there at all). Our interrogative engagement with the multiplicitous depth of the world is, I believe, the fundamental value for Merleau-Ponty: the value of being itself.

The recognition of different others which is so crucial to this engagement is at this point quite vague, however. In the following section I pursue some of the ethical and political implications of Merleau-Ponty's philosophy to elaborate the sense of this recognition in terms of our coexistence with others.

Ethics and Politics of Depth

A great deal of Merleau-Ponty's work directly addresses ethical and political issues. Although he developed penetrating and lucid critiques of some of the central ethical and political thoughts and practices of our age, however, the affirmative directions of his thought were left very far from being fully expressed. There are powerful and suggestive insights into these questions in almost every text he wrote, but they call for much further elaboration.

It is clear that Merleau-Ponty sought to develop his thoughts on perception, expression, and ontology in large part to provide us with fresh insights into how we might live together as political and social beings in ways that minimize "terror" in both its explicit and more insidious forms. It is no accident and of no small importance that in the prospectus of his work which he prepared for his candidacy to the Collège de France, he closes by noting that a successful elaboration of the "wonder" of expression "would at the same time give us the principle of an ethics" (*Primacy*, p. 11). Even the last work he saw published, a work on aesthetics and ontology which might seem far removed from ethics and politics, is in an important respect an attempt to reawaken the "brute" world of the painter as a first step in formulating an alternative to the nightmare of "operational thinking" and being which threatens us in modernity (p. 60).

But what exactly is the social and political nature of this nightmare and what might be the alternative? In this section I maintain that the power of illumination that Merleau-Ponty's writing lends to an exploration of these questions far exceeds his explicit attempts to address them directly. Hence (rather than limiting the present discussion to the latter) I wish to develop an interpretation of the ethical and political implications of the philosophy of depth elaborated in the previous section and bring into focus and distinction his more explicit ethical and political insights within this context. Only in so doing does the richness and depth of Merleau-Ponty's work—as well as the necessity of confronting it—become fully apparent.

Some historians of ideas will probably say that what follows is not a faithful remembrance of Merleau-Ponty; that one should stick to a more literal reading. But I do not wish—to use his own phrase—to condemn Merleau-Ponty to the "museum." In what follows, I take most seriously his view that art, philosophy, and politics thrive not in preserving the past by constructing identical copies, but through "the duty to start over again and to give the past, not survival, which is the hypocritical form of forgetfulness, but the efficacy of renewal or 'repetition,' which is the noble form of memory" (*Prose*, p. 68). Here I do not wish to record so much as to *continue* the philosophical effort that still lives and breathes on each page—so long as we do not treat them as artifacts to be dated and located in an entangled web of dead relations.[45]

In this section I attempt to draw out the ethical implications of his understanding of the artist in order to articulate a theory of the self and its relations to the surrounding world. Next I consider some of the social and political arrangements Merleau-Ponty believed fostered flattening and hence were untenable. I then proceed to explore carefully the affirmation of parliamentary democracy in an effort to gain ethical and political understandings that extend beyond the institution of parliament itself. Finally, I argue that an affirmation of the self as a work of art is essential to shifting the function of politics away from the imperative of ever-

45. See *Visible and the Invisible*, p. 198, for a related passage.

enhancing and legitimizing reified normalizing systems of productivity, toward an affirmation of diversity and agonistic dialogue that transcends "the existential requirements of a particular political order."[46] What are the implications of this gesture toward the affirmation of different others for ethical and political practice? On a superficial reading, one might argue for pure anarchical liberty: let everyone be absolutely free to express all "difference." Yet Merleau-Ponty is "not speaking in favor of an anarchical liberty" (*Humanism*, p. 35), for it simply denies the reality of—as well as the necessity of confronting—the violence that springs forth in the interaction between people who were not designed ahead of time to enter spontaneously into harmonious relations. It assumes that human society is naturally a "community of reasonable minds," whereas the task of both philosophers and political theorists is to "explain the upsurge of reason in a world that is not of its making and to prepare the substructure of living experience without which reason and liberty are emptied of their content and wither away" (*Phenomenology*, pp. 56–57). The anarchist solution to the problems of freedom and difference is simply to deny that they really are genuine problems of coexistence. Yet there is no reason to *assume* that there would be much recognition of otherness at all in a state of absolute anarchy. Indeed, what "difference" would there be to recognize in such a state of absolute freedom? As Merleau-Ponty has argued, "There is no freedom in submission to each shiver of opinion" (*Signs*, p. 349). Such an existence would, as Augustine realized, most likely cancel its efforts from one moment to the next; it would be more productive of nothing than of difference. The development of human difference that shines forth as visible and *demands recognition* is not "natural," but the product of careful elaboration of "styles" of individual and social existence. "*Liberty has to be made* in a world not predestined to it" (*Humanism*, p. xlii; my emphasis). We might say the same thing for the recognition of difference.

Self as a Work of Art

Merleau-Ponty's self dwells in the depths of an ambiguous world that "ceaselessly assails and beleaguers subjectivity as waves wash round a wreck on the shore" (*Phenomenology*, p. 207). Yet if at times we come

46. This apt phrase is William Connolly's (personal communication, Sept. 20, 1987).

across some remarkable echoes of Augustine—and would we not find substantial accord from Foucault here as well?—in his conception of this existence where humans so often are "not a strength but a weakness in the field of being,"[47] his conception of how we might understand and craft our lives is nevertheless very different from Augustine's in some fundamental ways. As we've seen, when Merleau-Ponty turns away from the objectified world of classical thought and toward a fresh study of the embodied self, he finds no "source of intrinsic truth," no "inner man" (p. xi). Rather, he uncovers only a self inextricably intertwined with the world-as-depth. There is no God to guide us, no nature in which we find hints of a design or transparent purpose for which to live. But neither is his position nihilistic and empty. To be sure, we do not discover a completely articulated theory of ethical values and practices through the ontological exploration of depth. In fact, the notion of a completed theory of ethics is antithetical to a philosophy of depth. Yet an understanding of the depth of being offers us a general ethical direction; it motions us toward a broad appreciation of difference and dialogue in light of which we might gather and push Merleau-Ponty beyond himself in order to fashion an ethos with more texture.

According to Merleau-Ponty, we are faced with living our lives and transforming our social world in ways that meaningfully articulate and creatively bring forth these general values that he finds rooted in our existence. And we must do so in the turbulent intercourse among the self, others, and the world at large. We creatively bring forth meaning and value in our lives in "actively being what we are by chance" (*Sense*, p. 40), in plunging into communication with this historical world of nature and others which penetrates us to the cores of our being, and in attempting to explore and pursue the limits and possibilities it presents as well as strategies for change that enhance freedom and the depth of being.

In an effort to further elaborate Merleau-Ponty's understanding of this task and the ethical understanding of our lives that emerges from his philosophy, I wish to explore and develop a notion of the self as a work of art, drawing extensively from his comments on style and the nature of artistic expression.

As our body makes its way in the world, it "gathers itself together and

47. Maurice Merleau-Ponty, *In Praise of Philosophy*, trans. John Wild and J. M. Edie (Evanston, Ill.: Northwestern University Press, 1963), p. 44.

begins to see, to understand, and to signify" (*Signs*, p. 240). Through our particular inscription in the social and natural world, through our successes and failures in our attempts to pick a path with our "fragile body, in a language which has already done so much speaking, and in a reeling history" (p. 240), we each develop a "style" of existence, sedimented habitual ways of perceiving, moving in, and conceiving of the world. It is this style through which the body interacts with the world and develops a degree of unity.[48] Through this style, others come to recognize and communicate with us. So fundamental is the notion of style to Merleau-Ponty's understanding of the body that he compares it to a "work of art" (*Phenomenology*, pp. 150–51), not because our life is the purely self-conscious elaboration of an absolute subject, but because each movement and perception is born in the wake of and colored by the style (primarily preconscious) that animates it.

Viewed from without, each manifestation of one's style reveals "a way of inhabiting the world, of handling it . . . in short, the emblem of a certain relationship to being" (*Signs*, p. 54). We witness this style in another's movement and perhaps even more profoundly in the paths left by the painter's brush as she attempts to capture, express, accentuate, and bring to explicit life on a canvas, the world that appears in her stylizing perception. From within, style does not appear *as such* but orients and gives form to the world one perceives in arranging "certain gaps or fissures, figures and ground, a top and a bottom, a norm and a deviation in the inaccessible plenum of things" (p. 54). Style submits things to a "coherent deformation" that bends the diverse elements of the world toward particular significations and establishes in one's movement and perception—one's work—a certain "system of equivalences," priorities, and privileged elements with respect to which the world tends to spring forth before us. Our style should be thought of not primarily as something that is governed by our consciousness but rather as what emerges at the point of contact between the self and the world through the practices and relationships into which the self enters. In turn, the world always appears to us through this style. Style at the most basic level is "preconceptual generality—generality of the 'axis' which is preobjective and creates the *reality* of the world" (*Prose*, p. 44). Intellectual and

48. Merleau-Ponty thinks here of a unity that is never total, not that of an entity subsumed under a law, and one that is continually disrupted by new experiences that challenge it in different ways.

artistic consciousness, as we shall see in more detail below, emerges out
of this preconceptual style, but it is not merely epiphenomenal, for as it
attempts to bring the preconceptual realm into explicit existence, it actively transforms this realm. Hence they exist in a relationship of circularity.

Though most of Merleau-Ponty's discussions of style are concerned
primarily with art and artists, and he makes little effort to develop explicitly an ethic around the notion of the self as a work of art, it seems to
me that when his few comments on the embodied self as art are thought
in relation to his more extensive discussions on the artist and style, we
can grasp and begin to tug on some interesting, broadly prescriptive
insights into the self and ethics. If we think of the self not simply as a
"work of *art*" (stylistic) but as a "*work* of art" (something we actively
participate in fashioning and elaborating), then Merleau-Ponty's work on
artists sheds insight on the artistic dimension of life; one's relation to self,
world, others. As embodied selves with sedimented ways of being in the
world, we are all essentially analogous to works of art, but we do not all
live artistically. It is only when one makes this understanding of the self as
art an integral part of one's existence, when one becomes self-conscious
of one's being as art and begins to fashion a life and an ethic around this
understanding, that the self starts to become a work of art in the fullest of
senses. The artistic self seeks not so much to *discover* the truth of itself
but to create meaning and elaborate a style of existence in the nexus
connecting the self, others, and the natural world.

Yet the artistic self is by no means to be the agent of an absolute
prescriptionless freedom for whom all ways of being are equally valid.
Merleau-Ponty's discussions of the artist are not merely descriptive, but
contain what is for him an exemplary notion of the artist and artistic
being more generally. They can be read as thoughts about an exemplary
style in light of which we might develop our various different styles. This
notion of artistic being does not give us meaning in and of itself, but
presents us with broad contours around which meaning ought to be
artistically brought forth. Let us turn to his discussion of the artist to gain
a better understanding of those elaborations of style Merleau-Ponty finds
problematical and those he holds in high esteem.

Thrown into the depths of the world, "caught up in the push and
shove of being . . . I take up a field and invent myself" (*Signs*, p. 14). But
what is the nature of this inventing? As his criticisms of Sartre illustrate,
it is not that of an originary subject—conceived as nothingness—who

chooses his existence with an absolute freedom. Rather, this "inventing" is that of a self whose being is bound up with numerous accidents—bodily, familial, historical—from which one cannot entirely escape; accidents that color our opening on the world. "In every life, one's birth and one's past define categories or basic dimensions which do not impose any particular act but which can be found in all" (*Sense*, pp. 24–25). The task of the artist and the self as a work of art is not to reject abstractly these givens in order to attain some Archimedian point of view that would witness existence without "distortion" and secure a pure freedom. Such a rebellion is an existential impossibility, and it is self-defeating insofar as it denies what is revealed through the particularities of oneself and one's situation.

Instead, the artist gathers the multiple aspects of his or her being together in an attempt to explore and express the possibilities they open. Of course, this "gathering" itself is not some abstract force, but always already motivated and infused with what it gathers. These "givens," however, do not impose on one's existence a determined, static meaning but rather, like the "accidents in Cézanne's life"—his nervous weaknesses, his troubled eyes—which "present[ed] themselves to him as *what* he had to live leaving *how* to live it undetermined" (p. 20), are the ambiguous text one has to decipher and elaborate. Cézanne's fits and depressions, his "schizoid temperament," instead of existing only as something that wrenched him and those around him, additionally acquires, when it speaks through his painting, a "metaphysical sense . . . a way of seeing the world reduced to the totality of frozen appearances, with all expressive values suspended. Thus the illness ceases to be an absurd fact and becomes a general possibility of human existence" (p. 20). Cézanne's temperament might have incapacitated him; he might have said nothing. But his artistic expression of the unusual world that appeared before his eyes brought forth and integrated this aspect into his existence in a way that enabled the peculiarities of his life to contribute to and shape a voice that continues significantly and interestingly to engage the historical world in which it is situated. Similarly, Merleau-Ponty writes: "The reason that Leonardo [da Vinci] is something more than one of the innumerable victims of an unhappy childhood is not that he has one foot in the great beyond but that he succeeded in making a means of interpreting the world out of everything he lived . . . he fashioned his corporeal or life situation into a language" (*Prose*, p. 75).

As the exemplary artistic self confronts the contingencies of existence, it does not allow itself to be simply determined by these factors, through either obedience or abstract denial, but instead carefully elaborates a style in a continual effort at expression that "always *goes beyond what it transforms by bringing it into a composition which changes its meaning*" (*Prose*, p. 69; my emphasis). In a sense, all expression, even the most basic perception, has this quality. Yet Merleau-Ponty seems to imply that in part great artists develop to a higher (which is also to say, deeper) level a potential born in our general perceptual being, one that in most people lies mostly undeveloped. Leonardo is Leonardo, but is there not still something we can learn here?

Let us consider more carefully the nature of this artistic "elaboration of style." Merleau-Ponty's discussions of style often accent the preconceptual level: "Perception already stylizes" (*Signs*, p. 54); it fashions the world that appears before us, and it is out of and with reference to this world that our intellectual and artistic consciousness develops. Yet is this to imply that all of the real work of existence is already accomplished at the preconceptual level? This would be strange, given that his discussions seem to indicate a conscious dimension of art important in its own right and not identical to perceptual style.

It is clear that in his discussions of the "primacy of perception," Merleau-Ponty does not seek to "renounce reflection" (*Primacy*, p. 19). While reflection itself is always vaguely portended—though not determined—in the perceptual field, intellectual consciousness plays an extremely important role in his philosophy. Indeed, "without reflection life would probably dissipate into ignorance of itself or in chaos" (p. 19). "That convergence of visible and intellectual vectors of the painting toward the same signification, X, is already sketched out in the painter's perception" (*Signs*, p. 54). The sketches one finds at the perceptual level, however, harbors only broad motives—beginnings with indeterminate outcomes—for artistic and intellectual expression. The stuff of artistic utterance does not lie completed in the perceptual realm, needing only to be recovered like a pearl at the bottom of a deep, murky sea, but rather must be submitted to yet another stylization—another giving of form— to be brought forth. This supplemental stylization at the level of artistic expression is "the 'coherent deformation' by which [the artist] concentrates the still scattered meaning of his perception and makes it exist expressly" (pp. 54–55). Hence the artist interacts with the world that appears before her; motivated by it, thrown by it, but also at the same time bending, orienting, and deforming it in the attempt to bring it into explicit existence for herself and others. For the body to get a perceptual grip on the world, it must participate in the "coherent deformation" of the plenitude of its surroundings, the establishment of depth, priorities, figures, and grounds. To get a grasp on this perceptual world itself— "making it manageable for the artist and accessible to others" (*Prose*, p. 58)—she must submit it to a similar transfiguration. Thus as the artist attempts to bring forth the perceptual realm, she also re-creates it and contributes to its making: "There is no pure absolutely unexpressed life in man; the unreflected [irréfléchi] comes into existence for us only through reflection" (*Primacy*, p. 30). The artist develops within this ceaseless circularity.

As long as the artist remains an artist, for her, her work is always in progress and never completed. Each expression of our encounter with the world fashions/brings forth out of the depths only a fragment of what there is to be said. To be sure, it is often an important fragment that really "says something," but the silences surrounding it, the transgressed elements driven from or subordinated within the work, speak of a tremendous plenitude of otherness that calls her to go further, to continue the dialogue between the self and the world which is the life of the artist. Indeed, the world that faces the artist every day is not so much what has already been caught in a phrase or on a canvas, but rather a "questioning" welling forth from the depths that exceed what she has been able to give voice to (*Signs*, p. 58).

This openness to the present and future is inherently an openness to the past and others as well. In an effort to express creatively what presents itself so elusively and in such a scattered fashion, what has been washed over and hidden by the currents of history; to engage that question that shines out of things in the world before her, the artist is thrown into a dialogue with the voices of the past and others.

In searching "beneath the imposed order of humanity" in an attempt to capture "the vibration of appearances which is the cradle of things" (*Sense*, pp. 16, 18), Cézanne no more abstractly denies tradition than he does his troubled eyes or his emotional makeup. Rather, he engages this tradition, listening to and examining its insights into the world in an effort to bend it toward new shapes and meanings that better express his existence and the appearance of the world to him—an existence and appearance that themselves are formed in part in the crucible of this uneasy conversation with tradition. When Cézanne is in Paris, Merleau-Ponty writes, he visits the Louvre every day. But he goes there as an artist, "in the joy of dialogue" and not with a "spurious reverence" (*Prose*, p. 72). He appropriates aspects of geometry, geography, impressionism, not in order to mimic, but to bring forth a world that goes significantly beyond what any of these traditions recognized. The exemplary artist engages the efforts of those who have come before her as well as her contemporaries, not as dead facts but as voices and actions that are entwined with and provoke one's own work and from which one cannot detach oneself; voices and actions that throw the self toward certain significations and away from others, voices with which we must wrestle since we exist as divergences in this historical conversation and struggle with others. To develop a style actively and partake actively in the historical dialogue requires a thorough knowledge of the history that penetrates us through and through. The past opens us to some possibilities for expression but also subjugates us and blinds us to others, and it is in our dialogue with it that we attempt to elaborate these possibilities further but also to explore what is denied. It is a question of discerning which limits enhance the depth of ourselves and the world and which ones act primarily to flatten.

Our existence as art is in large part the practice of bringing into mutual confrontation what has been said and done by others and the particular density of our own being—our difference—which has grown out of this social milieu yet exceeds it. "What we have to say"—both literally, in terms of immediate expression, and figuratively, thinking of the self as a work of art as a statement—"is only the excess of what we live over what has already been said" (*Prose*, p. 112). Our style attempts to express the things and dimensions of things we are or can see and embrace which seem important and empowering. It is by rearranging the elements of our milieu, changing figures and grounds, placing things in "compositions which change their meaning," using aspects of our history in new ways, abandoning others, juxtaposing terms that have been kept apart, highlighting tensions and contradictions that have been concealed, that we transfigure the past so that it may come better to express elements of our being—pleasures, powers, relationships, thoughts, desires—it has previously not expressed. Hence the artist "continues while going beyond, conserves while destroying, interprets through deviation" (p. 68).

Yet the transfiguring of this engagement between the self and its milieu is not one-sided, for the self is transfigured in the process as well. In its attempt to "say something," it comes to understand and create itself to an important extent in light of the other voices with which it is in dialogue. It expresses itself and takes form in a language—the terms of a tradition of understandings and practices—that it shares with others and the past, and in so doing not only bends this language toward new significations, but also is "coherently deformed" itself. As noted above, these words that others speak and have spoken—their works, their strivings, their gestures—"do not limit themselves to vibrating like chords the listener's machinery of acquired significations. . . . Their flow must have the power of throwing me in turn toward a signification that neither [they] nor I possessed before" (*Prose*, p. 142). Indeed, the artist is so intertwined in and so constituted by this dialogue that he is never able to say precisely "what comes from him and what comes from things, what the new work adds to the old ones, or what it has taken from others and what is its own" (*Signs*, p. 59). "The history in which the artist participates . . . is the perpetual conversation woven together by all speech, all valid works and actions, each, according to its place and circumstance, contesting and confirming the other, each one re-creating all the others" (*Prose*, p. 86). We elaborate ourselves—our style—in this agonistic interaction, and hence this is where the exemplary artist explicitly seeks to dwell: in continual dialogue with what precedes and surrounds her. It is through this dialogical attitude and activity that Merleau-Ponty's artists develop and exemplify the potential—born in our perceptual being—that lies mostly dormant in most people.

Yet the artist's interest, concern, and engagement with others is not that of an "I'm O.K., you're O.K." "validation" of everything surrounding her. No, it is much wilder, tougher, feistier than this. The artist listens carefully to, learns from, and is thrown by other voices. Indeed, Merleau-Ponty writes of an "obligation to understand situations other than my own and to create a path between my life and that of others, that is, to express myself" (*Signs*, p. 86). But her response is that of creative engagement, not flattery and polite accord. The exemplary artist pulls together the world that appears before her, the works and statements of others, in an effort to add a voice to the world which sheds a different and important light on the world in which we live—its depth and mystery, its pleasures, tragedies, subjugations, sufferings. When most successful, her work "throws our image of the world out of focus, distends it, draws it towards fuller meaning" (p. 78). From this angle, Merleau-Ponty's artist "moulds others much more often than follows them," is concerned "with others become such that he is able to live with them" (p. 74). Yet this "such that" should not be read as a tendency to make others "the same" as oneself. Such a world is a desert for all, offering little sustenance for creative life. The artist in part strives to fashion *artists*: distinct other beings who vitally contribute to, engage, enrich, and protect the diverse fabric that in turn contributes to depth and our entwined freedoms. A society and politics constituted around an ethic of the self as a work of art would see selves struggling within themselves and with each other in difficult, unending efforts to develop simultaneously strong, distinct voices and sharp, open ears. As we fashion our lives and the social fabric, we would strive to inhabit the tensions between an affirmation of difference and dialogical encroachment. Of the agonistic tensions between selves, Merleau-Ponty writes: "We have yet to learn the proper uses of this encroachment" (*Prose*, p. 13).

It seems to me, however, that at least a general direction is indicated in this discussion of the self as a work of art. The self as a work of art in the exemplary sense is aware of and actively deepens the dialogical dimension and possibilities of her style. She has a sense of the way in which self, others, and the natural world belong together in their differences, a sense that when the awareness of difference and transcendence wanes, so too does depth, art, and freedom. This involves a *care for* and nurturing of others and the natural world in their differences.

Yet let us not underplay the importance of identity here, for this ethic has historical meaning only to the extent that, as a society, we actually and practically affirm and nurture it in our thoughts and practices. It seems to me that society's *identification with* this ethic is as crucial to bringing forth the depth of the world and artistic existence as are the differences that depth and art entail. It is this very broad understanding of identity and difference toward which the artist attempts to move people.

What is involved, of course, is far more than simply the realm of understanding. Our lives are directly shaped on the everyday level by the institutions and practices in which we partake. Hence the effort to develop an ethics around a more artistic approach to life demands a very significant transformation of those institutions, which objectify and subjectify us around notions of truth that primarily enhance an often senseless, endless, disproportionately distributed productivity and control of flat things. These priorities and practices, as well as the larger systemic political and economic institutions with which they are interconnected, must be changed if the self as a work of art is ever to be more than an idea in the minds of a few philosophers. "The problem is to find institutions which implant this practice of freedom in our customs" (*Signs*, p. 349).

With this problem in mind, I turn to Merleau-Ponty's political writings to sketch the beginnings of a "politics of depth." First I explore his analysis of flattening social and political institutions, then his analysis of democratic politics in light of the discussion thus far.

Politics of Depth

We have already seen that Merleau-Ponty rejects anarchism, arguing that it is an untenable solution because it simply ignores the problems presented by the human condition. An equally superficial understanding of the politics of depth would be that capitalism, as that system supposedly thriving on the competitive struggle between "free" individuals, is the perfect social mechanism for bringing forth the difference and depth of others and the world. Merleau-Ponty is unsatisfied with capitalism as well, however, for under the guise of liberty, law, and individuality, he sees hierarchy, exploitation, unemployment, war, and imperialism. Far from simply leading to a mutual recognition of both the common humanity and the otherness of others, capitalism causes people to approach one another within the "free market" largely as objects reduced to use-value. Class divisions give birth not to an affirmation of others' differences, but rather to an obliteration of most people's difference, as society takes forms that fashion people around the goal of enhancing an endless productivity that is disproportionately allocated and even more disproportionately controlled. In contrast to an idealist humanism, which he thought functioned primarily to disguise capitalism's violence, Merleau-Ponty advocated a "*humanism in extension,* which acknowledges in every man a power more precious than his productive capacity, not in virtue of being an organism endowed with such and such a talent, but as a being capable of *self-determination* and *situating himself in the world*" (*Humanism*, p. 176; my emphasis except for "humanism in extension"). Even in his later political writings, where he becomes very critical of communist revolutionary theory and practice, he still emphasizes that "by this we in no way imply acceptance of the eternal laws of the capitalist order or any *respect* for this order."[49]

If not anarchy, if not capitalism, then what? For some years, particularly in the middle and late 1940s, Merleau-Ponty thought that Marxism offered not only the best critique of bourgeois society, but a tenable alternative direction as well. He believed with Marx that there was a possibility that the proletariat was a "class of men who, because they are expropriated in present society from their country, their labor, and their very life, are capable of recognizing one another aside from all differences, and thus founding humanity" (*Humanism*, p. xviii).[50] Though it is clear that he supported socialist production really governed by the workers and a breakdown of established hierarchies, the modes of organization that might best bring this about are not carefully elaborated. While he attempted to develop a reading of events within the Soviet Union which was sensitive to the way the contingency of history made itself felt in a single revolutionary country surrounded by hostile bourgeois states, he did not see an embodiment of the Marxian dream in Soviet reality. It did not appear to him that the Soviets were moving toward a greater recognition of humans by humans or proletarian power, (p. xx), though he left open the question of their future development.

Hence early Merleau-Ponty's affirmation of Marxism does not take us very far toward a more developed understanding of the political and ethical implications of his philosophical formulations. Nevertheless, it is worthwhile to emphasize that his Marxism was not one that was aimed at eliminating differences, but rather one that sought to create a world where a greater recognition of differences might exist. When he writes of the proletariat's "recognizing one another aside from all differences," this is, of course, not at all to say that we should do away with all of our differences. Rather, he had in mind a recognition of a common human

49. Maurice Merleau-Ponty, *Adventures of the Dialectic*, trans. Joseph Bien (Evanston, Ill.: Northwestern University Press, 1973), p. 227. Original: *Les aventures de la dialectique* (Paris: Gallimard, 1955). Further citations to the English edition are given directly in the text.

50. This position is ostensibly somewhat paradoxical for a philosopher who asserts that it is the *otherness* of an other that enables us to recognize the other as such. Apparently, as selves felt their own selves being squashed in capitalist society, they would be able to recognize others undergoing the same struggles. In this case, it is still a difference—class antagonism—that gives birth to recognition, not mere sameness. Merleau-Ponty never gives this paradox much consideration.

capacity for "self-determination" and the ability of each to "situate himself in the world." In short, to "recognize one another aside from all differences" is to recognize that other's differences are not, qua difference, the negation of their humanity—understood in terms of objectified norms or productive capacity—but rather expressions of humanity as the capacity for a degree of self-determination. If the exploitation of the proletariat was paradoxically to foster a common recognition, it was most fundamentally, on Merleau-Ponty's reading, a recognition that no one is free alone; that a greater level of self-determination is intrinsically intertwined with a greater mutual affirmation of others' freedom, their otherness. On Marxism and difference, Merleau-Ponty writes:

> To be a Marxist is *not to renounce all differences*, to give up one's identity as a Frenchman, a native of Tours or Paris, *or to forego individuality in order to blend into the world proletariat.* It is indeed to become part of the universal, but without ceasing to be what we are. . . . This will only happen through . . . a meeting at the crossroads of actual proletarians, such as they exist in the different countries, and not through an ascetic internationalism wherein each of them loses his *most compelling reasons for being a Marxist. (Sense,* p. 150)

Merleau-Ponty's belief that Marxism might lead to a greater recognition of the capacity for self-determination and difference did not last long, however. As he became aware in the early 1950s of the Soviet camps, the persistence of extreme hierarchy, authoritarianism in the workplace, and the tenacious unwillingness of the Soviet Communist party to allow a real opposition, his comments on the Soviet Union acquired an increasingly critical tone. His changing evaluation of the USSR culminated in a reassessment and rejection of what he argued were some of the theoretical foundations of Marxism as well.

Merleau-Ponty's critique of Marxism focuses on the manner in which it squashed the space within which a significant opposition could exist. He argues that its understanding of the relation between the proletariat and the party in the movement of history led it to deny the importance and legitimacy of any dialogical recognition of others who externally contest the party—indeed, to view all external opposition as a threat (to the development of a singular truth in history) that must be eliminated.

Merleau-Ponty maintains that at the center of Marxist theory is the idea that the proletariat is the universal class, which alone realizes the universality and self-consciousness that philosophers have previously only imagined. The proletariat is to transcend all particularity, and Marx argued that with its development, history has "finally put world-historical, empirically universal individuals in place of local ones."[51] Finally, history has made possible the universal subject. Marx and Lenin were, of course, well aware that this universal subject is only a "limit case," that in fact the proletariat is divided in a multiplicity of factions, uneven levels of development, and various stages of self-consciousness. "It is because of this that there is a need for a Party which clarifies the proletariat to itself, for a party of iron, as Lenin said" (*Humanism*, p. 117). In attempting to express the historical meaning of the proletariat, the party is to take the lead. It is never to get more than "one step ahead," however, for the proletarians "bring the seal of truth to the politics of the Party" and the party must maintain itself in a dialectical tension in which it "establishes itself as the expression of the working class by making itself accepted by the working class" (*Adventures*, pp. 52, 50).

Yet Merleau-Ponty argues that this tension is doomed to collapse into dictatorship, largely because of Marxism's conceptualization of the proletariat. For Marxism, as we have noted, the proletariat is universality-in-development, which is in a continual process of self-criticism and self-transcendence (*Selbstaufhebung*). Merleau-Ponty maintains that Marxism "concentrates all the negativity and all the meaning of history in an existing historical formation, the working class" (*Adventures*, p. 207). In so doing, in conceiving of one class as the locus of historically progressive critique, it lays the conceptual ground for denying the legitimacy of all those who do not speak and act as true representatives of this singular and exclusively genuine negativity. As universal negativity, the working class "would no longer need to be contested from the outside" (p. 206). Indeed, from this standpoint, *"all that is other is an enemy"* (p. 207), merely an attempt to thwart the true universal.

This, of course, leads to the exclusion of not only those who make no claim to speak exclusively for the working class, but also those members of the working class who understand their present conditions and desirable alternatives differently than those in the party who "truly" comprehend the "real" universality of this class. By conceiving of the working class as "universal in its truth" (even if it is not entirely self-conscious of

51. *The German Ideology*, quoted in Merleau-Ponty, *Humanism*, p. 116.

its universality), Marxism leaves no space for the articulation of a multiplicity of divergent perspectives, interests, and strategies within the working class—differences that it admits do in fact exist and differences that might require endless tensions and mediations. Rather, "universality" paves the way for a reduction of this multiplicity to its singular truth at any given moment, and since this reduction is not accomplished "naturally" within the working class itself (history does not give birth to a revolutionary proletariat in the optimistic fashion predicted by early Marx and early Lukács), it is brought about and "clarified" by a "party of iron." Through the elimination of certain tendencies and the accentuation of others, the proletariat is led by the party toward its true, unified meaning. Although there is supposed to be a continual dialectical interchange between the party and the proletariat, Marxism's conception of the latter is so singular that it cannot tolerate the plurality of negativities which is the essence of dialogue, and hence it abolishes the very space for the dialogical exchange that is to be the lifeblood and maximum guarantee of the revolution's legitimacy. This leads to a very truncated dialectic, or more accurately, a dialectic that is terminated in the party, which represents the genuine negative and has no need—or tolerance—for an opposition. The negative is driven out of existence as the party, in gaining power, becomes a positive entity that resists all criticism.

Perhaps, at least at the theoretical level, what lies at the heart of Merleau-Ponty's changed evaluation of certain important aspects of Marxism is the difference between his interpretation and what he finally believed to be the Marxist understanding of the passage we discussed above on the proletariat's "recognizing one another aside from all differences and thus founding humanity." For Merleau-Ponty, this recognition meant acknowledging the capacity of each to situate him or herself in the world; not simply to be a thing determined by the world, but, as a depth being, to transcend determinations, to proliferate the power of the negative in one's being in the world. The recognition that Merleau-Ponty had in mind was not one that flattened the depth and negativities of each into a universal negativity, but rather one that sought to affirm multiple loci of negativity and to build a shared social and political movement through "a meeting at the crossroads," which would articulate common interests that might enhance rather than erode the possibilities for different expressions of being. Such a notion was certainly not aimed at eliminating contestation.

For some time Merleau-Ponty thought this idea was Marxist, but his disillusionment with the historical development of communism and his consequent theoretical reassessment eventually brought him to a very different conclusion. Implicit in his later writing is a critique of the Marxist understanding of "recognition *aside from* all differences" as being part of a theoretical framework that concentrated negativity into a class— and the party representing it—while simultaneously denying multiplicitous expressions of its existence. In conceiving of recognition as "recognition *aside from* all differences," Marxism fails to establish the importance of difference at the center of its understanding. One finds instead flattened notions of the proletariat, negativity, and the party which, far from affirming depth, engender a situation in which "*the open depths close themselves*" (*Adventures*, p. 209; my emphasis).[52]

52. Merleau-Ponty has been criticized for placing the proletariat-party relation at the center of Marxism in a manner that misses the centrality of many contemporary Western neo-Marxist attempts to shift the primary level of analysis and focal point of change from state power to the structuration of everyday life. (Cf. Kruks, *Political Philosophy of Merleau-Ponty*, chap. 6; Dick Howard, "Ambiguous Radicalism: Merleau-Ponty's Interrogation of Political Thought," in *Horizons of the Flesh*, ed. Garth Gillan [Carbondale, Ill.: Southern Illinois University Press, 1973], chap. 7.) It is said that his criticism of Marxism misses what is most important about Marxism. It seems to me that as a defense of a certain type of Marxism interpreted along these lines, there is some truth to these criticisms. Merleau-Ponty's critique of Marxism was not intended as a wholesale dismissal of Marxism, however, and certainly it was not meant as a rejection of all Marxism of everyday life. Rather, it was a critique of the philosophical and political theoretical foundations of the historically most important communist developments of the twentieth century, foundations that Merleau-Ponty thought were rooted in Marx himself. At this level, I think, *Adventures of the Dialectic* remains a work of extremely valuable insight. Furthermore, insofar as any viable movement for change must confront the political realm as part of its strategy—we cannot wish this away—it is an important work for Marxism of everyday life as well.

It has been argued that *Adventures of the Dialectic* is insufficiently historical; that the collapse Merleau-Ponty describes which occurs when "the open depths close themselves" cannot be accounted for at such an abstract level (Kruks, *Philosophy*, chap. 6). Clearly, a textured historical account would have greatly enhanced his project. But again, this criticism largely misses the point. His discussion is not so much an effort to show what "caused" the particular development of twentieth-century communism, but more an attempt to illustrate the theoretical underpinnings and problems that contributed to this development. Of course, the dialectic between texts and interpretations is very important to this task, and this dialectic must be explored in a historical context to better show why certain readings of texts flourish and others do not at particular historical moments. Yet Merleau-Ponty argues quite persuasively that there is much in the texts of Marx, Lukács, and Lenin that contributed to the theoretical and practical developments of Soviet communism. At this level, his work remains very important, even if a historical account of other circumstances contributing to these developments would have made it more so.

Where does this critique leave us concerning our inquiry into the ethical and political understandings and practices that might lead to a greater mutual recognition of depth and difference? Merleau-Ponty's formulation of an alternative in *Adventures of the Dialectic* does not go very far in answering this question. Indeed, reflecting on his proposal, he writes: "This is not 'a solution' and we know it full well" (*Adventures*, p. 227). He is right; yet if considered closely and in conjunction with other elements of his philosophy, the alternative gestures further than many have realized—including, perhaps, Merleau-Ponty himself.

Of utmost importance in his defense against the closure he saw occurring in the communist left was his support of democratic parliamentary action, "for Parliament is the only known institution that guarantees a minimum of opposition and truth" (*Adventures*, p. 226).[53] In contrast to a politics that reduced negativity to singularity, Merleau-Ponty argued: "We expect progress only from a conscious action which will confront itself with the judgment of an opposition. Like Weber's heroic liberalism, it lets even what contests it enter its universe, and is justified in its own eyes only when it understands its opposition" (p. 226). The foundation of any attempt to improve things must be a recognition that no one has a monopoly on the negative, that there are different others with whom we must be dialogically and critically engaged. Parliament goes further in holding open this recognition than a "vanguard party."[54]

Yet Merleau-Ponty's support of parliament is not naively optimistic nor does it overlook the ambiguities and undersides of parliamentary action. In an essay published nearly a decade before *Adventures of the Dialectic*, Merleau-Ponty underscored the problems with this institution. "We know full well the means which the powerful have at their disposal— precisely under the aegis of freedom of the press—to stir up currents of opinion and manifestations which paralyze a parliamentary majority," assuming it is possible to obtain one (*Sense*, p. 115). He also warned against "comparing political democracy, in which everyone is called upon

53. This argument applies specifically to parliament, which is based on proportional representation with a minimal percentage of the overall vote enabling a party to gain representation. It applies to a far lesser extent, if at all, to our congressional system, in which the "winner takes all." This system operates to *exclude* minority voices and to minimize their chances for efficacious expression. It severely limits—one might say cripples, judging from the United States—political discourse.

54. In the most extreme situations (e.g., "starvation"), Merleau-Ponty admits that a "vanguard party" may be the best available alternative.

to give his opinion on abstract problems and, above all, where a whole series of influences . . . come between the voter and legislative decisions, with the daily management of business by workers." (p. 116). Furthermore, he was extremely skeptical about the possibility that an institution dominated by hegemonic economic interests could bring about significant change. At the time of this early essay, Merleau-Ponty maintained that a greater hope lay in a leadership like the one described by Lenin, which "presupposes a dialogue and exchange" with the people (p. 117). As we have seen, he later argued that this position is based on conceptions that work to undermine its best intentions. In affirming the importance of parliament, however, he did not forget or retract his earlier criticisms of this institution but rather urged the noncommunist left to work against those practices that undermined its proper functioning. He thought that they could do a lot to counter "parliamentary mystification," which consists in avoiding real problems or posing them too late or in ways that obfuscate far more than clarify. Beyond the problems resulting from abuses that might be remedied, however, Merleau-Ponty further recognized "the limitations of parliamentary and democratic action . . . which result from the institution" (*Adventures*, p. 226). Though he does not specify these limitations in *Adventures of the Dialectic*, he was probably in part referring to his earlier critical observations. These problems might be reduced, but never eliminated, as long as national parliamentary politics plays a significant role in political life. Nevertheless, he urges us to accept them as the necessary underside of a political institution that on the whole holds open the possibility for both effective governing by large groups of people according to a majority and recognizing different others, ambiguity, and contestation more than any other we know of—an institution that might contribute to maintaining and enhancing the depth of our coexistence.

Hence we see Merleau-Ponty's sketch of the manner in which parliament might be what we will call an "apparatus," which, with its arrangements that help guarantee the possibility of contestation from day to day, might help keep history open and demand a greater recognition among people. As an "apparatus," parliament (along with the rights that enable it to function) helps hold open a door through which people might enter and partake in the heated dialogical struggles over real life which actively contribute to our present and future, and as contestational acts, literally hold the social world open.

All this is of the utmost importance. Yet I suggest that in addition to parliament's being an "apparatus" helping to ensure the possibility of agonistic activity that contributes to bringing forth the world in depth, Merleau-Ponty's thought provides us with another way to understand the institution of parliament which is quite valuable as well; and it opens up fertile possibilities for thinking about human institutions and practices more generally. Here we must go beyond his explicit discussions of parliament to bring to the foreground some of the theoretical insights that probably shaped his view of it—and at any rate shape the argument that follows.

At about the same time that Merleau-Ponty wrote *Adventures of the Dialectic*, he also taught a course entitled "The Institution in Personal and Public History" at the Collège de France, in which he explored the notion of "institution" as a way of avoiding the problems that arise when philosophies of consciousness take the constituting subject and its object, the world, as the starting point of their investigations. Of particular interest to our current discussion of parliament is his conception of "institution." Most succinctly: "What we understand by the concept of institution are those *events in experience which endow it with durable dimensions, in relation to which a whole series of other experiences will acquire meaning*, will form an intelligible series or a history—or again those events which sediment in me a meaning, not just as survivals or residues, but as the invitation to a sequel, the necessity of a future" (my emphasis).[55]

This passage receives little further illumination that is helpful for us in the sketchy summary published in *Themes from the Lectures*. If we recall his discussion of dimensionality in *The Visible and the Invisible*, however, it begins to acquire a greater degree of conceptual texture. There he argued that all things are not simply objects within a perceptual field but also *dimensions:* meaning that they participate in clearing the perceptual field—in opening us to it and therefore presenting it—as well as appearing *in* the clearing. Yet while there is a dimensionality to all facts, not all facts are equally dimensional. Some facts or events may participate in the opening of the perceptual field only for an instant and then be swallowed up by a movement of the world in which they become utterly insignificant. Other things, however, things referred to above as "institutions"

---

55. *Themes from the Lectures*, pp. 40–41.

and elsewhere as "emblems," acquire such a significance that the disclosure of Being may take place through them throughout an entire lifetime. Merleau-Ponty describes this situation in a working note where he pursues an ontological reinterpretation of Freud in which he argues that "any entity [e.g., feces] can be accentuated as an emblem of Being" (*Visible and the Invisible*, p. 270). In other words, this entity or event can become "representative of Being"—a being that is fixated in such a way that the "investment of the openness to Being . . . henceforth takes place *through this Entity*" (p. 270). In such a manner an event, say of intense subordination or abandonment by someone deeply loved, may disclose all of our experiences henceforth in the light, or "atmosphere," of an inferiority complex or an inability to love.[56]

In these instances, the investment of the openness of Being in a thing is understood by Merleau-Ponty in a negative manner as a fixed opening that closes us to the multiplicity of the world by collapsing experience toward a single dimension that ceaselessly reactivates itself. Similarly, in the case of social institutions such as racism, sexism, authoritarian structures of power, sexual norms, etc., our field of perception is fixed in ways that flatten it. The depth of beings withers in these cases, and the dialogue between the self and the world is narrowly constituted or effectively terminated. Yet not all emblems are predominantly negative. Indeed, Merleau-Ponty elaborates his notion of the institution in a far more neutral manner. Institutions are events establishing relatively stable dimensions that create an atmosphere and illumination within which future events acquire meaning. Some institutions can fortify and enhance the depth and openness of the world by being emblems that significantly illuminate precisely these ontological qualities. It is in this sense of "institution"—in addition to the sense of "apparatus" discussed above—that parliament acquires a particular meaning within the context of Merleau-Ponty's philosophy.

Parliament, as a central institution in society which is connected to all citizens, can be an emblem that—at least in the best cases, elaborated more fully below—endows experience with a meaning that is less one of a particular being-event, and more one of the depth, openness, and resistance of the world; an emblem representative of Being not in collapsing it to a single dimension but by investing the clearing in a way that

56. Cf. *Phenomenology*, p. 442.

accentuates our experience of the most fundamental character of the clearing itself: depth. Said again in a slightly different way, parliament is an institution that in part discloses the openness and resistance of the "there" or "worldness" in the senses discussed in the last chapter. In this case, the meaning that attains durability and stability as it becomes a dimension is precisely that of the depth of people and the world, the incredible texturedness and transcendence of things fully present. As an emblem, parliament can contribute to a disclosure of the world that engenders a consensus around this ontological character of the world and the importance of recognizing different others. This is no small deed, for Merleau-Ponty's work—as well as that of others—has shown us the multiplicity of institutions, ethics, epistemologies, and practices whose effect is to flatten, reduce radically, and close being. In the best instances, the institution of parliament can be an emblem that counters these institutions of closure.

Insofar as the institution of parliament insists that we confront oppositions, it might foster a perception of the world as depth-being which always exceeds the definitions given it by one person or group. This is not to say that the best understandings and courses of action are necessarily compromises among several different positions, that is, moderate positions. In many instances, this is not the case, and at any rate there is no reason to assume it is. And parliament as Merleau-Ponty understands it makes no such assumption; it simply asserts that because the world transcends us, each must maintain an openness to the world and different others who may reveal dimensions of the world that we might never have seen or imagined alone. Furthermore, parliament discloses the importance of the interaction among different others in *bringing forth* the depth and fullness of the world into the clearing. It is through this interaction that we are continually confronted with aspects of the world, events, and proposals which remind us and enhance our awareness of the surplus of being that escapes our knowing. It is through these relations that some aspects of things are enhanced, multiplied, given greater texture, while others are crossed out and still others held in uncertain tensions—all of this rending and rendering the world "there" in an open fullness that is quite antithetical to the frozen figures of objectifying, normalizing practices.

Of course, none of this is unproblematic. We might with J. S. Mill view all genuine contestation primarily as a feature of "transitional ages" to be

transcended for the most part when we reach a consensus on all important issues in some unspecified future.[57] In this case, rather than revealing the depth of the world, parliamentary contestation would merely
reveal the deficiencies of our age. Or we might understand parliament
only in pragmatic terms as the best overall means of arriving at reasonable legislation to guide a nation.

Merleau-Ponty obviously rejects the former position, for reasons that
should be clear. Although he is sympathetic to the pragmatic argument, it
is not exhaustive of his position, in which parliament is important as an
institution emblematic of depth as well. Of course, the extent to which it
is emblematic of depth depends, in part, on the interpretations it receives. Hence the argument we are presenting is not simply a *description*
of things but part of an effort to bolster an interpretation that enhances
the extent to which parliament really is emblematic of openness and
depth. In this sense, the interpretation contributes to the realization of
what it describes.

However, if the understanding of parliament-as-emblem is to move
distinctly beyond being a mystification and legitimization of the present,
if it is to contribute to the deepening and opening of the world, it must
not only accentuate certain hopeful dimensions of our present, but alert
us to circumstances in our world threatening its further realization as
well. If parliament is to function as an institution of depth in a manner
that goes beyond mere reification and abstraction, then it must also be
operative and meaningful as an apparatus, and this depends not simply
on parliament, but on other social-historical factors as well. If parliament
is to be an authentic emblem of depth, it must be an institution that *in fact*
facilitates the expression of multiple voices. To the extent that it claims to
do this while doing something quite different, it in part becomes a bad
myth and takes its place in a regime of "truth" and power linked more to
subjugation than to freedom. Parliament cannot live up to its ideal of
ensuring the possibility of fair contestation as long as it is situated within
a society where wealth and many forms of power are extremely inequita-
bly distributed and yet play a very important role in the public sphere,
largely determining what issues are addressed, the limits of debate, who
speaks and who does not, who has access to certain information and who
does not, the way the mass media cover issues that help generate opin-

57. J. S. Mill, "The Spirit of the Age," in *Essays on Politics and Culture*, ed. Gertrude
Himmelfarb (Garden City, N.Y.: Anchor Books, 1963), pp. 1–44.

ions, etc. It cannot live up to its ideal of being a meaningful forum as long as the executive branch controls major foreign policy issues behind its back; as long as most of the really important economic decisions that affect hundreds of millions of lives in far-reaching ways are made behind the closed doors of multinational corporation boardrooms. It ceases to be meaningful when, as Theodore Lowi has described, decision-making becomes entirely fragmented inside "iron triangles" made up of congressional committee members, bureaucrats, and powerful interest groups with little concern for the consequences of their actions beyond their narrowly calculated balance sheets. It ceases to be meaningful when—as with the U.S. "winner take all" system of elections—minority voices are utterly shut out of Congress. It ceases to be meaningful when—for all these reasons and many more—most people stop voting and far fewer still are significantly engaged in political activity. In our current state of mass disaffection and political disempowerment in the United States, it is not clear how much an emblem of depth parliament really is or can be.

Nevertheless, the parliamentary emblem is not nonexistent, nor is it *simply* ideological. It also already functions to some extent as a lever of criticism and bolsters demands for changes toward a better world. The existing democratic ethos should not be underestimated. It stands as an ideal worthy of support, one that involves far-reaching reforms and major transformations in important areas of our society. The realization of the parliamentary emblem goes hand in hand with other changes that open our social world to participation by and empowerment of people over events that shape their lives; so too it involves creating greater space for different voices and ways of being to develop. As an emblem, parliament enhances the durability of the depth that emerges in this process.

In one of his last directly political essays, Merleau-Ponty alerts us to another issue concerning parliament which serves as an important caveat to the discussion thus far. In reflecting on parliamentary politics in France in the late 1950s, his criticism concerns not so much a lack of openness, but the lack of anything much at all. He writes sarcastically: "But what do checks and balances mean when there is no longer any action to check and balance? . . . today it is necessary, in continuing the criticism, to reorganize power. Many stupid things are said against 'personal power' or 'strong power': it is a genuine strength and personality which those in power during the Fourth Republic lacked" (*Signs*, pp. 348–49).

This passage provides us with both a political and an ontological clarification that is extremely important. While the world as depth is open to different renderings, it does not *equal*—it cannot be *reduced to*— "openness." Openness is not what is "there"; rather, what is "there" has a depth and is open. Like checks and balances without any action, openness alone is nothing. It is simply a recent form of that persistent dream harbored in Western metaphysics of being present—open—to the world everywhere and all at once. It is the latest form of nihilism. Furthermore, the effort to define the world as openness alone is yet another attempt to posit a world totally open to our efforts to transfigure and possess it: totally without resistance. If Merleau-Ponty has taught us anything, it is that, on the contrary, we always open onto the world *through* the specificity, difference, and limits of our historical bodily being, and likewise that others and things are "there" in a specificity that, in addition to being open, resists—is not open to—many renderings, and demands that we encounter *them*. Our openness to difference is not enhanced through annihilating the specificity and difference of our own embodiment in order simply to "be open to difference." Rather, it is by cultivating ourselves in a dialogue with the world and others which acknowledges and affirms the specificity, particularity, and difference of our own being that we open toward others. Our openness to the poly-phony and cacophony of the world is enhanced as we become *something "there"* with distinction—a distinction that both invites and is capable of participating in a profoundly dialogical existence with other distinct beings. Depth politics enjoins us not to eliminate our own voice, but rather to create a distinct voice in tension with one's distinct and open ears.

Hence parliament is an emblem not simply of openness, but of the depth of the world through which things are both *there and open*. Yet it can be this only to the extent that actions, initiatives, and programs are developed through this forum—to the extent that something is there. To the extent that no programs could be formulated in this arena, it would signify more a lack of any common world than a world of depth. Mer-leau-Ponty had in mind a vigorous politics, one that would strive in a powerful way to lead toward greater freedom and justice. The new "heroic liberalism" he advocated in his later works was not a variation of the self-effacing, fence-sitting-by-nature, hear-all-sides-in-absence-of-any-position liberalism with which we are all too familiar. Rather, it was to be an "initiative which gathers support . . . organizes its own pedagogy, and demonstrates as it develops" (*Signs*, p. 349). It was to attempt to shape the political world according to a vision of the common good (understood in large part as the creation of institutions and preconditions for dialogical existences) while remaining in agonistic tension and dialogue with those who contest this vision. Both there and open, it was to hear other voices, even be "thrown" by them. But its openness was to facilitate its development as a dynamic "living political power" (p. 349), forcefully shaping itself and the political world in dialogue, rather than using openness and dialogue as an excuse not to be present with distinction (more often than not, forfeiting power to hegemonic elements and structural tendencies of the status quo).

Both as an emblem of depth and as an apparatus for not only ensuring the possibility of contestation but also creating social, economic, and political conditions more conducive to the being of and creative interaction among different others, it is necessary that parliament actually draw enough differences *together* to generate action. Contestation is an extremely important part of Merleau-Ponty's understanding of parliament, but its importance stems from its place within the context of his philosophy of depth being. Contestation for the sake of contestation alone could destroy mutual recognition, communication and, in stifling all initiatives, could bring about the failure of parliament as an emblem of depth and as an institution capable of generating a politics of freedom. Contestation is an important element in bringing forth the social world that affirms depth, but such a world is the ultimate value for Merleau-Ponty and it is not reducible to contestation alone.

Hence along with and in tension with openness and difference in Merleau-Ponty's thought, there is a dimension of consensus building.[58] Yet the ethos around which Merleau-Ponty would have us attempt to achieve consensus is precisely one affirming institutions and practices that allow different selves to participate in creating themselves and each other in a dialogical context. Thus consensus becomes instrumental to ongoing dialogue, rather than being a self-expanding monologue of Truth or Reason.

Merleau-Ponty thought that for a short period the Mendez-France government approximated some of these ideas more than did the other

58. It is similar to what Ernesto Laclau and Chantal Mouffe refer to as the "project of hegemony" in *Hegemony and Socialist Strategy: Towards a Radical Democratic Politics* (London: Verso, 1985).

political alternatives in France. Nevertheless, he realized that the effort to
bring about a significant and sustained improvement in our political
culture would involve much more than parliamentary politics alone. It
would require important changes throughout society. "The problem is to
find institutions which implant this practice of freedom into our customs" (*Signs*, p. 349). Clearly, he was thinking here of institutions in their
capacity to elicit and organize certain dialogical forms of activity, and in
their emblematic aspect as well, though he does not specify what sorts of
institutions might enhance the freedom of which he writes.

Almost everything in Merleau-Ponty's philosophy gestures toward
changes in the institutions and practices of everyday life which would
both create spaces for and enhance people's capacity effectively to shape
their existences. Widespread workers' control of production is clearly
indicated in his early work (*Sense*, p. 116). Though he does not develop a
theory that emphasizes the importance of local and regional control of
major dimensions of economic, social, and political life, such de-
centralization seems essential to "implanting the practice of freedom."
Colossal institutions inhibit active participation because their sheer scale
makes one's efforts seem overwhelmingly insignificant. Yet our current
local institutions are often too irrelevant to solicit significant popular
involvement. Significantly empowered local democratic institutions
would likely go a long way toward confronting this problem. Crucial for
any effort to develop freer institutions is the multiplication and reforma-
tion of societal public spheres in ways that dampen structural asym-
metries.[59]

Yet institutions alone are insufficient. If we began this section on the
politics of depth by stressing the importance of developing institutions
that would enhance the possibilities of the artistic ethos, it is equally
important in closing to stress the circularity of this relationship. For a
politics of depth, it is vitally important that those inhabiting parliament—
and democratic institutions more generally—guide themselves in light of
the artistic ethos. That is, decisions should be aimed at furthering the
contextual preconditions and space for human beings creatively and dialogically to shape their existences. In absence of this ethos, democratic
politics easily becomes a more insidious pretext for a flattening politics.

We do not need to imagine this flattening politics, for it shadows much

---

59. See Jürgen Habermas, *The Structural Transformation of the Public Sphere*, trans.
Thomas Burger (Cambridge, Mass.: MIT Press, 1990).

of our contemporary world. We are driven in modernity by an ethos that identifies the "better life" with an endlessly increasing productivity. Growth, calculated in material terms, is seen as the solution for nearly everything. Yet, as we learn from Foucault, Adorno, and others, endlessly increasing productivity demands that more and more of the self be drawn into the productive apparatus, that the goal of productivity proliferate throughout more and more of the social (and nonhuman) world. And even if this can be done in ways that are not as normalizing per unit of output as those methods currently hegemonic, the pressures to *increase* will demand further absorption of the self, further normalization, and an eclipse of the space necessary to lead a creative existence. As long as we are governed by this god, it is very difficult to conceive of a flourishing politics of depth, even in a democratic society. Hence it is clear that we must tame the growth imperative and move in the direction of a relatively steady-state economy.

Yet this transformation requires a new ethos that both opposes mindless growth and provides an alternative sense of what is valuable. I believe the notion of the self as a dialogical artistic development is precisely such an ethos and that Merleau-Ponty had this ethos in mind when he wrote of "a *humanism in extension,* which acknowledges in every man a power more precious than his productive capacity . . . a being capable of self-determination and of situating himself in the world" (*Humanism*, p. 176). As we develop and inhabit democratic institutions, we ought to make decisions in light of this ethos, for it guides us toward an affirmation of difference and dialogue which is most appropriate to the world as depth. Just as democratic institutions are a precondition for the widespread proliferation of the artistic ethos, a lively and open democratic politics requires the sense of openness and distinction contained in the artistic ethos; for without it, debate flattens to the question of productivity—and the depth of being flattens in the productive apparatus. Instead of open forums, we will continue to have forums that are narrowly constituted and at war with what does not fit, forums that will be in great danger if their discourse exceeds that required by the goal of productivity.

Taken together, the democratic ethos and the self as a work of art set the stage for a grand human style, one that "embraces indivisibly all the order and all the disorder of the world" (*Humanism*, p. 189). We turn now to a more direct engagement of the three positions sketched in this book thus far.

5 · Conclusion: Possibilities and Dangers

I have argued that Augustine's turn toward an inward-seeking, hermeneutical deep self should be situated in the context of his understanding of the Roman pagan self. Inhabiting the center of a conceited ontology, the pagan self, in Augustine's view, was an imperialist, driven at every level to flatten others and the world to their being-for-the-self. In so doing, the space for what was not the self collapsed in a conflagration kindled and kept ablaze by the flaming gaze of vanity. By directing the self toward its depths in confession, Augustine sought to deflate this vanity and reinflate the depth of the world in which others and things could exist beyond the self as unique significations of God.

Yet it is too simple to view the confessing self and the self of ontological conceit as two types that Augustine sees merely in external opposition. While this opposition is extremely important and indicates what is at stake for Augustine, we must not lose sight of the fact—Augustine did not lose sight of the fact—that the struggle between the two selves is also one continually waged *within* the Christian self. Indeed, the confessing self is in large degree *defined by* its inward struggle with its "other." The confessing self is defined not so much by Truth and Goodness in and of themselves, but by the way in which one struggles on the side of these qualities to overcome the conceit, evil, sin, impurity within.

Whoever does not want to fear, let him probe his inmost self. Do not just touch the surface; go down into yourself; reach into the farthest corner of your heart. Examine it then with care: see there, whether a poisoned vein of wasting love of the world still does not pulse, whether you are not moved by some physical desires, and are not caught in some law of the senses; whether you are never elated with empty boasting, never depressed by some vain anxiety: then only can you dare to announce that you are pure and crystal clear, when you have sifted everything in the deepest recesses of your inner being.[1]

For Augustine, our fallen bodies and souls contain an endless multiplicity of lusts harboring ontological conceits that continually threaten to collapse the space in which others can be and appear in their glory as truly other, as God signifying. To the extent that one succumbs to these conceits, one ceases to participate in the glory of God. On earth, this struggle that is confession can never end.

This active struggle is important because it significantly defines the qualitative aspect of depth. Perhaps we should call the confessing self a being of *deepening* in order to draw attention to depth as activity, to draw attention to the effects of depth, which we must consider more carefully as we attempt to think about Augustine in the context of Foucault's work.

For Augustine, of course, the self that turns its gaze inward strives to discover, examine, decipher, and elaborate itself in light of God's truths, weeding out flattening conceits, purifying itself—in short, molding the deepest movements of its soul to participate in God's will. As we have seen, the confessing self relentlessly unifies itself around this task and God's truths. Augustine's faith in God and scripture is unflinching, and hence questions about the Christian morality to which one conforms never arise. To erase conceit is to discover God within and become receptive to the unique voices with which surrounding beings cry out, "He made us." To convert to an existence that signifies God and to see in all things his Word is not to *sacrifice* one's being or the being of things to God, but actively to affirm that which imparts being to all things. And this affirmation of the transcendental signified does not, in Augustine's view, entail a flattening or leveling of selves or things, for God's light on earth is infinitely polyphonous, each being manifesting it in a different

---

1. Saint Augustine, *Sermon*, 348.2, quoted in Brown, *Augustine of Hippo*, p. 432.

way. Of course, living according to God's light entails that the soul adhere to his injunctions and prohibitions, but these pull us precisely away from a flattened world and toward a truer experience, toward creation as a multiplicitous celebration of him. In God's light, the effects of confession can appear only as beneficial.

In an age when Christian metaphysics (and metaphysics in general) is losing its privileged position as the universal Truth, however—in an age when for many, God is dead—Augustine's confessing self now appears in a different light. The effects of confession as a mode of being must open themselves to questions that were concealed as long as being itself was unquestionably thought to be designed by God and Christianity was considered the only true story of the world.

For those who reject Christian metaphysics, there is a distinctly mono-logical quality to the confessing self. Augustine's polyphony becomes, for Nietzsche, monotony. In an important sense, from a postmetaphysical perspective there is only one significant voice (even if this voice enunci-ates endless phrases) in Augustine's relentless self-examination, and when he writes, "Help me so that I may see the truth about myself," his wish is ultimately to hear one voice in that cacophonous interior he calls the "great deep." From this vantage point, the quest for depth is a quest to rout out the last traces of other voices in his experience of the world, to surround them and penetrate them through and through to their deepest depths until they cease to speak, until they cease to be, until "you are pure and crystal clear." Of course, this purity was an unattainable end-point on earth (Augustine died "crying constantly and deeply" as he read penance), but as the confessing self deepened, it approached ever closer to monological being: a being no longer distracted by pleasures, desires, thoughts, or sensations that did not harbor the voice of the one True God.

This Nietzschean reading of early Christianity overstates the extent of the latter's reduction and elimination of otherness. It underplays (for strategic reasons I am not concerned with at the moment) the space Christianity opens for appreciating others as diverse expressions of God. Nevertheless, it contains an important insight that survives its own exag-geration. The space for being that is created by Christianity is—re-gardless of its merits relative to decadent Rome—thoroughly constituted by the one True Voice, by a single divine order in which the sense of all things is to be located. And this voice seems in many respects both wrong and narrowly defined, in light of postmetaphysical perspectives.

If there are many manifestations of the voice of Augustine's God, they all fall within a tightly limited range characterized by harmonious concord, the unchallengeability of Christian morality and scripture, and a conception of God as the transcendental signifier and signified (at best, signifying). Non-Christian difference becomes, for Christianity, discordance. Discord—indeed, even other philosophical perspectives that might lead in directions largely similar to those of Christianity—indicates error, and error is to be eradicated. The most fleeting desire or pleasure that might become lost in itself is a Problem. If the Being of God is finally ineffable for Augustine, it is nevertheless there for us enough to command an exceedingly insistent and demanding order of things. *Nothing* may be permitted which might point beyond God to an other that lies outside his totalizing order. In this sense, it seems to me that there is a great deal of truth in the claim that Augustine's mode of subjectivity is largely monological. Augustine's confessing self deciphers, re-members, and unifies itself according to God's truth in an effort to extirpate all voices that might be discordant with his voice. Within the self, God's voice meets the voice of the other as it confronts impure desires, thoughts, and pleasures. But that this meeting bears little resemblance to dialogue is indicated by the "nothing" to which all that is not in agreement with God is assigned. The confessing self is characterized more accurately as a site of inner confrontation than one of inner conversation (albeit often discordant), for the encounter in depth between God's light and what *is not* is marked by the aim of absolute hegemony of God's voice. *Within* the multiple manifestations of God's light is a dialogue in which the various dimensions of God commingle to give birth to deeper truth. Yet with respect to what lies beyond his Word, there is only a monological polemic—a ceaseless attempt to silence the other—and no possibility of a dialogue in which God is illuminated in the critical light of his other.

In a more postmetaphysical light, one might discern an ontological conceit in this confessing self, one of a different kind than the conceit Augustine so perceptively criticized in the pagans. In the conceit of the confessing self, human selves are no longer the implicit ground of Being; rather, God is the ground that establishes and secures the Truth, Goodness, and Being of all beings. Yet we are the highest elements of his creation and he made us capable of experiencing and knowing Truth and Goodness to a very high degree—even if there is an incredible extent to which much of Truth remains concealed and must be continually deciphered. Indeed, God has made us beings such that we harbor his truth *within us* and he is *concerned* enough for our fate that we can find enough truth to save ourselves if we truly will to do so. "Return within yourself," Augustine writes. "In the inward man dwells truth." Insofar as we should "*obey* the voice of unchangeable truth speaking silently within the soul,"[2] one perhaps can detect a certain humility, but it is a humility based on a conceited ontology that maintains that there is such a voice within us to obey. And it is precisely the singular centrality of this voice and this obedience which gives birth to the monological character of the confessing self, a character conceited with respect to its non-Christian other within and without. In short, the humility of obedience wells forth from a conceited ontology and returns to conceit when it repudiates even the possibility of that which is *utterly other* than His voice within (in the sense that this other, no matter how demanding, is "nothingness").

A new and distinct form of power begins to proliferate in the fabric of the discursive economy woven around this Christian version of ontological conceit.[3] Obedience isn't simply *suggested*, it is *demanded* by a textual tour de force that mobilizes responsibility, guilt, and death in a manner that aims at thoroughly extirpating others—the non-Christians within and without—which are constituted as "evil," "ignorant," and "vanity." A lot of difference becomes iniquity, and beneath iniquity there always lurks an evil will, evil desires that are guilty and deserving of reform, punishment, or both. We have seen the depth of this dynamic: there may be an evil will and iniquitous desires lurking even beneath Augustine's love of church music. This relentlessness fills the soul with God's noise, barring not only other voices but even silence. Augustine weaves the threads of God's voice tighter and tighter around himself and others. Wrapped in a confessional bundle or wrapped in a bundle of

2. Saint Augustine, *Of True Religion*, trans. J. H. S. Burleigh (South Bend, Ind.: Regnery/Gateway, 1959), sec. 110.

3. William Connolly's "A Letter to Augustine," in *Identity\Difference: Democratic Negotiations of Political Paradox* (Ithaca, N.Y.: Cornell University Press, 1991), pp. 123–57, explores this issue in an interesting manner. Though I disagree with parts of this essay, its influence is obvious in the following paragraph.

accusations and denunciations, we all, every one of us, face eternal life or eternal hellfire. Augustine's texts are an awesome mobilization of hope, fear, and guilt. The stakes are infinite, and we deserve what we get. Through immense enticement and gripping fear, Augustine lures others into confessional weaving.

The broad contours of this discursive economy should not be un-familiar to anyone, for they proliferate in our age. No longer bound to Augustine's religion, they take multiplicitous secular forms that crystallize around the work ethic, sexuality, mental health, political per-spectives. AIDS is the just punishment for those whose guilty wills are responsible for iniquitous erotic acts. In George Gilder's writing, wealth and poverty lurk like heaven and hell around selves who should willfully endorse the hegemony of the capitalist work ethic and deserve what they get if they don't. Capitalism is that totalizing system of enticements and fears which best lures selves into adopting the capitalist definitions of self, which he claims are the incarnation of the golden rule.[4] Capitalism, as Gilder notes, is about morality, and his text—along with the system it affirms—aims at constituting selves who will package themselves accord-ingly.

It would obviously be a serious mistake to hold Augustine "responsi-ble" somehow for these modern phenomena, whatever debt they may owe to his thought. And it would be a mistake as well, I think, to read Augustine mainly as one who was "responsible" for the new totalizing configurations of power proliferated by dimensions of his texts and his age: to see in Augustine primarily a power-mongering *evil will* inten-tionally setting traps everywhere. The mistake here is not only that of overlooking the profound extent to which Augustine's thought prolife-rates openings and freedoms as well as closures. Clearly, when one considers his thought with the slightest care, Augustine appears in an entirely different category of thinkers than the one in which we find ideologists like Gilder. (Of course, Augustine was not pure and he knew it. And it is difficult to read about his silencing of his religious com-petitors without sensing in him some evil of which he was perhaps less aware than he was of the possibility of perversion during church hymns.) Yet the mistake I am thinking of here involves more than overlooking the fecundity and complexity of Augustine's thought. It is that of reading

4. George Gilder, *Wealth and Poverty* (New York: Bantam Books, 1981), p. 8.

Augustine primarily as a "responsible will." Such a treatment of Augustine would—far from moving beyond him in a positive manner—deploy the darkest moments of his own philosophy against him. To do so would be to fail to learn from Augustine's best moments and to fail to explore sufficiently the meaning of his mistakes as well.

Rather than constitute Augustine as an "evil other" (to be extirpated in order to purify a "postmodern" age), we might attempt to read Augustine's errors *in a tragic mode* as the errors of a human being who, like all of us, submerged in the depths of being, could comprehend only a fraction of the proliferating strengths, weaknesses, and meanings of his work. We live and write on the tip of an iceberg, and there is a dimension of tragedy to our life and work that is ineliminable. Augustine's grasp of the tragedies of the world was eclipsed by an overriding effort to see responsibility and deeply buried willful intentions behind all things, combined with a sense that in the end everything that happens is in the large picture good and just. We get what we deserve; and if we have a truly bad fate, it is because we have a truly evil will: vanity of vanities. Yet perhaps it was precisely his lack of a deep sense of tragedy—a deep sense of how our intentions, actions, and lives so frequently assume horrific shapes and consequences we never willed or planned—which allowed and indeed encouraged him confidently to launch such a totalizing project. Would not a sense of ineliminable tragedy at least partially have tamed Augustine's own ontological conceit, or at least the comprehensiveness of its imperatives?

If we are truly to venture beyond totalizing theory and practice toward positions capable of entertaining a wider spectrum of questions and ways of being, we will need, among other things, ears more able to hear other voices. Such listening will require at once a remarkable degree of audacity and humility. A sense of tragedy is important for both these qualities. For it spurs us beyond ourselves and simultaneously gestures toward the necessity of other voices, without which this transcendence is impossible. Creon could not hear Antigone. Augustine could not hear the pagans. If we attempt too simply to leap beyond Augustine into the "postmodern," perhaps our own tragedy will be barbarism. The inaugural acts of wiser philosophical and practical positions—such as our critique of Augustine—should themselves contain the wisdom they hope to embody after they have displaced the Gods they oppose.

A sense of the essential tragic dimension of life—the tragic dimension

of Augustine—will not eliminate tragedy in our future efforts. But perhaps it will reduce it. For often what is most tragic—for example, what is
most tragic in Augustine—emerges when we act in oblivion to the possible errors and limits of our own voice. Perhaps this oblivion is the
common home of multiple forms of dangerous conceit? If we can grasp
the tragedy in Augustine's voice, as well as the possibilities remaining
there, we might begin to think in a way that takes a significant step
beyond him.

In addition to oblivion, the lack of a sense of tragedy is closely connected to an imperative: the imperative to drive relentlessly toward the
perfectly purified self and world; to view all discord, discrepancy, difference as unnecessary, therefore evil, therefore to be extirpated. This
imperative is intertwined with straitjacketing forms of subjectivity and
administration. The alternative to this imperative cannot be simply to
"let tragedy be." There is no impulse for freedom, dialogue, diversity, or
art in such complacency. Perhaps we should explore the possibility of an
ethos of freedom that vigorously seeks to create a better world while
recognizing that though the effort to reduce tragedy is admirable, worthwhile, and necessary, it tends to turn into its opposite when it believes it
can—and seeks to—eliminate all tragedy. For the drive to eliminate
tragedy altogether ushers forth demands for purity and control with
tragic consequences for life. If this is the case, then part of the task of
freedom that aims at a better world is to seek to discern that line—and
create just this side of it—beyond which the will to reduce tragedy begins
to create a situation worse than the one it seeks to better. Such an ethos
may be misconstrued to be remarkably close to the one Gilder and other
proponents of contemporary capitalism affirm, but this construal would
fly in the face of everything said thus far. For the current capitalist ethos
errs simultaneously on the side of complacency (regarding homelessness,
poverty, environmental destruction) and on the side of the purification
imperative (regarding modes of social control illuminated by Marx,
Foucault, Adorno, and others.) In contrast, the tragic ethos gestures
toward a marked reduction in both these forms of complacency and these
forms of control, for both thwart the possibility of enhancing dialogical
artistic freedom.

Augustine's confessing self is an ambiguous phenomenon. For he
argues quite convincingly that what I have identified as its specific conceit and monologue—its relentless inward journey—provides a space for

appreciating others and things which was rapidly disappearing for the pagan self in late antiquity. Within what Foucault calls the modern episteme, however, the conceit that lingers on from two thousand years of Christianity is indirectly implicated in a rapidly narrowing closure. Foucault makes the case that we are still thoroughly attached to the belief in a Truth that can and must be discovered and obeyed. Yet with the recession of God from our world, man himself becomes the uncertain ground of this truth—uncertain because he inhabits a world, drained of its telos, that continually threatens to cut him off from truth. Driven by both his desire for truth and the centrality of his uncertainty, man in modernity endlessly seeks to objectify and normalize the social and natural world around him—to make the other the same. (At a more concrete level, this dynamic is entwined with and driven by socioeconomic and political imperatives for profit and productivity.)

One could argue that there is a sense in which modernity unites two ontological conceits that bear an interesting resemblance to those emerging from our discussion of Augustine's work: the belief in a largely discoverable universal truth and the belief that man is the ground of the truth of things. This combination, and the fact that "man" cannot in fact discover a truth that is able to sustain claims to universality for very long, provides the "truth," the "norm," with a mutability that allows it to shift as it is employed in various power strategies. (E.g., sex is that which must be carefully regulated, psychoanalytically deciphered, and freed—in advertisements and commodities all across the nation.) Put somewhat differently, the combination makes truth relevant to the latest demands of man's productive apparatuses and circumstances.

Yet this restless proliferation of norms and the instability of truth is only one outcome of the interplay between the two conceits. Another frequent consequence of this uneasy marriage of modernity which Foucault is less concerned with is separation and the destruction of one of the members: namely, universal truth. Sometimes the atomistic self is unable to tolerate even the claims to universality which help establish his hegemony. What is left, then, is man as his own ground—or rather *men*, in the absence of universals uniting them. This leads to atomistic struggles and the most severe reduction of those who cohabit the social world to beings-for-the-self. Augustine described this process with remarkable acuity in general terms. Hegel and Marx analyzed this dynamic extensively in its particular modern form. Thus far, humans without metaphysical truths have most often been self-aggrandizing humans, un-limited by past morals. Their social action—lacking all grounds—has in the worst cases been "justified" by the senseless and horrifying forms of fascistic aesthetic decisionism by which Habermas, Richard Wolin, and many others are rightfully haunted.

Both these outcomes—the restless searches for truth and various forms of nihilism-egoism—are among the defining features of our age. And both play an important role in the regular functioning of power. As the former surveys, regulates, and coerces people around norms that enhance productivity, the latter frequently deflects criticism and thwarts a sense of responsibility for and commitment to anything that lies beyond the self. The former obliterates and codifies differences while the latter fosters an oblivious indifference. Foucault, it can be argued, has not paid enough attention to the salience and dangers of the latter in his critical writing. That "man" may be "erased like a face drawn in sand at the edge of the sea" is dangerous and frightening as well as potentially attractive and provocative.

Augustine, writing in an extremely different age, had a profound sense of the dangers of the ontological conceit that recognizes nothing beyond the self, and we would do well to listen to his warnings carefully—even if his alternative contains its own problems and much that is untenable for us. As we stand near the edge of a world without universal truths, we cannot wish away or take lightly the problems that tormented him. Beyond metaphysics there are various paths. If we dance too lightly over the edge, we may again discover the horrific instead of the possibility of our freedom. Some recent theorists (Deleuze and Lyotard, for example) often seem insufficiently aware of this risk.[5]

Yet is it possible to provide both an awareness of those dangers and an alternative to them without Augustine's metaphysics? Can we separate Augustine's critical insight from the totalizing dimensions of his morali-ty? Better still, is there a position from which we can recognize both the importance of Augustine's critique of ontological conceit and his limits and insufficiencies as well? A position from which we can take and fortify what is best in Augustine's morality—a concern with flattening and a

5. Cf. Gilles Deleuze and Félix Guattari, *Anti-Oedipus: Capitalism and Schizophrenia* (Minneapolis: University of Minnesota Press, 1983); Jean-François Lyotard, *The Postmod-ern Condition: A Report on Knowledge*, trans. Geoff Bennington and Brian Massumi (Min-neapolis: University of Minnesota Press, 1984).

move toward a greater appreciation of difference than the decadent version of Roman paganism—while avoiding its monological character and arbitrary limitations?

I have argued that Foucault's work contains an ethical alternative to the search for metaphysical truths which avoids nihilism, egoism, and indifference (in spite of the fact that he rarely focuses on the second and third problems in his critical writing). His artistic ethos should be distinguished from the decisionism with which some would like to associate him. Because Foucault's understanding of artistic activity is inextricably connected to a great appreciation of dialogical encounters with others who are different, his artistic ethos is closely linked to creating the self, as well as social, economic, and political practices, in forms that would allow and indeed engender such experiences. This process involves fashioning the self and social world in ways that increase the space for different others and affirm the value of our differences and their dialogical relations. Far from leaving Foucault without any positive directions, this position provides a most important voice in the discussion of which values should govern personal and societal change.

Foucault's ontology and ethics work counter to both conceits and provide us with a particular humility, not that of humble obedience to metaphysical truths, but instead, respectful regard for the importance of the dialogical engagement with those who are different and differences within the self. Foucault offers us the outlines of a notion of the self as a work of art which would not generate a monological process within the self aimed at establishing the One Truth in depth, but rather fashion the self in part through a careful internal conversation that would consider many dimensions of the self and its multiplicitous experiences. And if, as we noted above, one dimension of Augustine's humility wells forth from a certain conceit, we *might* say that Foucault's ethic is characterized by a peculiar audacity rooted in an ontological humility (though what unexpected crashing tides await this claim?). Not being the stuff of deep truth, nor being self-sufficient, Foucault suggests that we dwell at the edge of our being, carefully questioning who we are in a historical social ontology of ourselves aimed in part at determining where a transgressive crafting of our existences might enhance the possibilities of our freedom and better our lives. Within Foucault's ethos, distinction is both appropriate to the self (there is no ontological providence that predisposes us to the "norm") and important if we are to be valuable interlocutors for others in their own attempts to shape their lives and the shared social milieu artistically.

Within the Foucaultian ethos much of what Augustine analyzed perceptively in his discussion of the confessing self remains, albeit in a radically transfigured sense. Augustine's turn away from the immediacy of a present that ceases to be, toward memory as a dimension for the mediations of critical reflection, finds echoes in Foucault's "history of the present" and "historical ontology of ourselves." For Foucault, however, this memory is decentered and spills beyond Augustinian interiors partially illuminated by God's word, to encompass the world of institutions and practices in genealogical ways only broached in the *City of God* and generally truncated by Augustine's excessive focus on evil wills. Augustine's analysis of the gathering and unifying dimensions of reflection likewise has its analogue in the artistic stylization of the self. Yet with Foucault, the stylization imperative is tempered by reflections on the obliterating dimensions of any unity.

These dimensions of Foucault's thought have been missed by most of his interpreters, for a few important reasons, I believe. Foucault put forth little effort to make his ethics explicit until his later writings, and even there he was quite subtle about the matter. For strategic reasons, he carefully avoided writing from a position that could be construed to rest on another "truth claim." In his "final interview" in *Raritan*, he again made clear that he opposed the idea of a single morality applicable to everyone.[6] He was not terribly concerned with those who wished to dismiss him as a nihilist and hence did not guard against passing phrases that could be construed in this way.

Moreover, Foucault's ethical strategy in many of his works was one that sought not to define an explicit ethical position so much as to *practice* an ethics; to explore an ethics by actually perceiving, questioning, establishing an actual relation to the world through it.[7] For Foucault, much of what mattered in ethics lay in this activity rather than in general formulations. Here he is close to Adorno in *Negative Dialectics:* "The crux [of philosophy] is what happens in it, not a thesis or a position—the texture."[8] In works such as the preface to *Herculine Barbin* or *Discipline and*

---

6. Michel Foucault, "Final Interview," *Raritan* (Summer 1985).
7. Conversations with Michael Shapiro were very helpful on this issue.
8. Theodor Adorno, *Negative Dialectics*, trans. E. B. Ashton (New York: Continuum, 1973).

Punish, we find Foucault's ethics not in a set of explicit principles, but rather as a group of concerns that are addressed, a style of addressing them, a choice of words.

Foucault was not a nihilist, and the ethical stance central to his work is precisely an attempt to stake out a strategy between universal morality and nihilism. It is not a strategy that has been well received in a world where many are still yearning to discover metaphysical solutions to our problems. And it is a strategy whose merits are barely audible in a world where dialogue and difference are rigorously marginalized.

The differences between Foucault and Augustine are quite easy to discern in some respects. Those between my readings of Foucault and Merleau-Ponty, however, are more difficult to grasp. Indeed, I draw them closer together than would probably make either of them very comfortable.[9] (The Merleau-Ponty I describe bears little similarity to the Merleau-Ponty—yearning for an originary subject or trying to reduce the world of difference with a phenomenological body—to which Foucault occasionally made cryptic references.)[10] In fact, I think in many respects—far from being at odds with each other—the notions of an artistic ethos which can be discerned in each thinker actually provide an interesting and textured theory when they are brought together. Nevertheless, there are differences between the two thinkers, and they are important and illuminating. I explore these differences as they are manifest in three areas: first, through a brief analysis of the rhetoric of "depth" in Merleau-Ponty and Foucault's frequent attacks on this word; second, through a discussion of the ontological differences between the two thinkers; and finally, by exploring loose affiliations that might be drawn between these two differences and those in the political tendencies of the two philosophers.

Foucault, as we have seen, consistently avoids the rhetoric of "depth." He is extremely conscious of its deployment within Christian metaphysics and within the numerous attempts in our age to resuscitate a metaphysical understanding of the world. To touch the word is, for him,

9. Nonetheless, others have also given readings of the antagonistic traditions stemming from Husserl and structuralism which show them converging. For example: Schmidt, *Merleau-Ponty;* Christopher Norris, *Deconstruction: Theory and Practice* (London: Methuen, 1982).

10. Michel Foucault, *The Archaeology of Knowledge,* trans. A. M. Sheridan Smith (New York: Harper and Row, 1972), p. 203; Foucault, "Theatrum," p. 170.

to risk triggering all sorts of resonations that might insidiously reinscribe his discourse back into those he opposes as sham: confession, Truth, teleological unities that cohere naturally around the depths of their singular centers, codified-normalized subjects, discoverable essences—the secret whispers of God. Depth is too inextricably tied in with this constellation of things to be of any use for either criticizing this constellation or working toward different discourses and practices.

Of course, Merleau-Ponty also aims his philosophy in part against notions of preexisting truths that we need only reflect or discover and prefabricated unities that are predestined to come into existence. But for him, "depth" is both an important term and a vital metaphor. In large part, Merleau-Ponty employs "depth" in a manner that is not concerned with whatever echoes the term may import from its use within Christian metaphysics. He employs it for its spatial significance, in order, as I have recounted, to return us to dense living space, space born in and wildly intertwined with time. Depth is the dimension that pushes us most forcefully toward a reconsideration of our being in the world, a reconsideration of the birth of our experience of space itself ("originality of depth"). While using the spatial connotations of "depth," he simultaneously and quite consistently attempts coherently to transform the word, reinscribing it as a central figure in a philosophy that reverberates with such words as "polymorphism," "latency," "transgress," "express," "wild," "invisible." At some point along the way, spatial depth comes to signify a living thickness—both sensible and sensing—"overlapping" and "transgressing" itself, a dimension born simultaneously with our intercorporeal mingling with others, a dimension in which things remain distinct and other as opposed to the dimension in which things are objectively contained, displayed, and possessed in entirety.

Yet Merleau-Ponty does more with the word than use and coherently deform its spatial intimations. He engages certain resonances "depth" has acquired in Christianity as well. Echoing Augustine, Merleau-Ponty writes that "depth is the dimension of the hidden." Reawakening our sense of the hidden, of the invisible, which lines and is an integral aspect of the sensible world is a central theme for Merleau-Ponty, and "depth" plays a vital role in unraveling this theme. Of course, what is hidden is not "deep Truth"; rather, it is "hidden-ness" itself that Merleau-Ponty wishes to bring before us in an effort to reveal an ontology that recognizes the "obstacles" and "resistance" that belong to things, a protean world with ineliminable pregnant reserves. Beyond mere hidden-ness, however, "depth" colors the hidden as wondrous and motions us in the direction of a particular attitude toward the hidden: that of "wonder." And accompanying this wonder is a certain reverence, a profound awed respect for Being and flesh. Albeit this reverence is not for "His voice," Merleau-Ponty employs a word steeped in two thousand years of Christianity, a word saturated with wonder, mystery, reverence, as he calls us toward different relations with the world.

In spite of his important departures from metaphysics—in the broad sense in which it is commonly employed today, not the sense in which he sometimes worked with it[11]—Merleau-Ponty employs the rhetoric of depth, in part to salvage a sense of mystery and awe: a dimension of respect for otherness which Christianity contained far more of than we typically find in the secular regions of the modern world. For Merleau-Ponty (with Weber), "depoeticization" and "disenchantment" are central to the problems of modernity. A new and better ontology and ethics would have in part to evoke poetic—even reverent—attitudes. Foucault, on the other hand, is more suspicious. He conscientiously avoids such things in his writing, even as he describes for us as well as anyone ever has the methods that depoeticize our bodies and disrespect our differences. Reverence seems in his view to have been too dangerous, too likely to rekindle teleological conceptions, universal truths, secret strategies for subjugation, sugary disguises for violence. In his later work on Kant and enlightenment, there are traces in his rhetoric of something like reverence—we find words such as "belonging" and "respect"—but even here he is sparing. Indeed, perhaps my development of these themes in his thought pushes Foucault "further than he wished to go himself."

This rhetorical difference between these two theorists is, I think, entwined with differences at the ontological level. In an effort to highlight these differences, let us carefully consider the following passages.

The first, by Foucault, is inescapably self-explicit:

> We must not imagine that the world turns towards us a legible face which we would have only to decipher; the world is not the accomplice of our knowledge; there is no prediscursive providence which disposes the world

11. Cf. "The Metaphysical in Man," in Merleau-Ponty, *Sense.*

in our favour. We must conceive discourse as a violence which we do to things, or in any case as a practice which we impose upon them.[12]

The second, by Merleau-Ponty, is more difficult:

> The phenomenological world is not the bringing to explicit expression of a pre-existing being, but the laying down of being. Philosophy is not the reflection of a pre-existing truth, but, like art, the act of bringing truth into being. One may well ask how this creation is *possible*, and if it does not recapture in things a pre-existing Reason. The answer is that the only pre-existent Logos is the world itself, and that the philosophy which brings it into visible existence does not begin by being *possible;* it is actual or real like the world of which it is a part, and no explanatory hypothesis is clearer than the act whereby we take up this unfinished world in an effort to complete and conceive it.[13]

We must read carefully here, for if we do not, we may come to the mistaken conclusion that on the very fundamental issue of "the world," Foucault and Merleau-Ponty stand as complete antagonists: the former denies that the world is Logos, let alone legible, whereas the latter discovers in the world a "pre-existent Logos." Those in search of transcendental breath are allured to these words, a comforting rhetoric that settles us back into our chairs after all that blather about violence, illegibility, indecipherability, imposition, and lack of favors. So comforting, in fact, that "pre-existent Logos" may be the only words one remembers or thinks about on this entire page.

This construal would be unfortunate, however, for Merleau-Ponty's line of thought runs in a very different direction than the one indicated by this phrase when isolated. Consider first the "world" that is this preexistent Logos. He refers, of course, to the "phenomenological world," the perceptual field or clearing, which we always inhabit, which, as he writes in the first sentence of the quoted passage, is itself *not* an "expression of a pre-existing being, but the laying down of being" that emerges—in his later terminology—through the intertwining of our flesh and that of things and other beings. So this world we experience does not preexist *us*, but is laid down through our existence. (And let us not forget, as I noted earlier, that for Merleau-Ponty, "perception is a violent act.") The

---

12. Foucault, "Order of Discourse," p. 67.
13. Merleau-Ponty, *Phenomenology*, p. xx.

phenomenological world is preexistent only with respect to *philosophy,* and philosophical activity does not mirror the Logos of this world—the correlations, discrepancies, consistencies, continuities, distinctions revealed at the intersections of my various experiences and those between myself and others—but "brings it into being" as philosophy attempts to complete an unfinished world (with respect to explicit conceptualization). Philosophers "do not rediscover an already given rationality, they 'establish themselves' and establish it, by an act of initiative which has no guarantee in being, its justification resting entirely on the effective power it centers on us of taking our history upon ourselves."[14] As with perception, the philosophical reflection that further gives form to the world does not simply express possibilities of this world, it also transgresses others, and as Merleau-Ponty writes in the closing sentence of this paragraph: it "is a violent act that is validated by being performed."[15]

Yet although Foucault and Merleau-Ponty are closer than first appearances may suggest, the rhetorical differences remain. Just as Foucault banishes "depth" from his discourse, one cannot imagine him touching "pre-existent Logos"—even in a somewhat defensive paragraph like Merleau-Ponty's—with a ten-foot pen. There simply is no space within Foucault's ontology for this type of trope. For Foucault, discourse is a violence we do to things. It is, of course, violent for Merleau-Ponty also, but it is not *simply* violence. Central to Merleau-Ponty's understanding of our embodied perceptual and conceptual relation to ourselves and the world is the notion that in the best cases, things that were—in some sense regarding their coexistence with us—"unfinished" and "incomplete" can be "brought into being" and "expressed" in our intercourse with them. In spite of (he would say *because of*) his awareness of "encroachment," "transgression," "concealment," he can still write that the best speech "frees the meaning captive in a thing."[16] He can write of the "miracle of related experiences."[17] There *is* a certain complicity between our body and the world for Merleau-Ponty. In the overlapping of flesh on flesh, the world solicits our gaze and our gaze responds. Solicitation and response are fraught with an ineliminable dimension of discord and violence, but there is the possibility, and some-

14. Ibid.
15. Ibid.
16. Merleau-Ponty, *Signs,* p. 44.
17. Merleau-Ponty, *Phenomenology,* p. xx.

times the occurrence, of a certain circumscribed justice here as well. Merleau-Ponty's rhetoric—and the ontology that reciprocally calls this rhetoric forth and is illuminated by it—instills an awareness of the turbulence in our existence, but simultaneously it never allows us to forget the experience of miracles, profundity, and poetry. "It is a view which like the most fragile object of perception—a soap bubble, or a wave—or like the most simple dialogue, embraces indivisibly all the order and disorder of the world."[18]

The profundity of our experience is not the expression of a "deep truth" that would be our guarantee, justification, and measure. It is brought into being in a dialogue between human lives and a partially indeterminate surrounding world, in which we do not discover a reason we could obey—even as we experience miracles—but rather "become responsible for our history."

It seems to me that Merleau-Ponty's rhetoric and ontology, in which expression and transgression are intertwined, are existentially and experientially much more appropriate than Foucault's nearly exclusive emphasis on violence and obstacle. One cannot read a book like Barry Lopez's *Arctic Dreams*, with its sensitive portrayal of the people, animals, and plants of the arctic, the ice, the sun, and not be struck by the fact that in this discourse there is a certain justice, an expression of things in which truths and poetry intermingle. It is a text that calls attention to the limits and potential violence of its own and various other perspectives— but it is not a perspective one could summarize as a "violence done to things." And there is the civil rights movement, the antiwar movement, the socialist movement linked with Eugene Debs. None of these can be summarized adequately as violence, and I doubt Foucault would disagree. Nevertheless, I still have difficulty imagining how I could "prove" the superiority of Merleau-Ponty's approach or even what a "proof" might look like at this level, given their philosophies.

The status of their philosophical agreements—their points of overlap—seems a bit easier to define. Both agree that there is an ineliminable degree of otherness, recalcitrance, pregnancy to all things we experience. Everything that we sense, conceptualize, and act on harbors a surplus beyond what we acknowledge—a surplus that is continually given birth to, spills beyond, and is transgressed by the identities we formulate in an

18. Merleau-Ponty, *Humanism*, p. 189.

effort to capture things in their entirety. The sense of this view does not rest on some sort of "correspondence" between it and some thing in the world that it signifies which would guarantee its truth. Rather, its sense rests on our sense of the perpetual failure of concepts, categories, significations, norms totally to grasp things. Two tactics Foucault repeatedly uses for provoking this sense of bankruptcy are, first, to call our attention to what is obliterated or mutilated by our categories and practices (those who do not work fast enough, those who do not obey, hermaphrodites, those who masturbate, etc.) and, second, to expose the way in which they actively and forcefully impose themselves on the world. Of course, this argument does not prove the (at least partial) inadequacy of totalizing concepts and norms per se, but only that of those norms and concepts he debunks (or those related). By showing us repeated efforts and repeated failures, however, Foucault seeks to prod us into questioning the sense of this history of Truth-without-excess more generally. Still, his counter to this history—the notion that otherness and at least a degree of violence are inescapable aspects of existence we must dialogically confront in our choices—can claim to be no more than a working assumption.

Merleau-Ponty also proceeds in part by bringing to our attention what is unacknowledged in hegemonic conceptions (for example, in his criticisms of liberalism and Marxism). But because he also addresses questions of perception and ontology in ways that are more rigorous, sustained, and, in some senses, more basic, it seems to me that he more successfully "secures" the points on which he and Foucault agree. He focuses much of his writing on the inadequacies of objectivist/identifying thought *per se*, showing persuasively that it cannot account for our most basic perceptual experiences—or more simply, experience itself. He has convincingly demonstrated that some notions of excess—background, depth, the invisible—are necessary if we are to begin to formulate an understanding of our existence in which experience is at all possible. He has shown us, at a far more general level than Foucault, that every revealing implies concealment; every expression, transgression.

But has either shown that perception, discourse, and action are "violent acts"? Here their footing is more difficult, and any attempt summarily to characterize the relation of the visible to the invisible, the spoken to what remains unsaid seems highly questionable. For it is possible to think of perceptions, conceptions, and practices in which what is eclipsed is so relatively insignificant or the eclipse so temporary that "violence" hardly seems to capture what is going on. Indeed, as I have argued, to use "violence" in some cases (we can each conjure our favorite examples) seems to begin to drain an important word of much of its significance. Hence it seems to me that if we wish to stick to what we can know about the underside of what happens whenever anything appears, we must be satisfied with a word like "eclipse"—which may take the form of an utter disgrace or may mean only that a part of the moon is deprived of sunlight for a few seconds.

I do not think that either Foucault or Merleau-Ponty chose his metaphors simply in an attempt to shed realistic light on perception or ontology, however. Beyond what they both know about "eclipsing," their rhetorical choices are tightly bound up with questions of ethics and politics. Through his employment of certain metaphors to describe our fundamental relation to the world (in the broadest sense: self, others, nonhuman beings, things), each theorist attempts to draw us toward what he perceives to be most important yet most lacking in modernity. For Foucault, who had one of the most acute eyes for subjugation in this century, this effort entails a sense that "everything is dangerous." Succinctly: "I think that the ethico-political choice we have to make every day is to determine which is the main danger."[19] The rhetoric of discord that colors his ontology is aimed at instilling this lesson so we never forget it.

Merleau-Ponty also thinks that objectification and the "terror" associated with it—both overt and insidious—define the modern age to a great extent. In a period when denial is a chief mechanism by which violence is rendered less visible and perpetuated, he employs ontological metaphors that summon us to recognize the degree of violence in every perception. In an age when violence is disguised, he gestures us with Foucault toward a hypersensitivity to both the encroachment and the responsibility intrinsic in existence. Yet this insight shares the stage with another. For this age of objectification that denies its violence is at the same time one of "depoeticization and disenchantment," a time when both our categories and our experiences of their failure are draining away our sense of the openness of the future and the possibility of creating a world with more justice and grandeur. Merleau-Ponty worries about a "*bad existen-*

19. Foucault, "Genealogy," p. 232.

tialism, which exhausts itself in the description of the collision between reason and the contradictions of experience and terminates in a consciousness of defeat."[20] His perceptual and ontological metaphors of "depth," "expression," "miracle," "overlapping" are attempts to re-poeticize our experience at a most basic level—attempts to color our existence with the profundity of possibility.

Viewed at this level, I think that Merleau-Ponty's rhetoric and ontology are more suited than Foucault's to the dialogical artistic ethos I believe they share. A sense of danger and discord alone is not sufficient—for most people at most times—to provoke and call forth great creative deeds. Great acts usually require a sense of positive possibility as well. Insofar as the world Merleau-Ponty evokes is a *"pregnancy* of possibles"[21] irreducible to transgression, "possibles" that allow and call for better expressions of existence, it elicits our creative engagement in a way that Foucault's world does not. It summons us to the task of constructing as well as deconstructing. Of course, Foucault himself calls us to create our existences as works of art, but the world he describes at the ontological level harbors little space for the inspiration of possibility which would help sustain this ethos—an ethos that requires an enormous degree of fortitude. In short, I think the tenability of this ethos rests on a sense of the possibility of a certain *degree of complicity* in our relations with others and the natural world, along with the recognition that this complicity always involves an element of transgression.

Of course, I've argued above that Foucault was often much more interested in ethics as a textual and political practice than he was in being able to articulate a consistent and explicit ethical position. Given this strategy, one might maintain that elaborating an ontological position suited to his ethics is relatively unimportant since the focus of his ethics is more on "what happens" than on "why." Yet in spite of the importance of Foucault's practical strategy, I suggest that ethico-political questions require continual interrogations at *both* levels, each illuminated by and undergoing a constant modification in the light of the other. This is not to move toward some transcendental terra firma, but simply to initiate and perpetuate one kind of circular questioning that can help us make ethico-political judgments. A crucial dimension of the ethico-political project involves the question "what happens": how our discourses and

20. Merleau-Ponty, *Humanism,* p. 188.
21. Merleau-Ponty, *Visible and the Invisible,* p. 250.

practices constitute the visible and invisible, the normal and abnormal, the desirable and undesirable. Yet as we attempt to make decisions in light of these questions, it is important to draw on the sense we can make of what it is to be a human being in the world in very basic dimensions. Our positions will always be significantly bound to historical contingencies; we should have no illusions otherwise. But this qualification should not inhibit us from explicitly engaging these questions, for our practices are always bound to tacit positions, and an ethos of questioning should encourage a dialogue that makes them explicit objects of inquiry: affording us the degree of enlightenment possible for human beings. The process of explication opens us to the other and is, I think, a precondition for a dialogical ethical project. Later Foucault becomes more explicit about the ethics that animates his writing, but his comments sometimes sit uneasy in the context of a literal reading of his ontological gestures. If this paradox between an utterly discordant ontology and a dialogical aesthetic ethos is in some sense essential in its starkest form (it remains, but not as starkly, in Merleau-Ponty), we need a better account of why, or at least a presentation of the paradox itself which is more capable of holding sway.

There are important political implications in the present distinction as well. The centrality of discord and danger in Foucault's perception of the world is entwined with a focus on "local" strategies designed to thwart the exercise of power at specific sites. This is partly due to the fact that this perception has given rise to a heightened understanding of the importance of these sites in the subjugation of selves. Yet it is also because this perception has given rise to a skepticism that leads one to shy away from attempts to construct plausible alternatives. In absence of such alternatives, resistance tends to be consumed in local struggles against current modes of power.

That Foucault's rhetoric and ontology largely discourage the attempt to formulate alternatives is extremely significant, for such alternatives would involve an articulation of different social values, visions, and concrete directions that might catalyze significant coalition building with other people struggling against other sites of power. In addition, the formulation of alternative practices would tend to raise more "global" issues as well, as people attempted to consider the broader circumstances required to realize their goals. These global issues could provide another focus for creating solidarity.

None of this is necessarily excluded by the ethic that governs

Foucault's work. In fact, I think these things are *called for* at the level of his ethics as I developed them in Chapter 4. But his ontology and rhetoric tend to inhibit their development. Although his ethics provides an extremely valuable position from which to begin to formulate positive alternatives to the contemporary practices he has criticized, Foucault very rarely actually took these steps. One will say that it was a strategic choice, that Foucault was simply more concerned with playing the "fool" and "problematizing" than with offering us concrete solutions. In part, that is true—he has said so himself[22]—and he was able to raise important questions from this position in ways that others had not done. Yet we should not endow Foucault with an agency that he and others have persuasively debunked. Foucault partly chose his rhetoric and ontological formulations, but at the same time his language and fundamental experiences of the world guided and limited his choices. They dissuaded him from formulating concrete alternatives even as an ethos emerged in his writings which provides an original and fascinating perspective for beginning this task. If we are to grasp and develop creatively the most profound dimensions of Foucault's thought in the direction of a more adequate political theory, it seems to me that we would do well to shift toward ontological formulations and rhetorical configurations that are closer to those of Merleau-Ponty as I have developed his thought in this text. (This is not to deny that there is no society imaginable that would not benefit from the presence of "fools." It is simply to assert that this benefit hinges in part on those who take up their insights in ways that are not "fool-ish.")

Merleau-Ponty—as inadequate and unoriginal as his thoughts on politics often are—continually calls us to formulate alternatives to the given visions and practices of violence and subjugation. His vision of a "third way" was aimed not only at criticizing and avoiding the hegemony of the two superpowers, but also at working out a path toward a more dialogical and just world. If we are able to inform this impulse (and the ontology that supports it) with Foucault's insights into the workings and dangers of power in modernity, and develop it in light of the dialogical artistic ethos that emerges in the writings of both, there may be great possibilities.

If this text has thus far for the most part remained at the level of ontology and ethics, if I have avoided throwing out many anchors that

---

22. Foucault, "Genealogy," p. 231.

might "ground" and "bring down to earth" what is admittedly an abstract journey, it is in no way to avoid either the necessity or the desirability of working out the implications of what has been said for our everyday practices. Yet while theory and practice, ethics and politics, exist in a relationship of circularity which partially constitutes the nature of each, I am extremely wary of those who demand that the circle be drawn tightly. The circumscription implied too often leads to both bad theory and bad practice. If I have exploited for the moment a margin of autonomy for theory, it has been to allow it the possibility of developing in a manner that might shed a different light on the practices and commitments out of which it sprang.

There is another issue as well. If theory runs the danger of being excessively constrained when it is tied too tightly, frequently, or carelessly into the everyday, practice also suffers. The way we live is too textured and important to be shaped and governed by quick leaps out of theory, too complicated for there to be much justice in glib theoretical references affirming this practice, denying that one. As Foucault illustrated and articulated on numerous occasions, the task of creating our lives is an activity requiring profoundly historical analysis. Discerning the practical implications of theory requires the same. Leaping over historical analysis blunts the possible contributions of theory, making it of little value to the world, and stifles the possibility that the world might speak to and transform theory. The very possibility of a dialogue between theory and practice requires more care than I am capable of in passing remarks and examples. What is needed at this point (in addition to further work on the ethic at an abstract level) is historical analysis proceeding with the values and insights that surface in the ethos shared by Merleau-Ponty and Foucault and social movements that act in dialogue with these insights.

With these caveats, I suggest that one of the most fertile sites for this analysis is that of our relations to the nonhuman world. I began this book with a discussion of ecotones, and though I quickly extracted the word from its specifically ecological context, it seems to me that this context poses questions about the relationship between self and other in an especially dramatic form. For some time, modernity has reduced the nonhuman world to an object for human use, and the resulting rape of the earth has consistently demanded that humans be ordered and subjugated to an imperative to master the earth and enhance productivity. In our civilization practices of mastery over other people and the earth reciprocally reinforce each other in a manner that intensifies objectification. To confront the current ecological crisis deeply is to face the problem of elaborating an ethics of self and other at the point where, in important respects, they face each other at their most radical alterity. To begin to formulate a dialogical ethics and practice with this other-that-does-not-speak is to confront, where it is at once most difficult and most necessary, both the questions of our entwinement with what is different and our ability to affirm a greater degree of difference.

It seems to me that the ecological crisis is a crucial site for a few other reasons as well. First, it strikes me as one of the places where the questions raised in this book are pushed closest to the surface by the practical historical course of events. While our history does not in any way make these questions inevitable (for example, we could go off the brink into oblivion, or we could become more successful *managers* of the earth), it appears that a discursive space is emerging for them which will have widespread appeal, given the extent and intensity of ecological issues for people all across the planet and the poverty that our current discourses and practices exhibit when dealing with them. Second, because social structures and institutions are so central to ecological issues, such matters have the potential to bring to the fore questions of the relations between human selves and others in fundamental ways. Third, because ecological issues generally are either larger or smaller than our ecologically oblivious institutions, they raise additional questions about how we might restructure the scale and functioning of human social, economic, and political practices as well as the self's relation to these practices.

If we were carefully to inhabit and expand the spaces ecological issues make possible, and link them to other crucial areas where the questions of self and other desperately need to be addressed—such as race, gender, sexuality, class—we could begin to imagine that Foucault's "patient labor [that gives] form to our impatience for liberty" might assume a more genuine and lasting social significance. Of course, it is difficult to muster a great deal of optimism here, except, perhaps, to say that such times have never been expected. And this is no insignificant principle of hope.

Bibliography

PRIMARY SOURCES

Augustine. *An Augustine Synthesis*. Arranged by Erich Przywara. New York: Harper and Row, 1958.
——. *City of God*. Translated by Henry Bettenson. Harmondsworth, U.K.: Penguin Books, 1972.
——. *The Confessions*. Translated by F. J. Sheed. Kansas City: Sheed, Andrews, and McMeel, 1942.
——. *Of True Religion*. Translated by J. H. S. Burleigh. South Bend, Ind.: Regnery/Gateway, 1959.
——. *On Christian Doctrine*. Translated by D. W. Robertson Jr. Indianapolis: Bobbs-Merrill, 1958.
——. *On Free Choice of the Will*. Translated by A. S. Benjamin and L. H. Hackstaff. Indianapolis: Bobbs-Merrill, 1964.
——. *The Political Writings of St. Augustine*. Edited by Henry Paolucci. South Bend, Ind.: Regnery/Gateway, 1962.
Foucault, Michel. *The Archaeology of Knowledge and the Discourse on Language*. Translated by A. M. Sheridan Smith. New York: Harper and Row, Colophon Books, 1972.
——. *The Birth of the Clinic: An Archaeology of Medical Perception*. Translated by A. M. Sheridan Smith. New York: Random House, Vintage Books, 1975.
——. "Christianity and Confession." Lecture delivered at Wesleyan University, November 24, 1980.
——. *Discipline and Punish: The Birth of the Prison*. Translated by Alan Sheridan. New York: Random House, Vintage Books, 1979.

———. *Final Foucault.* Edited by James Bernauer and David Rasmussen. Cambridge, Mass.: MIT Press, 1988.

———. *The Foucault Reader.* Edited by Paul Rabinow. New York: Pantheon, 1984.

———. *The History of Sexuality, Volume 1: An Introduction.* Translated by Robert Hurley. New York: Random House, Vintage Books, 1980.

———. *The History of Sexuality, Volume 2: The Use of Pleasure.* Translated by Robert Hurley. New York: Pantheon, 1985.

———. Introduction to *Herculine Barbin: Being the Recently Discovered Memoirs of a Nineteenth-Century French Hermaphrodite.* Translated by Richard McDougall. New York: Pantheon, 1980.

———. "Kant on Enlightenment and Revolution." Translated by Colin Gordon. *Economy and Society* 15 (February 1986): 88–96.

———. *Language, Counter-Memory, Practice: Selected Essays and Interviews.* Edited by Donald Bouchard. New York: Cornell University Press, 1977.

———. *Madness and Civilization: A History of Insanity in the Age of Reason.* Translated by Richard Howard. New York: Random House, Vintage Books, 1973.

———. *Mental Illness and Psychology.* Translated by Alan Sheridan. New York: Harper and Row, 1976.

———. "The Order of Discourse." In *Untying the Text,* edited by Robert Young. New York: Methuen, 1981.

———. *The Order of Things: An Archaeology of the Human Sciences.* New York: Random House, Vintage Books, 1973.

———. *Politics, Philosophy, Culture: Interviews and Other Writings, 1977–1984.* Edited by Lawrence Kritzman. New York: Routledge, 1988.

———. *Power/Knowledge: Selected Interviews and Other Writings by Michel Foucault.* Edited by Colin Gordon. New York: Pantheon, 1980.

Merleau-Ponty, Maurice. *Adventures of the Dialectic.* Translated by Joseph Bien. Evanston, Ill.: Northwestern University Press, 1973.

———. *Les aventures de la dialectique.* Paris: Gallimard, 1955.

———. *Consciousness and the Acquisition of Language.* Translated by H. J. Silverman. Evanston, Ill.: Northwestern University Press, 1973.

———. *Humanism and Terror.* Translated by John O'Neill. Boston: Beacon Press, 1969.

———. *Humanisme et terreur.* Paris: Gallimard, 1947.

———. *In Praise of Philosophy.* Translated by John Wild and J. M. Edie. Evanston, Ill.: Northwestern University Press, 1963.

———. *Phénoménologie de la perception.* Paris: Gallimard, 1945.

———. *Phenomenology of Perception.* Translated by Colin Smith. London: Routledge and Kegan Paul, 1962.

———. *The Primacy of Perception and Other Essays.* Edited by James Edie. Evanston, Ill.: Northwestern University Press, 1964.

———. *The Prose of the World.* Translated by John O'Neill. Evanston, Ill.: Northwestern University Press, 1973.

———. *Sense and Non-Sense.* Translated by H. L. Dreyfus and P. A. Dreyfus. Evanston, Ill.: Northwestern University Press, 1964.

———. *Sens et non-sens.* Paris: Gallimard, 1948.

———. *Signes.* Paris: Gallimard, 1960.

——. *Signs.* Translated by R. C. McCleary. Evanston, Ill.: Northwestern University Press, 1964.

——. *Themes from the Lectures at the Collège de France, 1952–1960.* Translated by John O'Neill. Evanston, Ill.: Northwestern University Press, 1970.

——. *The Visible and the Invisible.* Translated by Alphonso Lingis. Evanston, Ill.: Northwestern University Press, 1968.

——. *Le visible et l'invisible.* Paris: Gallimard, 1964.

SELECTED SECONDARY SOURCES

Baudrillard, Jean. *Forget Foucault.* New York: Semiotext(e), 1987.

Bonner, G. I. "Libido and Concupiscentia in St. Augustine." *Studia Patristica* 7 (1962), 307–26.

Brown, Peter. *Augustine of Hippo.* Berkeley: University of California Press, 1967.

——. *Cult of the Saints: Its Rise and Function in Latin Christianity.* Chicago: University of Chicago Press, 1981.

Connolly, William. "A Letter to Augustine." In *Identity\Difference: Democratic Negotiations of Political Paradox.* Ithaca, N.Y.: Cornell University Press, 1991.

Cooper, Barry. *Merleau-Ponty and Marxism: From Terror to Reform.* Toronto: University of Toronto Press, 1979.

D'Arcy, S. J., et al. *Saint Augustine: His Age, Life and Thought.* New York: Meridian, 1957.

Dreyfus, Hubert L., and Paul Rabinow. *Michel Foucault: Beyond Structuralism and Hermeneutics.* 2d ed. Afterword by and interview with Michel Foucault. Chicago: University of Chicago Press, 1983.

Gillan, Garth, ed. *Horizons of the Flesh: Critical Perspectives on the Thought of Merleau-Ponty.* Carbondale, Ill.: Southern Illinois University Press, 1973.

Gilson, Etienne. *The Christian Philosophy of St. Augustine.* New York: Random House, 1960.

Hoy, D. C., ed. *Foucault: A Critical Reader.* Oxford: Blackwell, 1986.

Jaspers, Karl. *Plato and Augustine.* Edited by H. Arendt. Translated by Ralph Manheim. New York: Harcourt, Brace and World, 1957.

Kruks, Sonia. *The Political Philosophy of Merleau-Ponty.* Brighton, U.K.: Harvester Press, 1985.

Madison, Gary Brent. *The Phenomenology of Merleau-Ponty: A Search for the Limits of Consciousness.* Athens: University of Ohio Press, 1981.

Mallin, Samuel B. *Merleau-Ponty's Philosophy.* New Haven, Conn.: Yale University Press, 1979.

Markus, R. A., ed. *Augustine: A Collection of Critical Essays.* Garden City, N.Y.: Anchor Books, 1972.

Miles, Margaret R. *Augustine on the Body.* Missoula, Mont.: Scholars Press, 1979.

Poster, Mark. *Foucault, Marxism, and History: Mode of Production versus Mode of Information.* Cambridge: Polity Press, 1984.

Rabil, Albert, Jr. *Merleau-Ponty: Existentialist of the Social World.* New York: Columbia University Press, 1967.

Rajchman, John. *Michel Foucault: The Freedom of Philosophy*. New York: Columbia University Press, 1985.
Schmidt, James. *Maurice Merleau-Ponty: Between Phenomenology and Structuralism*. New York: St. Martin's Press, 1985.
Sheridan, Alan. *Michel Foucault: The Will to Truth*. London: Tavistock, 1980.
Whiteside, Kerry H. *Merleau-Ponty and the Foundation of an Existential Politics*. Princeton: Princeton University Press, 1988.

SOME SIGNIFICANT BACKGROUND TEXTS

Adorno, Theodor W. *Negative Dialectics*. Translated by E. B. Ashton. New York: Continuum, 1973.
Cochrane, C. N. *Christianity and Classical Culture*. New York: Oxford University Press, 1940.
Connolly, William E. *Politics and Ambiguity: Rhetoric of the Human Sciences*. Madison: University of Wisconsin Press, 1987.
Dallmayr, Fred R. *Twilight of Subjectivity: Contributions to a Post-Individualist Theory of Politics*. Amherst: University of Massachusetts Press, 1981.
Deleuze, Gilles, and Félix Guattari. *Anti-Oedipus: Capitalism and Schizophrenia*. Minneapolis: University of Minnesota Press, 1983.
Derrida, Jacques. *Of Grammatology*. Translated by G. C. Spivak. Baltimore: Johns Hopkins University Press, 1976.
——. *Speech and Phenomena and Other Essays on Husserl's Theory of Signs*. Translated by D. B. Allison. Evanston, Ill.: Northwestern University Press, 1973.
——. *Writing and Difference*. Translated by Alan Bass. Chicago: University of Chicago Press, 1978.
Descombes, Vincent. *Modern French Philosophy*. Translated by L. Scott-Fox and J. M. Harding. Cambridge: Cambridge University Press, 1980.
Gadamer, Hans-Georg. *Truth and Method*. Translated by Joel Weinsheimer and D. G. Marshall. 2d ed. New York: Crossroad, 1989.
Habermas, Jürgen. *Knowledge and Human Interests*. Translated by J. J. Shapiro. Boston: Beacon Press, 1971.
——. *The Philosophical Discourse of Modernity*. Translated by Fredrick Lawrence. Cambridge, Mass.: MIT Press, 1987.
Hegel, G. W. F. *Phenomenology of Spirit*. Translated by A. V. Miller. Oxford: Oxford University Press, 1977.
——. *Philosophy of Right*. Translated by T. M. Knox. Oxford: Oxford University Press, 1967.
Heidegger, Martin. *Basic Writings*. Translated by D. F. Krell. New York: Harper and Row, 1977.
——. *Being and Time*. Translated by John Macquarrie and Edward Robinson. New York: Harper and Row, 1962.
——. *Identity and Difference*. Translated by Joan Stambaugh. New York: Harper and Row, 1969.
Horkheimer, Max, and Theodor W. Adorno. *Dialectic of Enlightenment*. Translated by John Cumming. New York: Seabury Press, 1972.

Husserl, Edmund. *Cartesian Meditations: An Introduction to Phenomenology*. Translated by Dorion Cairns. The Hague: Martinus Nijhoff, 1977.
——. *Crisis of the European Sciences and Transcendental Phenomenology*. Translated by David Carr. Evanston, Ill.: Northwestern University Press, 1970.
——. *Ideas: General Introduction to Pure Phenomenology*. Translated by W. R. B. Gibson. New York: Collier, 1962.
Kant, Immanuel. *Critique of Practical Reason*. Translated by L. W. Beck. Indianapolis: Bobbs-Merrill, 1956.
——. *Critique of Pure Reason*. Translated by N. K. Smith. New York: St. Martin's Press, 1965.
——. *On History*. Edited by L. W. Beck. Indianapolis: Bobbs-Merrill, 1963.
Lenin, V. I. *The Lenin Anthology*. Edited by R. C. Tucker. New York: Norton, 1975.
——. *Materialism and Empirio-Criticism: Comments on a Reactionary Philosophy*. New York: International, 1927.
Lukács, Georg. *History and Class Consciousness*. Cambridge, Mass.: MIT Press, 1971.
Lukes, Steven. *Marxism and Morality*. Oxford: Clarendon Press, 1985.
Lyotard, Jean-François. *Just Gaming*. Translated by Wlad Godzich. Minneapolis: University of Minnesota Press, 1985.
——. *The Postmodern Condition: A Report on Knowledge*. Translated by Geoff Bennington and Brian Massumi. Minneapolis: University of Minnesota Press, 1984.
Marx, Karl. *Grundrisse: Introduction to the Critique of Political Economy*. Translated by Martin Nicolaus. New York: Vintage Books, 1973.
Marx, Karl, and Friedrich Engels. *The Marx Engels Reader*. Edited by R. C. Tucker. 2d ed. New York: Norton, 1972.
Nietzsche, Friedrich. *The Gay Science: With a Prelude in Rhymes and an Appendix of Songs*. Translated by Walter Kaufmann. New York: Vintage Books, 1974.
——. *On the Genealogy of Morals and Ecce Homo*. Translated by Walter Kaufmann and R. J. Hollingdale. New York: Vintage Books, 1967.
——. *The Will to Power*. Translated by Walter Kaufmann and R. J. Hollingdale. New York: Vintage Books, 1968.
Poster, Mark. *Existential Marxism in Postwar France: Sartre to Althusser*. Princeton: Princeton University Press, 1975.
Rawls, John. *A Theory of Justice*. Cambridge, Mass.: Harvard University Press, 1971.
Rorty, Richard. *Philosophy and the Mirror of Nature*. Princeton: Princeton University Press, 1979.
Sandel, Michael J. *Liberalism and the Limits of Justice*. Cambridge: Cambridge University Press, 1982.
Taylor, Charles. *Hegel*. Cambridge: Cambridge University Press, 1975.
Weber, Max. *The Protestant Ethic and the Spirit of Capitalism*. Translated by Talcott Parsons. New York: Scribner's, 1958.

Index

Library of Congress Cataloging-in-Publication Data

Coles, Romand, 1959-
    Self/power/other : political theory and dialogical ethics / Romand
Coles.
      p. cm.
    Includes bibliographical references and index.
    ISBN 0-8014-2609-X (pbk. : alk. paper)
    1. Political ethics. 2. Social ethics. 3. Individualism.
4. Community. 5. Augustine, Saint, Bishop of Hippo—Contributions
in political science. 6. Foucault, Michel—Contributions in
political science. 7. Merleau-Ponty, Maurice, 1908–1961—
Contributions in political science. I. Title.
JA79.C64 1992
172—dc20   91-55546

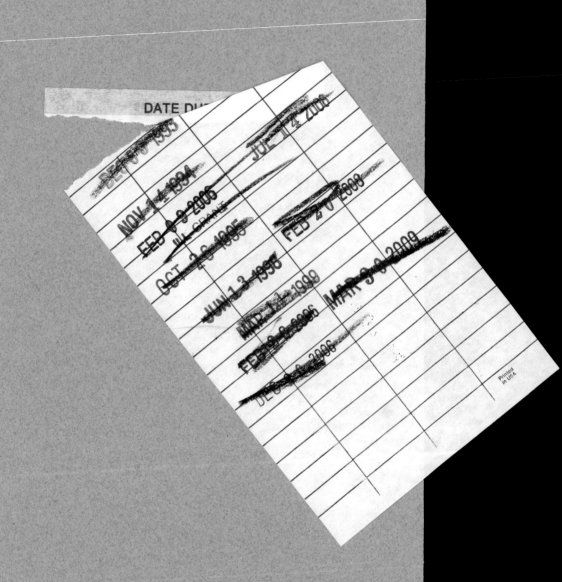

DATE DUE